UNDER SURVEILLANCE

Under Surveillance

Being Watched in Modern America

RANDOLPH LEWIS

University of Texas Press

AUSTIN

Requests for permission to reproduce material from this work should be sent to:
Permissions
University of Texas Press
P.O. Box 7819
Austin, TX 78713-7819
utpress.utexas.edu/rp-form

♾ The paper used in this book meets the minimum requirements of ANSI/NISO Z39.48-1992 (R1997) (Permanence of Paper).

LIBRARY OF CONGRESS CATALOGING-IN-PUBLICATION DATA

Names: Lewis, Randolph, author.
Title: Under surveillance : being watched in modern America / Randolph Lewis.
Description: First edition. | Austin : University of Texas Press, 2017. | Includes bibliographical references and index.
Identifiers: LCCN 2017003541
        ISBN 978-1-4773-1243-8 (cloth : alk. paper)
        ISBN 978-1-4773-1380-0 (library e-book)
        ISBN 978-1-4773-1381-7 (non-library e-book)
Subjects: LCSH: Electronic surveillance—Social aspects—United States. | Social control—United States. | Privacy, Right of—United States.
Classification: LCC TK7882.E2 L49 2017 | DDC 363.1/063—dc23
LC record available at https://lccn.loc.gov/2017003541

doi:10.7560/312438

Contents

UNDER SURVEILLANCE

Introduction

A grateful parent listens to a sleeping newborn through a baby monitor. An excited teenager uses an app to locate her friends at the mall for some holiday shopping. A worried family relies on a security camera to safeguard an elderly relative in a nursing home three states away.[1] A hip young couple, ever so ironic, giggles at the private lives of the rich, famous, and decadent who have been caught on a paparazzo's camera. A shy second-grader boards a bus, looks into an iris scanner, and receives instant confirmation that he's in the right place.

This is surveillance—and it doesn't sound so bad.

But then imagine something else: A hotel maid continues to go full tilt near the end of her shift, even when her feet start aching, because she's being electronically monitored for maximum sheet-changing efficiency.[2] A retiree is enjoying the privacy of his backyard, until he spots a small, video-equipped drone hovering overhead, gawking at him for no apparent reason. A call-center worker chooses his words carefully, painfully aware that his voice is being filtered through an automated emotion detection system that can sense an "inappropriate" tone of voice directed at a customer.[3] An undocumented migrant sees security cameras pointed in her direction and feels the wariness, exhaustion, and uncertainty that come from being vulnerable to deportation. A young woman cringes because her laptop has been enslaved by malware that allows a criminal on the other side of the world to take illicit bedroom photos, which he ransoms back to her. A Muslim couple is yanked off a JetBlue flight on a Florida runway because their eighteen-month-old daughter is on the No Fly List, seemingly for no reason other than the fact that her mother, born and raised in New Jersey, wears a hijab and has a Middle Eastern name.[4]

This is surveillance, too, and at times it's enough to make someone put on a tinfoil hat and hide underneath the sofa. CCTV cameras, Transportation Security Administration (TSA) scanners, National Security Agency (NSA) databases, Big Data marketers, Predator drones, stop-and-frisk police tactics, Facebook algorithms, hidden spyware, workplace monitors, and even old-fashioned nosy neighbors armed with the latest in monitoring technology—Big Brother now has many different faces, some designed to intimidate, others designed to entice our cheerful participation. Although surveillance has a long history that precedes its latest high-tech incarnation, it has a new prominence in our world today, so much so that one scholar, Kevin Haggerty, has called it "the dominant organizing practice of late modernity." Like many other scholars who write in the emerging field of Surveillance Studies, Haggerty suggests that we are in the midst of a "world-historical transformation in terms of the emergence of new practices, dynamics, and technologies of surveillance."[5] The NSA leaker Edward Snowden put it even more dramatically when he warned a potential collaborator that "every border you cross, every purchase you make, every call you dial, every cell phone tower you pass, friend you keep, site you visit and subject line you type is in the hands of a system whose reach is unlimited, but whose safeguards are not."[6]

Never before has so much been known about so many. As the sociologist William G. Staples wrote in 2000, "We seem

to be entering a state of permanent visibility where attempts
to control and shape our behavior, in essence our bodies, are
accomplished not so much by the threat of punishment and
physical force but by the act of being watched—continuously,
anonymously, and automatically."[7] Almost two decades later,
we are much closer to that unprecedented "state of permanent
visibility" in which our secrets—what we say, what we buy,
what we want—are constantly laid bare to various monitoring
systems with very long memories. The vast infrastructure of
surveillance is still an imperfect system with disparate parts
working for disparate purposes, but these distinct state, corporate, and personal systems are likely to become increasingly
interwoven in the near future. Yet even as I write in 2017, the
first year of Donald Trump's administration, the capabilities of
state, corporate, and peer surveillance are enough to give most
anyone pause.

Some representative examples should give you a sense of
what I mean: the NSA scoops up almost every electronic utter-
ance and stores it in a vault built to hold thousands of yotta-
bytes in the Utah desert. Customs and Border Protection flies
Predator drones over the United States that are identical to the
ones in Afghanistan, minus the missiles. Across the pond, in a
program with the fiendish code name Optic Nerve, the British
intelligence service known as MI6 collected millions of images
from Yahoo! Chat, including naked selfies, from people who
were never suspects in any investigation.[8] Other US allies are
equally adept at surveillance practices. A soldier in an Israeli
unit charged with monitoring Palestinians "whose only crime
was that they interested the Israeli security system for various
reasons" explained that "all Palestinians are exposed to nonstop monitoring without any legal protection."[9]

The situation is not that different back home in the United
States, where law enforcement is investing in sophisticated
surveillance tools once reserved for soldiers and spies. While

the Federal Bureau of Investigation (FBI) runs surveillance planes over US cities for unspecified reasons, police cars are equipped with automated license-plate readers that can record our whereabouts at an astonishing rate, fast enough that more than 36 million scans were entered into a database for the San Diego area over a two-year period.[10] Other police departments in the United States are using cell-phone tracking devices called Stingrays to arrest people for tax fraud and other humdrum crimes, though they won't admit that these devices even exist without legal pressure from civil-rights groups like the ACLU.[11] A mind-set of constant surveillance is also spreading into American public schools, where some principals, even in small towns in Iowa, are wearing police-style body cameras to record their interactions with fourteen-year-olds.[12]

If it sounds like government agencies are driving the spread of surveillance technologies and techniques in contemporary America, it's important to remember that the private sector is an equal partner in this lucrative business. In addition to working with government agencies to create backdoors into our private communications, corporate America sells the drones, cameras, sensors, computers, and expertise needed to run a surveillance-obsessed society. While one US bank experiments with retina scans for ATM identification, another uses biometric voice-printing during customer service calls to confirm a customer's identity, though it didn't bother to let anyone know.[13] ("MILLIONS OF VOICEPRINTS QUIETLY BEING HARVESTED AS LATEST IDENTIFICATION TOOL," a headline in the *Guardian* reported ominously.)[14] Credit-card companies can lower our credit scores the moment we make a purchase in a neighborhood where repayment histories are sketchy, while stealthy marketers track our behaviors with increasingly unnerving precision.[15] A woman whose pregnancy ended in the sixth month received an unsolicited package of Enfamil baby formula with the message "You're almost there!"—an agonizing intrusion into one woman's private grief that resulted from a random marketer exploiting the fact that she signed up for something on an unrelated pregnancy website.[16] Meanwhile, so-called smart thermostats, TVs, coffeemakers, door locks, washing machines, and other devices for home, office, and health and recreation are sending huge quantities of information about what we watch, eat, buy, and even say to their manufacturers, who share our data with unknown third parties that we might find disturbing if it were not happening behind a thick wall of legal fine print and corporate double-speak.[17]

Not surprisingly, some of the biggest companies of the twenty-first century are getting rich off monitoring and sharing vast quantities of personal data that we happily (and perhaps not-so-happily) divulge in the name of community, connection, and convenience.[18] Facebook and other social-media sites have become essential and often joyful tools for modern living, even if we recognize the occasional creepiness with which chairman Mark Zuckerberg conducts his megabillion-dollar business. When not engaged in experiments to shape the emotions of its users, for which it was roundly denounced in 2014, or assembling the world's largest private database for facial recognition, Facebook is watching how users read its News Feed feature and is recording whenever we linger over a particular story—even if we don't click the Like button.[19] Zuckerberg's employees even have the ability to identify people in photos that don't include faces—posture, clothing, or even the back of one's head is enough to tag us.[20] Of course, some alternatives to Facebook aren't much better about protecting privacy. The popular Brazilian startup Facegloria looks just like the original, but it filters out anything "sinful" that offends its conservative evangelical owners.[21] Sorry, gay Brazilians—no friends for you in God's Panopticon!

Yet Facebook and other social media are offering something that many people want: the ability to keep close tabs on friends, family, coworkers, pets, and property. This is why we should be aware of the smaller players in the surveillance landscape—all the Little Brothers monitoring one another in the nervous age of President Trump. Much of it is harmless or even a source of joyful connection between family and friends, teachers and students, pastors and parishioners; but some of it can feel burdensome and strange. Whether it's an automated home-security drone that zips over your property whenever it detects a threat, an app for jealous lovers trying to spy on their partners (yep, there's an app for that), "CIA-backed surveillance software" marketed to public schools to track social-media accounts of teenagers, a facial-recognition system that allows ministers to know who's sitting in the pews on a given Sunday, or a Duke University professor who secretly films women in cafés in the name of art—it is clear that surveillance confronts us from almost every direction, not just from faceless government agencies and multinational corporations.[22] As a *Guardian* article posed the question: "Just how easy it is to uncover the intimate details of a complete stranger's life?" Very easy, it turns out—especially when we constantly share our location, sometimes inadvertently, with friends and strangers. In 2010, as social media was exploding in user numbers, the website PleaseRobMe.com launched to highlight how much people reveal about their whereabouts, often in ways incredibly useful to thieves on the lookout. "The issue with location-based information," said the site's founder, "is that it exposes another layer of personal information that, frankly, we haven't had to think much about: our exact physical location at any time, anywhere."[23] Clearly, it's not just the government watching where we are, what we are saying, what we are buying, and who we are with. Increasingly, we are exposed to one another—friends, family, strangers—in ways that we have only begun to understand.

None of this should come as a shock if you've been following the news in the years since Edward Snowden's extraordinary leaks and related stories that seem to arrive with mind-numbing frequency—or if you've been watching television shows like *Black Mirror*, the popular British series that imagines the strange outcomes of existing technologies in the not-so-distant future. But what does it all mean? What will it feel like to live in a society making unprecedented investments in surveillance? Are we enhancing human happiness or undermining it? Will we be able to preserve pockets of dignity, autonomy, and privacy in a world of ubiquitous monitoring? I'm cautiously optimistic that we can learn to use surveillance technologies in a more thoughtful manner; that we can make better decisions about our personal privacy and home security; and that we can make wiser choices for investing our limited emotional and financial resources as individuals and as a country—but only if we start to ask difficult questions about the weirdness and weariness of living under the blanket of surveillance technology in the years ahead.

One can offer, at best, only a partial report on a sprawling phenomenon such as surveillance in contemporary society. The part that I have chosen to report on is not what interests most politicians or the mainstream media outlets, most of which prefer stories about looming threats that "require" new security measures, new fortifications, new secret archives. Almost nothing in the mainstream conversation about surveillance touches upon the thing that interests me: *the soft tissue damage* that it inflicts. What I mean by this is the sustained and often subtle impact of surveillance, its unintended consequences, and the intimate ways that it changes how we think and feel about the world. That is why this is not a book about Edward Snowden's revelations, nor the inner workings of the NSA, FBI, or Google, nor the constant peer scrutiny that drives our online lives on Snapchat, Instagram, Facebook, and similar apps. Instead, I'm chasing something far more slippery but no less consequential: the ethical, aesthetic, and emotional undercurrents that course through a high-tech surveillance society. What are the implications of living with these rapidly proliferating surveillance technologies and practices? What are the hidden costs of living in a society in which surveillance is deemed essential to governance, business, and ordinary social life? What are the emotional burdens and benefits of living in a surveillance-obsessed culture? And ultimately, what is driving the vast market for surveillance on an emotional and ideological level in ways that often transcend logic and reason? These are the central questions in a book that weighs some of the subtle impacts of surveillance in the United States.

Each of the six essays in this book provides a different angle on America's expanding surveillance regime. At times I put myself into the story, writing about my own experiences and going to places like London, New York, Colorado Springs, and Walden Pond that help me explore the strange shape of surveillance culture today. At the same time I draw widely from cultural history, popular culture, literature, and philosophy, relying on books, films, and ideas that bring the subject to life in new ways.

The book starts with a wide-ranging chapter ("Feeling Surveillance") that considers the emotional burdens of living under multiple layers of scrutiny. From the creepiness of cyberstalkers to the frustrations of citizen surveillance to the violent antidrone rage of Texas libertarians, the chapter explores the darker side of surveillance. Chapter 2 ("Welcome to the Funopticon") focuses on the joyful and participatory side of surveillance culture, something that might seem at odds with dour concepts such as Big Brother and the Panopticon, two powerful metaphors that continue to resonate in the twenty-first century. (The Panopticon design for penitentiaries allows a single watchman to put inmates on constant display without detection, a concept that has become crucial to the modern understanding of surveillance.)

In the two chapters that follow, I look at surveillance where it might seem out of place. In chapter 3 ("Growing up Observed"), I write candidly about the psychological and familial roots of surveillance sensitivity, often in a very personal way that suggests that biography can explain a great deal about our surveillance aversions (or the lack thereof). In chapter 4 ("Watching Walden"), I go off-road with Henry David Thoreau as my guide, hoping to escape the tentacles of modern surveillance systems for a brief moment of bucolic calm and autonomy. (Spoiler: it's not easy.)

Chapters 5 and 6 explore the strange business of surveillance in a very literal sense. In chapter 5 ("A Mighty Fortress Is Our God"), I fly to Colorado Springs to see how churches in the United States are being courted by Christian security companies that market their services primarily to their spiritual brethren. Finally, in chapter 6 ("The Business of Insecurity"), I land in New York City, not far from the 9/11 Memorial, to look at what is happening at sales conventions for the security industry, where a vast surveillance-industrial complex is emerging to market and manage technologies that range from nanny cams to video-equipped aerial drones for law enforcement.

I recognize that surveillance technologies are often useful, necessary, and well intentioned at some level: in the best-case scenarios, someone is trying to protect their home, their child, their colleagues, or their citizens from harm. Yet even a well-intentioned technology can have unexpected consequences, unwelcome byproducts, and subtle aftershocks that far exceed what is outlined in a user manual for a biometric scanner, CCTV camera, or drone. What if, at least *sometimes*, surveillance culture operates with a quiet inhumanity, eroding the "emotional liberty" that geographer Nigel Thrift has beautifully evoked? What if, at least *sometimes*, it functions like an orthodoxy machine, efficiently producing docile subjects that have internalized the needs of the system in which they are stuck? Such questions once seemed like the exclusive province of paranoid minds filled with visions of black helicopters—but not any longer. Even if they do not yet work flawlessly, even if they are sometimes run by people who are more like the bumbling Mr. Bean than James Bond, surveillance systems are already working to monetize our social interactions, to harvest our data, to render us predictable, and to make our passions and energies yield to those in charge. Often when schools, governments, companies, and neighbors wire up their property for electronic monitoring, someone is implicitly telling us *don't steal, don't speak your mind, don't run the light, don't leave THC traces in your urine, don't sign the petition, don't wear a Guy Fawkes mask at the mall, don't drive while black, don't relax, don't forget who's watching.* For some privacy activists, the election of Donald Trump added a new wrinkle: just after the 2016 election results were announced, an NSA whistleblower fretted that "the electronic infrastructure is fully in place ... and ripe for further abuse under an autocratic, power-obsessed president."[24]

Yet many people wonder: Why worry about surveillance if I'm not doing anything wrong? Why fret about it if I've got nothing to hide? To my mind, *I've got nothing to hide* has become one of the most disingenuous phrases in the English language. Often spoken with a privileged voice that assumes it can hide what really needs to be hidden, that it has the power to pull the curtains when the need arises, it is generally a hollow boast. Those who utter it are rarely prepared for someone to start burrowing into every forgotten email, late-night purchase, speeding ticket, or ill-considered Twitter message that will outlive their corporeal selves. Even a strutting exhibitionist has something to hide: certain diary entries, genetic predispositions, financial mistakes, medical crises, teenage embarrassments, antisocial compulsions, sexual fantasies, radical dreams. We all have something that we want to shield from public view. The real question is: *Who gets to pull the curtains?* (And increasingly: *How will we know when they are really closed?*)

Despite all this, you still might think that surveillance has nothing to do with you, that it's someone else's problem, that it's far from whatever you're doing right now. You might think that it's something that normal people can simply tune out, that it's just part of the background noise of modern living, that it doesn't feel like much of anything to people who aren't in a maximum security prison or hiding from an overseas drone strike. You might even think it has little impact on the healthy functioning of a democratic culture. This book will suggest otherwise.

CHAPTER ONE

Feeling Surveillance

One episode of the TV drama *Breaking Bad* begins with a wonderful surveillance moment. Walter White, a high-school chemistry teacher who has traded his soul for a meth empire, is sipping coffee and looking unusually pleased with himself. He is alone in some sort of industrial basement, standing amid shining air compressors and filtration systems that, as one of his criminal associates puts it, wouldn't be out of place at Pfizer or Merck. Certainly the high-tech equipment is more than adequate to supply what the show calls the "scabby tweakers" of Albuquerque with an astonishingly powerful high.

On this particular morning Walter has good reason to eye his underground lab with satisfaction. Driven by a toxic blend of hubris and humiliation, he is rising quickly in the drug underworld. No longer a broken middle-aged man reduced to moonlighting at a car wash, where he is mocked by high-school seniors with sweet rides and healthy bodies, he is now feared and in control. In some twisted fashion, the drug trade has helped him to discover what he imagines as his long-lost *cojones*, along with a previously undetected aptitude for savagery and deceit. This perverse quest for masculine autonomy is essential to his story: he craves independence, respect, power, and dignity. If he can't have it as a law-abiding teacher with a beater car and a terminal diagnosis, he'll have it as a gangster PhD with endless cash buried in the desert.

But on this occasion, still in the opening seconds of a characteristically taut episode, Walter's manly reverie is disturbed by an unexpected whirring sound. He walks a few puzzled steps before hearing it again. Suddenly he spots a new CCTV camera looking down at him, providing his criminal associates with a high-resolution view of his work habits. His body rigid with anger and humiliation, Walter storms around the lab like a great ape in senseless captivity, quickly realizing that there is no place to hide, no spot from which he is out of view. No matter where he goes, the security camera tracks his movements like a sniper with a scope—a visual parallel that the cinematography seems to emphasize. Gazing down at him from the elevated perspective of the CCTV camera, the viewer is invited to consider the great Walter White as a puny figure, impotent to avoid our scrutiny. Apoplectically helpless, he rushes toward the camera and thrusts a defiant middle finger at it, the very last thing we see before the opening credits roll.[1]

Walter's hatred of being monitored in his secret lair is palpable. For him the security camera is not just intrusive; it's emasculating in the most intimate way he can imagine. Later in the episode he hears complaints that he's "not man enough," to which he responds with raw anger, a symptom of his fragile masculinity—he can't stand being unmanned by another man's controlling gaze. Just as a crucifix on a wall is a symbol of hope and redemption for Christians, the CCTV camera is an icon of humiliation and anxiety for someone like Walter White, and perhaps even those who are far from the moral shadows where he plies his trade. Even for regular people with the proverbial *nothing to hide*, the rituals of surveillance culture can feel humiliating and exhausting—but what else does surveillance feel like?

We know it's not just what Walter White experienced. We know it's not simply the bummer of Big Brother, the post–9/11 tightening in the chest, the anxious sense of an alarm half-sounded. It's not simply the nervousness of living with imminent threats, or the shame and discomfort of negotiating the small indignities of the TSA and Facebook. It's not simply the panic of reading about the latest privacy scare, the latest drone strike, the latest police atrocity caught on camera, the latest breach of some perimeter somewhere. It's not even the shock of learning that our government is sucking up every speck of personal information in our digital lives and storing them somewhere in the Utah desert on a server farm straight out of *The Matrix* or some other sci-fi dystopia. Such revelations might wallop us into a permanent funk, as we forever wince at the weird fate of the republic, not to mention that loss of personal privacy, dignity, and autonomy. But that's only one way in which the machinery of modern surveillance touches our bodies and souls.[2]

Surveillance: it's also light as a feather. It overflows with libidinous energy. It makes us laugh at some innocent *Candid Camera* moment or leer at a celebrity caught in lurid wardrobe malfunction. It lets us hope that our property, and our loved ones, are a little safer from harm. It lets us imagine that the government can stand between our bodies and random acts of terror. Because surveillance tends toward the serious, anxious, and unpleasant side of life, we can forget that it can also bring happiness, love, and reassurance—we can forget that it has many forms, textures, and resonances. Depending on who you are and where you sit in relation to various systems of surveillance, it can feel very different indeed. This chapter sketches some of the heavier ways of *feeling surveillance*: boredom, rage, indifference, anxiety, and even madness. (Of course there are many other feelings to be considered, and chapter 2 looks at some of the happier experiences that are driving the expansion of surveillance culture.) We've become so habituated to the presence of surveillance that we hardly seem to notice its bodily impact, the way it roils the senses, the confusing and contradictory ways that it encourages us to feel.

One thing is increasingly clear: we live in its world now. As we move through this maze of sensors, monitors, and electronic archives, trading scrutinizing glances with people and machines, dimly aware of the traces we leave behind everywhere, we experience a dizzying array of security-related feelings: confusion, fear, delight, relief, desire, concern, reassurance, safety, certainty, weariness, wrath, exhaustion, hope, melancholy, indifference. While surveillance in the vein of *1984* (George Orwell's dystopian novel that introduced the world to Big Brother) can feel ominous, creepy, or brutally invasive, most forms of surveillance evoke a blasé shrug. *Whatever*. Some even thrill us with the miracle of seeing and hearing from afar—their Dick Tracy powers of detection. Think about how much has changed. Two hundred years ago, optical surveillance meant peeking through a keyhole. Now anyone can order a video-equipped drone to hover above sunbathing neighbors, creating a Peeping Tom's delight to which there is no legal remedy, only ethical queasiness and YouTube. Meanwhile the rest of our bodies are increasingly exposed to various forms of sensing, sorting, and archiving. Voiceprint technology might be handy for accessing one's bank account without a card, but it also raises the possibility of surreptitiously being identified whenever one speaks in public.[3] Some airlines are monitoring passengers' food intake—but not because they're concerned about our health. It's to keep track of requests for halal meals to expose the hidden link between lamb chops and terror.[4] Not even the invisible realm is safe from surveillance. Hoping to use subtle biological cues to flush out nervous terrorists in a crowded public space, China's government is developing an emotional X-ray machine that uses "hyperspectral imaging to detect the amount of blood in oxygen and calculate stress levels."[5] Even banal objects are turned against us. Enter a hotel elevator with a towel you're trying to permanently "borrow," and a sensor will notify house-keeping and you'll have a very awkward conversation at reception.[6] Ratted out by the microchip in the bath towel? What a strange new world.

Our culture is vibrating with the feelings of surveillance, and they are more various and subtle than the best novelists can imagine. Still, the bodily impact of surveillance demands attention now—even if we are not quite up to the task. If we have produced the most elaborate, cross-referenced multi-modal system of observing, sorting, and remembering in the history of the world—a system far beyond the best efforts of Joseph Stalin or the most censorious ministers of Puritan New England—why wouldn't this omnipresent system have subtle effects that we have only begun to understand? Why wouldn't it register on our flesh, shaping its internal contours in ways that are not necessarily welcome, and not necessarily in the best interest of our liberty, autonomy, and dignity?[7] We have become masters of high-tech surveillance, culturally speaking, but it has also mastered us, working its way into our bodies in ways that are powerful, mysterious, and often insidious.

After all, surveillance invites us to share its worries. It wants us to screen potential dating partners on websites that can expose criminal records. It requires our bodies to wait in a line while our bags are scanned for bombs. It asks us to wonder if *what we type* and even *how we type* might give away our identity to an authoritarian regime eager to stamp out dissent, now that keyboards can identify anyone from their unique "keystroke dynamics."[8] It asks us to think about the pattern that our VISA purchases suggest, at least if we know that credit-card companies make interest-rate adjustments depending on how and where we use our cards. It invites us to feel self-conscious about how we appear to someone who may be watching, to flush at the realization that our discreet under-wear adjustments were recorded on CCTV and might end up on YouTube or *America's Funniest Home Videos*. It asks us to produce the ideal face of a compliant, nonthreatening citizen—the furthest thing from a terrorist—whenever we spot the TSA or law enforcement. It asks us to modulate behavior in light of *how things might appear* rather that just being in the world without second thoughts. In short, it asks us to internalize an exhausting regime of predictability, to repress chaotic human urges and organic feelings, all to make sure the system doesn't misread us in a way that might cause problems. It even invites us to wonder how well the system knows who we are. As the novelist Philip K. Dick famously put it in *A Scanner Darkly*:

> What does a scanner see? Into the head? Down into the heart? Does it see into me, into us? Clearly or darkly? I hope it sees clearly, because I can't any longer see into myself. I see only murk. I hope for everyone's sake the scanners do better.

Living in a surveillance culture invites such existential queasi-ness: *Am I safe? Am I free? Am I wrong? Am I bad?* Such queasiness about the emotional experience of surveillance is not something easily tuned out, at least not entirely, even while sitting on a very privileged perch that offers the illusion of control over the crudest forces of regulation. No one can tune out the background noise of modern life, the subtle grinding sound that isn't always heard until we stop to listen—at which point we might hear something unsettling: a digital blip, a wire being pulled taut, a mechanical whirr, a heel coming down the corridor. Like an air conditioner, it's always work-ing on our bodies, shaping our environment, always in motion even when we're not. But what if we were free from the intru-sion of security-mindedness or the glare of the social-media spotlight? What if we were free from the feelings of watching and being watched in the age of Snowden, Snapchat, Google Analytics, and Homeland Security? In other words, what if we were really free from all this scrutiny?

Perhaps surveillance narrows the options, creating a particular emotional path to follow whether we want to or not, whether we realize it or not. Perhaps it's a path that power has cleared, a path that is antihuman, antirevolutionary, antihope, antisolidarity, antidemocratic, antidignity, anti-autonomy, antiliberty, antiserenity, antiprivacy. If so, then we are creating ways of feeling "safe" that work against our own best interests.[9] In the aftermath of the *Charlie Hebdo* shooting in Paris in late 2014, the philosopher Slavoj Žižek described how the "terrorist attacks achieved the impossible: to reconcile the generation of '68 with its arch enemy in something like a French popular version of the Patriot Act, with people offering themselves up to surveillance."[10] Who could blame us? We live within a system that rewards the pose of maximum compliance. "In contemporary society, fear has taken the place of moral norms," writes the scholar Hille Koskela. "The question of 'what is suitable' has been replaced by the question of 'what is safe.'"[11]

Naked Rage

FIRST VIDEO. A middle-aged man is talking on a phone in front of a store in the Seattle area. Although he's sipping coffee, he seems engaged in something important. Suddenly an uninvited videographer sits at his table and trains his camera on the stranger's face. From his voice he seems young, maybe twenty-five, not more than thirty. He's calm, soft-spoken, and weirdly polite—yet extremely upsetting to the people in his viewfinder, the people that I now see on YouTube.

"Why are you taking a video of me?" the man with the coffee wants to know.

"Why not?"

The man looks at him in disbelief. "I'm just trying to have a private conversation."

"It's just a video, man."

The man with the coffee seems to ponder what a physical assault would entail, but then settles for storming off in disbelief.

SECOND VIDEO. Now it's later in the day or maybe another day. An athletic young white man is walking out of a drugstore with his bike helmet in hand when he notices the camera pointed at him. "What are you doing?" he asks, skeptical and a little tense.

"Oh, I'm taking a video." It's the only explanation the cameraman ever provides, and despite the lack of affect in his voice the phrase is rendered as if it has vast explanatory power, as if he's saying, "It's all right, I'm a medical doctor." Playing with the semantic possibilities of this stock phrase— "I'm taking a video"—seems like it's part of the game.

The cyclist looks unhappy. "Why are you taking a video of me?"

He gets a calm, almost philosophical reply. "Why not?"

The cyclist studies him for a long moment. "I don't really care for other people just taking a video of me."

"Didn't you just come out of the drugstore?" the cameraman asks with utter calm, seemingly unconcerned by the rising threat of violence. "They have cameras in there."

"So?" The point is lost on the cyclist, who puts on his helmet and pushes past the videographer with less violence than some of his other subjects. Other people want to arrest the videographer or even beat him for recording their presence in a public place. An African American woman exits her downtown office when she realizes she is being filmed through the glass doors of the building. She walks up to the camera, puts her hand on her heart, and looks at him with a mixture of dignity and dismay: "It's not okay. You didn't ask me if you could take a picture of me, sir. . . . That's not okay with me. That's an invasion of my privacy and time. Why are you taking a picture of me, sir? This is America and I have a choice that you not take a picture of me." Other people seem even angrier when he approaches with his camera—people of color seem particularly irate at his antics. If he continues this project with random people on the street, he will almost certainly be harmed, so much so his subjects resent the presence of his camera. It's obvious in his videos that many people *hate* being filmed by a stranger, at least when they're prodded to really think about it.

We don't know much about the mysterious man with the camera. It's not clear if he's a provocateur performance artist willing to take a punch for his art or just a voyeuristic nut job. All we know is that he uploads his footage under the name Surveillance Camera Man and that, since 2013, his YouTube channel has gotten hundreds of thousands of views and a great deal of impassioned commentary, much of it intensely negative. No doubt, his videos are often painful to watch. Half of his unwilling subjects threaten to smash his camera, if not the face behind it. The other half look freaked out and scared. "Some mute creep taking pictures" is how one person describes him after just a few seconds of being filmed. Others imply that he's just been released from a mental institution. Hurt, angry, scared—those are the typical responses.

What is going on with Surveillance Camera Man? At best, it's a cruel social experiment to see how much people hate being filmed in public without their permission. (Answer: a *lot*). At worst, he's an asinine prankster without a conscience. Whatever he is, he's right about one thing: what he's doing is not that different from what the other security cameras are doing all day long. What's interesting is how most people want to maintain a distinction between the indignities of Surveillance Camera Man and the normal flow of surveillance in our lives. In a Twitter conversation called "Why Does Everyone Hate Surveillance Camera Man?," one person said, "There's a big difference between a camera passively recording everything and some dude actively shoving a camera in your face."[12] What is the fundamental difference? Is the drugstore or post office somehow more trustworthy, more transparent, more innocent in the purposes to which it puts its security footage? I don't think we have the ability to make that judgment in most cases. It's just that we're accustomed to institutional surveillance that almost blends into the background. When cameras come into the foreground, we seem to remember how much we dislike their presence. And if we can't do much about the security cameras in public places, we can push back against a single individual with a camera. We remember how much it pisses us off.

Some people are doing more than pushing back against surveillance—some are shooting back. In 2012, a group of libertarians gathered in central Texas to make a political point with semiautomatic weapons and a few drones from an online store.[13] These were tough-talking men who railed against the surveillance state through magazines, websites, and videos devoted to their project of maximizing individual liberty. Their hatred of state surveillance is visceral: you hear it in their language, and see it in their bumper stickers and t-shirts. *They're sick and tired of the surveillance state. They're not going to take it anymore.* On this sunny morning in the beautiful Hill Country not far from Austin, these young and middle-aged white men are engaged in a symbolic protest against surveillance drones: they're filming a video in which they blast drones out of the sky. With cameras rolling to record their antisurveillance rage, their guns start popping until a drone explodes midair. The men cheer one another like it's the Boston Tea Party for the age of viral video. These are middle-class men donning war paint, raging against imperial schemes, enjoying a vandal's orgy–cum–street theater in order to strike a blow against Barack Obama's surveillance state, as they see it. "The answer to *1984* is *1776*," one of them says darkly, before posting the video online (where it received a half-million hits and counting).

What makes these men so angry about the perceived Panopticon in their midst? For these men, state surveillance is slavery, not freedom. While they talk less often about corporate or peer surveillance, government surveillance is imagined as a form of abjection, degradation, and even emasculation (especially true, it seems, during the Obama administration). To listen to them talk on the radio or online, it's clear that the bars on the cage are shutting tight on men with deep investments in words such as *freedom, autonomy, privacy*, and *individual rights*. For many of them, I suspect that privacy and masculinity are inextricably linked. Confronted with the prospect of their own impotence, these men find it empowering to rage in the dark against perceived abuses by the system. Their collective rage creates an imagined community of resistance, a symbolic rebel army of brash patriots. Putting up a symbolic fight against the surveillance regime preserves an old-fashioned illusion of individual control for these men, just as embracing the latest spyware and CCTV applications does for other people.

As their old bête noir, Bill Clinton, used to say, I feel their pain. There's an element of pathos to their outsized protest. These blustering men are engaged in more than a lost cause— it's a sentimental enterprise that is symptomatic of their collapsing faith in social norms. Alienated from mainstream politics and the state that derives from it, these men have embraced a fantasy of last resort: maximum individual sovereignty. In many ways it's a masculine fantasy of empowerment (guns are no different). Shooting down drones (especially those they purchased), raging about Orwellian conspiracies, screaming about Obama's violations of person and property, imagining themselves at the center of a vivid political melo-drama—it's not changing the proliferation of actual surveil-lance technologies. It is, however, registering the humiliations of living within a culture of intense surveillance.

More than a decade ago, well before omnipresent drones and TSA screenings, the sociologist William Staples wrote insight-fully about the quasi-pornographic qualities of what he called "bodily surveillance." At its core modern surveillance is a "sys-tematic, methodical, and automatic" effort to control human bodies and their movements. It pushes toward constant ex-posure, a "state of permanent visibility" in which the threat is "the act of being watched" in either a literal sense (CCTV) or figurative (Big Data). Not only is the "methodical, technology-driven, impersonal gaze" quickly becoming an essential tool for postmodern social control, it is doing so in a way that casts the net of potential "deviance" ever wider. As we witness a "his-torical shift from the specific punishment of the individual de-viant to the generalized surveillance of us all," what separates the "criminal" from the "non-criminal" when both are sub-jected to the exact same monitoring? Staples is quick to note that surveillance regimes are far from egalitarian. In thinking of the inherent biases in surveillance architecture, he points out that we are not "all necessarily subject to the same quan-tity or quality of social control." But the net is being cast much wider than in the past, and middle-class white men cannot use race or gender privilege to circumvent the security screen-ing at the airport or CCTV at the bank. Indeed, they are feel-ing a form of political shame that is unfamiliar: the shame of exposure.

Underneath the macho posturing, something else is hap-pening among these libertarian men. If their response to surveillance is infused with various sorts of race and gender privilege, it is also a legitimate response to "social sadism made explicit," to borrow a phrase from the scholar Claire Bishop.[14] They're quite right to object to a government that treats one's very existence as criminal and in constant need of reassessment. *You weren't a terrorist yesterday*, it seems to suggest, *but you might be one tomorrow. After all, who knows what lurks in the depths of your soul?*[15] I understand why libertarians, or anyone else, would find this offensive and degrading. The fact that many antisurveillance libertarians are white men accustomed to the privilege of being relatively unmonitored only fuels their anger. Even if they're exempt from the worst abuses of a racialized security apparatus, white men are increasingly subjected to invasive monitoring.

Women have even more reason to feel angry about surveillance, which, as Torin Monahan puts it, "operates much more on the masculine and controlling end of the gender spectrum." More interested in ogling than providing security, CCTV operators watch one out of every ten women for prurient reasons. TSA body scanners are often experienced as a humiliating form of sexual harassment.[16] "I feel like I was totally exposed," said one woman, who was told by airport security that she had a "cute figure" before asking her to return to the full-body scanner. "They wanted a nice good look," she complained, prompting Texas State Representative Lon Burnam to say, "I think it's sexual harassment if you're run through there a third or fourth time."[17] What if ogling ("the giving of admiring, amorous, flirtatious, or lecherous looks") has more in common with surveillance than has been previously understood? Casino operators, cops, and security guards have all been charged with using CCTV for licentious purposes. Perhaps the surveillance gaze has something in common with the cinematic gaze that feminist film-studies scholars have described in classic films such as Hitchcock's *Rear Window*, Powell's *Peeping Tom*, and other films that depict the camera as a "weapon of phallic power."[18] I suggest that surveillance brings the cinematic "male gaze" out of the theater and into the streets, where it is applied whenever it suits the needs of government bureaucrats, corporate profits, and creepy individuals. But men who might have relished the leering, asymmetrical male gaze in *Rear Window*, or even on a security camera, now find themselves the unwilling subjects of a similar gaze from the state and other institutional forces, all of which direct far more cameras and recording devices at them than Hitchcock ever commanded. For anyone assuming that racial, class, and gender privilege provides greater freedom from social scrutiny, it's no surprise that new forms of surveillance are often experienced as disempowerment, humiliation, and tyranny.

Invisible Men

On August 19, 2014, less than two weeks after a police officer's high-profile shooting of Michael Brown in the St. Louis suburbs, a young man named Kajieme Powell shoplifted two energy drinks and a donut from the Six Star convenience store in a nearby community. When the police arrived, Powell paced in circles and then started yelling "Shoot me!" After he allegedly failed to drop a small knife that he held in his hand, two inexperienced officers let loose a hail of bullets at the young man. *Pop-pop-pop-pop-pop-pop-pop-pop-pop*! And that was that: his body crumpled from a dozen shots from cops who had been on the scene for less than twenty-three seconds. Powell spent his final moments dying on the sidewalk in broad daylight.

There are two reasons we outside of the St. Louis area know something about this case. First, Powell fell to the ground just a few miles from where police left Michael Brown's corpse on the hot summer pavement for more than four hours.

Like Brown, Powell was a young African American in a poor neighborhood. Like Brown's death, Powell's death would receive more attention than most police shootings in the United States. But Powell's story was short-lived in many ways. Cable news had little to say about the shooting, other than to note its eerie similarity to the Brown case. Powell became a mere footnote to the Brown shooting, which attracted a month of consistent national and international media coverage.

A second reason sets Kajieme Powell apart from Michael Brown: a bystander recorded the whole tragic event on a cellphone camera.[19] When I first read about this graphic video of a man's last minutes on earth, I didn't want to watch it. But I had been thinking about the extraordinary attention given to a similar video in late August 2014—the beheading of American journalist James Foley in Iraq. Nothing rattles American journalists like the death of one of their own, which may explain why Foley's execution received an extraordinary amount of coverage, while almost no one heard about Kajieme Powell. There were two gruesome videos of Americans being killed in the same week, but the attention of the corporate media went to Foley. What was less important, less awful, less tragic about the Powell case? That he may have been mentally ill? That he was in the American Heartland rather than some exotic locale? That he was black?

I searched for the Powell video with some hesitation. Although I refused to watch the Foley beheading, I had seen the infamous Rodney King video on several occasions and even showed it while teaching a class. I assumed I could put on my scholar's hat and bear witness to whatever happened to Kajieme Powell without it hitting me too hard. But that's not what happened: I felt a spasm of grief as I watched the video. Watching a human life ending so abruptly and so needlessly is an agonizing experience. I've long been inured to the horror of make-believe death that we see in Hollywood action films and on police procedurals like *CSI: Miami*. I don't know that I've seen an actual death on film, at least not the death of someone whose name I knew, someone I was watching from street level. Like most people, I've seen some footage from a drone strike on the evening news, in which we are looking down on targets (actually, human beings) who suddenly are maimed or killed for geopolitical justice (or so we are told). The footage inevitably draws a comparison that I detest—*it was like watching a videogame*. But nothing about the shooting of Kajieme Powell is like a videogame. It is raw, sudden, shaky. It has narration, a very poignant play-by-play from the eyewitness with the camera. It has visceral impact.

"Powell looks sick more than he looks dangerous," the journalist Ezra Klein observed about the video, lamenting the fact that the St. Louis police seemed primed for deadly force rather than patient negotiation with an apparently sick man. "If the police had been in their car, with the windows rolled up, he could have done little to hurt them," Klein noted. "There is no warning shot, even. It does not seem like it should be so easy to take a life."[20]

Surveillance conducted by citizens, or *sousveillance*, is supposed to shield us from the worst abuses of the state. It's supposed to act as a deterrent, as well as a way of making law enforcement accountable to the communities it serves. For this reason, community activists often sound optimistic about the corrective power of sousveillance—it *feels* like one of the great tools for curbing police misconduct and safeguarding the lives of the most vulnerable among us. As Black Panthers founder Bobby Seale recently said, "I tell the youth today, ever since Rodney King, I say today, you don't need guns. Let's use the technology to observe the police."[21] But he picks a tricky example to inspire faith in citizen surveillance: despite the bystander video, and in some ways *because* of the infamous video that showed King charging the officers along with their horrific beating of the unarmed motorist in 1991, all of the LAPD officers were acquitted in the highly publicized case.

Of course, citizen surveillance may have other benefits, and some of these seem genuinely hopeful. Writing in *MIT Technology Review* in 2016, Ethan Zuckerman notes that citizen surveillance can inspire and inform even when it does not prevent police misconduct. "Sousveillance offers fuel for the activists who are trying to turn powerful images into justice and systemic change," Zuckerman writes. "And most critically, ubiquitous cameras and viral video means we are now all aware of America's epidemic of civilian death at the hands of the police."[22] In other words, sousveillance might not stop police misconduct from happening, it might not lead to an arrest or conviction, but it might educate the public about these tragic interactions between African Americans and law enforcement.

That is cold comfort to the family of Kajieme Powell and others like him. While it is encouraging to realize that citizen cameras can instantly connect to YouTube, or to wonder if police will feel differently about the use of force when they are required to wear body cameras, we shouldn't forget the extent to which power is asymmetrically wielded against impoverished communities of color in the United States. In cases such as Powell's, sousveillance seems far from its utopian promise to level the playing field. Mostly, what we get from his video is knowledge, not justice—a documentary record, not a preventative measure that stops the abuse. Because of the video, we know the police were on the scene for only twenty-three seconds before discharging their weapons. We know that Powell did not have his knife overhead in a stabbing gesture as police claimed, but down by his side as he walked erratically toward the cops. We know what witnesses were saying as the tragedy unfolded. We know something of what people were feeling, their fear, anger, and even resignation, as these gruesome events went down. We hear the distraught voice of the man filming the scene from before the arrival of the cops, through the shooting, and for several minutes afterward. We hear him talking to other African American men in the street. "Here we go again. They just killed this man. He's dead.... I've got everything on camera. Oh my God.... I got everything on tape. They could have tased him or shot him in the leg. Oh my fucking God, this again?" Later in the recording we see at least four African American men holding up their cameras as the police approach them to clear the street. The camera is their only protection against the police, but it's not enough, at least not for someone like Kajieme Powell, at least not yet. No matter how much we might feel the stirring of utopian possibility when we think about citizen surveillance, right now it's not enough to save a young black person. For people historically pushed into the sort of social invisibility that Ralph Ellison explored in the 1952 novel *Invisible Man,* electronic visibility is not always enough.

Citizen surveillance is in its infancy, and its real power is not yet known. If we have faith in the power of ordinary people to document the truth of their lives, we should have a sense of hope and possibility about sousveillance, as long as it's not seen as a high-tech panacea for chronic social ills. After all, not everyone has the same ability to deploy citizen surveillance. The Italian sociologist Andrea Brighenti recalls protests in which visibility was the essential issue for him and his radical friends. "I personally remember more than one anticapitalist demonstration where one of the culminating points was someone climbing up to a bank's CCTV installed well above the street level in order to put a thick black plastic bag around it — in a kind of postmodern version of the blinding of Cyclops."[23] The celebrated street artist Banksy might feel similarly empowered, as might the Bay Area firebrands who run the "Filming Cops" project. But the politics of visibility are much trickier for poor and working-class people of color in America, people for whom blinding the Cyclops is often an impossibility.

Nanny-Cam Horror

The surveillance camera, as if bored with nothing to do, began to scan the house in close-up. The superb lenses, representing the most advanced optical technology, showed every detail with unnerving clarity. The camera panned along the plate-glass windows of the lounge and dining room. The undisturbed furniture could be clearly seen, even a clock registering 8:20 on a mantelpiece.

—J. G. BALLARD, *RUNNING WILD* (1988)

"There's always the crazy thoughts you get from watching the news stories about people catching their nanny on the 'nanny cam' doing terrible things to their kids," said one young mother in Colorado to Fox News. "It can be pretty scary."[24] No doubt, it often feels scary for parents who are watching the news—nanny-cam horror stories are everywhere. Almost 400,000 views for a Fox News clip called "What Is Really Going on When You Are Away." Two million hits for "Home Invasion in Millburn NJ Caught on Nanny Cam—Brutal Beating in Front of Daughter June, 2013."[25] Nine million views for "Child Abuse—Nanny Caught on Tape," in which the mother explains, "I probably never would have suspected if not for the camera.... It scares me to think what could have happened to my children."[26] Far less attention is paid to the statistical rarity of nanny abuse.[27] Far less attention is paid to the story of a Florida nanny wrongfully imprisoned because a nanny cam, which records at 5.5 frames per second instead of the normal thirty, made it appear that she was violently shaking a child. After two and a half years in prison, the nanny, a Peruvian immigrant named Claudio Muro, was cleared of any wrongdoing and filed suit against the camera manufacturer.[28] Instead, the stories pile up on tabloid television and online: "Monster Nanny," "Killer Nanny," "Abusive Nannies Caught on Video," "You Can't Be Too Careful," "Horrific: 96-year-old Elderly Woman Tortured," "Babysitter Swings Infant into Door Frame," "Nurse Caught Peeing on Kitchen Sink." One ethnographer has shown how parents in Brooklyn use nanny cams, cell phones, and parent blogs with names like "I Saw Your Nanny" to watch their West Indian employees with almost as much vigilance as their own children.[29] This is how race, class, gender, and immigration status can conspire against someone: bad-nanny videos are circulating like crazy in the news media and online, while their abusive employers remain almost invisible. In the first category are many working-class people of color and recent immigrants, almost all of them women; in the second category is generally the white middle class. (As one scholar noted, "Race and ethnic differences between the employer and the employee are distinctive characteristics of domestic service in the United States.")[30] Fear is pushing these devices into the homes of millions of Americans, with little regard for their impact on children being raised under new forms of surveillance, on parents feeling obliged to monitor the home front while at work, or on domestic workers who must labor under increasing scrutiny. One product review of these devices in the *Wall Street Journal* alluded to "the apparent creepiness of having a running Web recording of our private living spaces," as well as the danger of having endless video footage uploaded to the Cloud with only a password to shield it from hackers, but the author quickly decided that it was worth the risk for the "peace of mind" that the camera allegedly provides its owner.[31]

Yet the nanny cam sees more than just the nanny, of course: others ignore its gaze at their peril. Realtors are warned to look out for surveillance devices in the homes they are selling: "You and your buyers should walk through every home like there is a nanny cam recording your private conversations. If you are recorded, the information gleaned from your private conversations with buyers could be used against you in negotiations."[32] Spouses are not safe from scrutiny. "I've been spying on my husband for a month now," confesses one puckish English writer.

> Ever since our house was fitted with a home safety device called Piper, all domestic privacy has been eroded. It's not so much a nanny cam as a husband cam — a boredom cam that I can call up on my tablet from anywhere in the world, allowing me to watch our sun-blanched sitting room in Beverly Hills from sodden London, curse my husband for leaving the TV on standby, and myself for allowing our bird of paradise plant to die.[33]

Not every parent uses surveillance technology to watch their nanny, as I know from my mother's work in several private homes in the 1990s and early 2000s, though you can never know for sure — cameras are hidden inside teddy bears, clocks, and baskets (as one Airbnb user discovered, to his distress).[34] And not every parent imagines the nanny as a figure of imminent monstrosity — but I suspect that nanny cams are creating a climate that often works against such humane relations. Prescient as ever, J. G. Ballard imagined the impact of such technologies more than a generation ago: "With its passive and unobtrusive despotism, the camera governed the smallest spaces of our lives," he wrote. "Even in the privacy of our own homes we had all been recruited to play our parts in what were little more than real-life commercials."[35] It's a sobering vision of the future of the wired American home, but it seems hard to avoid when the news is filled with sensational headlines like

"NANNY CAM CATCHES WOMAN ATTACKING INFANT, POLICE SAY." Describing events in the Bay Area in 2016, the ABC affiliate article is accompanied by a mug shot of a dark-skinned Latina, yet another nanny horror story to keep white, middle-class parents in the market for high-resolution cameras to protect their kids from an overhyped threat.[36]

Vigilance Fatigue

Writing in *FBI Law Enforcement Bulletin* in 2012, a psychologist named Meredith Krause described the risk of what she called "vigilance fatigue" for law enforcement and other professionals charged with threat detection, risk assessment, long-term surveillance, and "decision making under uncertainty" in the years since 9/11. With an eye toward the creation of "proactive countermeasures designed to bolster vigilance," Krause looked at four factors that contribute to vigilance fatigue: "overwhelming pressure to maintain exceptional, error-free performance," "prolonged exposure to ambiguous, unspecified, and ubiquitous threat information," "information overload," and "faulty strategies for structuring informed decision making under conditions of uncertainty and stress." Although Krause summarizes existing research that "underscored the negative impact of stress on vigilance" in order to find ways to make security professionals more efficient in their jobs, we might think about the converse for a moment: the negative impact of vigilance on stress. Moreover, we might think about ordinary people instead of simply considering the plight of security professionals. If some FBI agents lack the "mature tradecraft" needed to avoid the state of "degraded vigilance," as Krause coolly puts it, they can always choose another line of work if the burdens of surveillance are too onerous. The rest of us are not so lucky. Lacking proper training or even the vocabulary to describe the emotional burden of surveillance culture, ordinary citizens might be even more vulnerable to vigilance fatigue. Regular people are often stuck in a condition of "prolonged exposure" to "information overload" about proliferating threats that require "informed decisions" and "error-free performance" to keep us safe from the danger du jour (al-Qaeda, cyberstalkers, online pedophiles, hackers, or micromanaging bosses). In this sense we might suffer as much vigilance fatigue as burned-out security professionals, who at least have some control over the corporate or governmental surveillance systems they operate.[37] By contrast, citizens are often pawns struggling to survive a wearisome game that they barely understand.

What would it be like to be Asad Dandia, an idealistic young Muslim activist (and US citizen) living in Brooklyn, who learned that the NYPD was monitoring his charity work, even to the point of sending an informer to infiltrate his circle of friends, whose main activity was distributing food to the poor? In early 2012, Dandia invited a friendly stranger to his parent's home, fed him dinner, and invited him to stay the night as a guest of the family. When he later learned the man's true identity as a police informant, Dandia was horrified to have offered him hospitality and intimacy. The experience changed him. He lost trust in his neighbors and began to worry about his photo being taken. "I used to try to be as inclusive and public as possible about my charitable work," he lamented in a blog post. "Now, I communicate mainly with people I know personally."[38] For simply feeding the poor—or, more specifically, for being a young Muslim in Brooklyn—he now has to look over his shoulder, second-guessing even his most benevolent impulses before they can be used against him. What an exhausting way to live—yet not that different from what many people experience in post–9/11 America. Accidents of birth and circumstance might intensify the emotional burden of surveillance for those without means, without documents, and without certain forms of racial and gender privilege, but nothing exempts us entirely from having to swim against the vast tide of uncertainty and vulnerability that surveillance is designed to manage.

In true twenty-first-century fashion, the responsibility for our salvation is ours alone: if only we choose the right service, the right security system, the right password, the right neighborhood, the right school, and the right fortification, we might reach the nirvana of total security, that elusive place of serenity and bliss that beckons to our insecure souls like a tropical island resort in the dead of winter. In this cruel fantasy, we're asked to deal with insecurity on our own, secure the perimeters on our own, endure the endless vigilance on our own. We're not huddled together like Londoners in a tube station holding firm while the Luftwaffe did its worst to the streets above. Instead, we're atomized, disconnected, free-floating, privatized, insecure creatures with an immense social weight balanced on our individual backs. One scholar has written about the way in which people in the United Kingdom internalize widespread fears about terrorism or crime, making them their own personal responsibility, requiring each citizen to "vigilantly monitor every banal minutia of [their] lives," since "even mundane acts are now viewed as inherently risky and dangerous."[39] In an individualistic country such as the United States, the burden of personal responsibility must be even greater, even crueler.

For all of these reasons, surveillance is often exhausting to those who really feel its undertow: it overwhelms with its constant badgering, its omnipresent mysteries, its endless tabulations of movements, purchases, potentialities. Its rituals of compliance would test the patience of a saint—take off your shoes, stand in that line, remember the password, avoid the speed trap, go through the metal detector, hide from the boss, keep the hoodie down, don't make eye contact with the cops, don't joke with the TSA, don't act in a way that could end up on your permanent record. How could we not have vigilance fatigue from dealing with surveillance culture? How could our nerves not be frayed at times? How could our emotions be untouched? Yet almost no one in power asks how we're bearing up in the years since 9/11: they just add more cameras, more data collection, more scrutiny, more drones, more surveillance. Consequently, no one seems to notice that many people are tired of being wired up, inspected, counted, distrusted, and asked to sit still for whatever monetized, securitized, racialized, nationalized outcome someone has planned for our lives. While some young people seem more accustomed to the pressures and pleasures of a surveillance-obsessed culture, a lot of us are tired of what might turn up in our urine, tired of security guards at kid's sporting events, tired of metal detectors in high schools, tired of geo-locating RFID tags in our employee ID badges, tired of smart cookies that stalk us from site to site, tired of undercover cops in our mosques, tired of Russian hackers that rip off our credit cards, tired of civil servants reading our metadata in the name of freedom.[40] (Insecurity is the new banality.) Many of us are tired of the whole securitarian show, tired of second-guessing, tired of performing civic virtue for the camera and the omniscient database, even tired of how bad it must look to someone with a bird's-eye view of the sad little scramble toward safety and security.

In a bravura bit of cultural criticism, the African American novelist Colson Whitehead imagined the burden of living in a mundane surveillance culture. In an essay published in 2015, he envisioned just how dismal our visible lives would appear on camera, especially the dull and sometimes shameful bits that comprise the majority of our time between Facebook boasts about how well it's all going. In the language of reality TV, when someone is kicked off a show like *Big Brother* or *The Bachelor*, the most embarrassing bits are compiled into a "loser edit" that provides an ignominious farewell. At least in some poetic sense, Whitehead imagines the shame of visibility that the ultimate "loser edit" would elicit:

> The footage of your loser edit is out there as well, waiting. Taken from the surveillance camera of the gas station where you bought a lottery ticket like a chump. From the A.T.M. that recorded you taking out money for the romantic evening that went bust. From inside the black domes on the ceiling of the train station, the lenses that captured your slow walk up the platform stairs after the doomed excursion. From all the cameras on all the street corners, entryways and strangers' cellphones, building the digital dossier of your days. Maybe we can't clearly make out your face in every shot, but everyone knows it's you. We know you like to slump. Our entire lives as B-roll, shot and stored away to be recut and reviewed at a moment's notice when the plot changes: the divorce, the layoff, the lawsuit. Any time the producers decide to raise the stakes.[41]

Living on camera, even in a metaphorical sense, is draining because these systems add a level of scrutiny that is wearying, whether it's utterly abstract ("I have a feeling that the NSA might be reading this!") or utterly concrete ("I just found out our houseguest was a police informant!").

Michael Haneke makes this point beautifully in the opening sequence of his film *Caché* (2005), one of the great inquiries into the emotional stress of life under surveillance. A mystery in many senses, the film begins with a simple question: *Who is watching?* In the first several minutes, which include the title sequence, Haneke gives us a static shot of a quiet street in a European city. Nothing interesting is happening, not even by the standards of European art cinema, until we learn that we've been watching surveillance footage from a videotape that a French television personality and his book-publisher wife have received. Not only are the tapes appearing on their doorstep without explanation; the front of their house is the subject of the footage, which has been recently recorded from very nearby. The sudden awareness of being watched throws the family into increasing turmoil: *What have we done to deserve this scrutiny? Why are they watching us? Who is watching?* At first the videotapes are not particularly threatening, but the mere idea of being under surveillance is enough to unsettle the family, eventually knocking it from its secure bourgeois perch at the height of French society into contact with all sorts of hidden histories and memories (the English title of the film is *Hidden*). The film scholar Todd Herzog has observed how the main character, and perhaps the audience as well, internalizes the gaze of a CCTV camera over the course of the film, writing that the main character learns "to view his life after the end of privacy through the lens of the surveillance camera that has become a standard feature of twenty-first-century urban life: detached, objective, unemotional, unedited." Or, as another film scholar has noted about *Caché*'s ability to raise questions about the emotional strangeness of surveillance, the film imagines the phenomenon as "a visual model of 'intimate alienation' in that, although it represents an intrusion of the camera into once private spaces, it is also characterized by boredom, ambiguity and a lack of expression."[42] By often inviting us to share the unblinking POV of the security camera, Haneke's film suggests the fatigue of dealing with the subtle ubiquity of surveillance, the cold eye of a machine that infects one's sense of the landscape whether we know it consciously or not. In this sense contemporary surveillance culture creates a constant burden that is not quite Orwellian in scope, but rather something quieter, less dramatic, and less stark, but often equally exhausting.

What do we make of this endless vigilance that never lets us rest in the calm state of *security achieved*, that never lets us turn off the surveillance cameras and biometric sensors? In many cases people simply spin their wheels in noncomprehension, feeling overwhelmed and uncertain about what is really happening. At other moments they are surely overcome by its wearisome inevitability. Writing in the *Guardian* in late 2013, journalist John Naughton lamented the way in which surveillance has spread into our lives: "And yet the discovery that in less than three decades our societies have achieved Orwellian levels of surveillance provokes, at most, a wry smile or a resigned shrug," he marveled. "And it is this level of passive acceptance that I find really scary." He then quoted his colleague Henry Porter, who had expressed a similar thought: "Today, apparently, we are at ease with a system of near total intrusion that would have horrified every adult Briton 25 years ago." He continued, "We have changed, that is obvious . . . and, to be honest, I wonder whether I, and others who care about privacy and freedom, have been left behind by societies that accept surveillance as a part of the sophisticated world we live in."[43]

Yet most Americans are not quite "accepting" of surveillance. Surveys reveal a widespread sense that government and businesses are invading our privacy in very troubling ways.[44] They know something is wrong. Whether it's a traditional landline, cell phone, text, email, chat, or social media, "there is not one mode through which a majority of the American public feels 'very secure' when sharing private information with another trusted person or organization," according to a November 2014 Pew Research survey. The same survey revealed that 91 percent of Americans "believe that consumers have lost control over how personal information is collected and used by companies," and "a further 80 percent also felt that Americans should be concerned about government surveillance."[45] People clearly dislike a great deal of what is happening—yet they seem relatively compliant, even docile, in the face of new surveillance technologies and methods. How can we explain the apparent disconnect between how we feel and how we act?

Some of it may be an understandable choice to save one's energies for a foe less abstract, less omnipresent, less subtle. Fighting surveillance feels so overwhelming: should we stay home, disconnect our computer, get rid of our phone, and close the curtains? What are we supposed to do? Perhaps we can avoid vigilance fatigue by deciding not to get worked up about surveillance, by simply choosing not to dwell on the implications of new surveillance technologies, or by embracing the securitarian politics behind them. Why would we not look for an emotional survival strategy that can get us through these strange times of rapid change? In his influential essay "The Metropolis and Mental Life" (1903), the German sociologist Georg Simmel described the risk of living in the overstimulation of modern cities. He claimed that many people would, quite naturally, turn their backs on the noise and chaos of the urban environment and retreat into what he called a "blasé outlook" that resides, as I imagine it, somewhere between resignation and apathy.[46] More than a century later, many Americans seem to have adopted this sort of blasé outlook to deal with surveillance culture: it's easier to shrug in sadness than to shout in opposition, especially when confronting a phenomenon so ubiquitous, subtle, and potent.[47] Perhaps people are resigned to being on camera—or resigned to not thinking about it.[48]

It's easier to feel other ways. *I'm sure they have a good reason for whatever they're doing. If I've got nothing to hide, I've got nothing to worry about, right?* Perhaps this is why the most common response to the latest development in surveillance capabilities, from hummingbird-size drones to televisions that automatically monitor our private conversations, is a collective shrug of the shoulders. Surveillance seeps into another realm that had been behind the velvet rope of privacy, and few have the energy to kick up any real dust. Politicians don't talk about it, pundits don't pontificate about it, rappers don't rap about it: like global warming, the sheer size of the problem has an immobilizing effect. It's just something "out there," constantly humming in the background, an impossible enemy and an uncertain friend. It's implicitly sold as an electronic salve for vulnerabilities, a vast machinery of protection and defense, a necessary evil for a world filled with innumerable threats. It promises freedom from fear and at least some relief from risk, yet it delivers the opposite in equal measure: a gnawing sense that something is wrong, that people are vulnerable and exposed, that their perimeter is not quite secure, that they must remain forever vigilant.

Surveillance Anxiety

There is almost no way of talking about surveillance without talking about anxiety, a condition that has exploded in public and private consciousness in recent decades. And one way to get at the possible connections between these two defining features of contemporary life—anxiety and surveillance—is to consider the work of Scott Stossel. In his 2014 book *My Age of Anxiety: Fear, Hope, Dread, and the Search for Peace of Mind*, he shows how anxiety has been a debilitating part of American life throughout the postwar era, with its symptoms seeming to spike after 9/11.[49] I say "seeming" only because concrete data about mental health across time and place is often elusive. Yet we know this much for certain: America is an anxious society. Anxiety is higher here than in other countries.[50]

In fact, anxiety is now the most common mental illness in the United States, with one in seven Americans in its grasp and its sufferers outnumbering those with all other mood disorders. Although Stossel doesn't address surveillance, he does

provide some information that is relevant.[51] For instance, social phobics, some 15 million strong in the United States, are
exquisitely attuned to potential signs of negativity in their environment. Anxiously monitoring facial expressions, vocal
tones, and body postures that could suggest any hint of criticism or threat, social phobics run endlessly on a hamster wheel
of insecurity that rarely pauses. According to a National Insti-
tute of Mental Health study, their brains even respond differently to perceived (as well as imagined) criticism in the environment. Recent fMRI studies have recorded their amygdalas
firing with unusual intensity, even in response to *nonconscious*
stimuli, in a way that produces feelings of shame, anxiety, and
negativity.[52] Could omnipresent CCTV, invasive workplace
monitoring, and ambitious data-mining be part of the conscious or even nonconscious stimuli that make some people
feel judged and insecure? Could the general atmosphere of
surveillance add to these distressing feelings of being judged?
I can't help but wonder about the inherent anxiety of living inside a surveillance system that expects submission to its needs:
*don't steal, don't jaywalk, don't slack off at work, don't cheat on
the test, don't screw up your credit score, don't make that Facebook faux pas, don't bring scissors on the plane, don't let your
data get hacked, don't let the boss see that email.* With increasing frequency and stealth, surveillance systems are evaluating
our behavior in ways that can have a real impact. Whether sitting at home alone with the computer or walking to the bank,
people are being evaluated by corporations, state agencies,
and peers about their worth and suitability. Speeder? Credit
risk? Twitter follower? Terrorist? Facebook friend? Lacklus-
ter employee? Mediocre student? Home buyer? Some of it is
very Willy Lomanesque: *Are we well-liked?* Successful, trustworthy, legitimate, appropriate? A good person, a good customer, a good American? These are the implicit questions of
the surveillance systems in which we live. Is it any wonder that

15 million Americans suffer from social anxiety disorder—the excessive fear of being judged in public?[53]

But there is a solution—a pharmacological remedy for the ills of the system. Millions of prescriptions are written each year to quell social anxiety with powerful selective serotonin reuptake inhibitors (SSRIs). In the year I took one of these medications—while in my middle forties, as a two decade-long marriage was slowly unraveling—I found that it made a tremendous difference in my experience of the public sphere in general and surveillance in particular. I went from feeling the stereotypical anxieties of the surveillance-averse to being a chilled-out subject in the kingdom of calm. It produces a kind of chemical confidence in strangers, a blasé sense that being watched is no big deal. I sometimes wonder if we would have ever heard from Edward Snowden and learned about the over-reach of the NSA if he had been taking Zoloft.

Totalitarian Feelings

One of the best illustrations of the emotional price of living in a culture of deep suspicion can be found in the loosely auto-biographical work of the English writer Patrick McGuinness, whose beautiful first novel, *The Last Hundred Days*, follows the uncertain path of a young expatriate academic into a bizarre teaching post in the waning moments of Nicolae Ceau-sescu's Romania in 1989. "This is a country where fifty per-cent of the population is watching the other fifty percent," the protagonist is told. "And then they swap over."[54] As the young man feels his way into a corrupt surveillance state during the final implosions of the Cold War, the reader is given poetic insights into the experience of being watched from afar (and not so far away), both in the casual surveillance of neighbors peering between curtains as well as the more ominous forms of government intrusion into the lives of private citizens (if such a designation has any meaning in a totalitarian state). Even on his first day, as he negotiates the unfamiliar smells of Bucharest—"petrol fumes, the juice of rubbish bins, the sharp, empty scent of hot dust"—he is constantly reminded that he is being watched, as when a neighbor pretends to fumble with her keys after he notices her stare. "Nothing had changed, yet everything had that slight emphasis that comes from an awareness of being watched, as if the whole street were now suddenly in italics." (I love that sense of *emphasis* and *italics* as the byproduct of surveillance). As he senses the surveilling gaze on his body through his first weeks in Romania, he almost appreciates the "clandestine savour" as "another of life's minor reassurances, like regular bus service or dependable weather forecasts."[55] In a place like this, you can count on being watched, on never quite being alone in the world.

Soon, however, McGuinness suggests a darker side to the psychology of being watched. Once he had been living in a society of ubiquitous monitoring, "there was no need to watch me all the time," he explains, because "I would be watching myself. That was how it worked: you ended up doing the job for them."[56] The impact is subtle, at least to an external observer: "starting to sing in the kitchen, I stopped; in the shower I closed the bathroom door, even reaching to bolt it shut. This is what surveillance does: we stop being ourselves, and begin living alongside ourselves." In a sense, McGuinness is fleshing out what Jeremy Bentham and Michel Foucault predicted about the internalization of surveillance, giving it human palpability and psychological shading in a way that makes the novel a useful source of insight. "Human nature cannot be changed," McGuinness goes on to say, "but it can be brought to a degree of self-consciousness that denatures it." Of course, what festers as an internal state of self-consciousness does not remain exclusively within the self but rather is reflected back upon the world in dispiriting ways: "So it was that the feeling of guilt and furtiveness that had suddenly grown in me I now projected over the whole indifferent street." In the movies, the sense of being watched is part of a "ratcheting of tension that must always lead somewhere," but in reality it is "an aimless affair, a pedestrian shaggy dog story with no beginning, middle, or end."[57]

After reading such lines, those who are complacent about the proliferation of surveillance in Western democracies might wonder if this shift in consciousness, this lessening of social trust, is what is really being sold under the red, white, and blue banner of security. How different is modern America from the old surveillance states of the Eastern Bloc? Americans sometimes imagine they exist in a separate category of human experience, yet they now live under the watchful eyes of a violent state run by a thin-skinned billionaire with authoritarian tendencies, along with the increasingly constant supervision of Big Data and various forms of peer surveillance. In McGuinness's novel, a wizened Romanian intellectual, whose own memoirs are constantly being redacted and rewritten by state censors, asks the young protagonist: "You've heard of the Freudian talking cure, where the mere art of saying something to someone who is listening is sufficient? Well, we always have someone listening here, we are the Freudian state."[58] Surveillance is an extension of the violence that undergirds the Ceausescu regime, and only the few impotent souls who are too old and feeble to pose a threat are exempt from its inquiring eye.[59] "Retired technocrats, ex-apparatchiks, *bonjouristes* from the pre-communist era ... the police wasted little time watching them." To not be watched, however, was its own psychic burden, for it was a clear sign of being beneath contempt. The protagonist muses darkly, "It never occurred to me that irrelevance might feel much the same [as being watched]."[60]

Are Americans that different, or anyone living in democratic nations who imagine themselves in a star-spangled world quite unlike Ceausescu's Romania? And can a democratic culture thrive under the weight of constant monitoring? Will we shift our behavior when we sense that we're being watched—especially with the threat of violence behind that gaze? We can see the impact on the narrator of Octavia Butler's *Kindred*, a sci-fi novel about an African American woman who time-travels from contemporary Los Angeles to the antebellum South, where she risks certain death if she doesn't acquire the most acute form of surveillance consciousness. "As the days passed, I got into the habit of being careful," she explains after some harrowing experiences with slave masters. "I played the slave, minded my manners probably more than I had to because I wasn't sure what I could get away with."[61] This grinding awareness of being scrutinized was one of the most difficult lessons for a modern woman to accept in early-nineteenth-century America. "See how easily slaves are made?" she muses at one low point in her journey into the past.[62]

It doesn't require time travel to the Old South to instill the fear of being seen, the exhaustion of watching and being watched, the degradation of being monitored and judged, always aware of the results of nonconformity: bullying, insults, exclusion, scorn, blows. Surveillance consciousness is shaped in the most quotidian confines: school, church, home, shopping mall. It can come wrapped up with, or enabled by, anxiety, depression, and torturous forms of self-consciousness and mental illness. And it teaches all but the bravest or craziest to buckle to its demands, to do what is expected, to dance for the master somewhere at the center of its circuitry. "See how easily slaves are made?" And still we could ponder Octavia Butler's question about surveillance culture in its myriad forms today. See how easily obedient children are made in the domestic Panopticon? See how easily obedient friends are corralled on social media, where users quickly realize what sort of posts, what sort of pictures get the most likes and shares? See how easily obedient subjects are made under the whip of CCTV? Under the drones of Homeland Security? Under the pressure of surveillance, the prying eyes of bosses and colleagues at work, the withering scorn of angry parents, bitter priests, and cops writing citations for the mysteriously problematic "manner of walking along roadway," to cite the notorious statute in Ferguson that was applied almost exclusively to African Americans?[63] It all fits together. Self-consciousness, anxiety, depression—all exacerbated by living in a culture of constant monitoring, where at the far end of the spectrum is madness, the place where surveillance paranoia, no matter how justified in origin, spirals out of control. Let me end this chapter with a visit to eighteenth-century London—not to encounter Jeremy Bentham and his Panopticon, but instead a fellow Londoner from Bentham's world.

Surveillance and Madness

The Welshman James Tilly Matthews, an erstwhile architect and political reformer, could feel that he was being watched. Less than a thousand feet away, nefarious agents operated a secret machine that did more than keep tabs on his movements through King George III's London. Matthews was being subjected to something worse than what a CCTV camera could pick up today: he was wracked by a diabolical form of surveillance emanating from a mysterious machine that could track him personally, plant foreign ideas in his mind, and immobilize and even poison his body—whatever was required to undermine his self-assigned mission to broker peace between England and France. He called this machine the "Air Loom," believing it to be run by "spies" without mercy.

Because of such troubled beliefs, Matthews was imprisoned in London's notorious Bethlem (Bedlam) asylum, enduring harsh treatment that included the withering scorn of the asylum's apothecary, John Haslam. Despite the protests of political allies and a few doctors who attested to Matthew's sound mental health, Haslam refused to release his controversial patient. In 1810, perhaps to silence a campaign for Matthews's release, Haslam published a damning account of his patient's condition, ridiculing his fears of being watched and controlled by secret agents pushing buttons and pulling levers on a fantastical machine. As a result of Haslam's remarkably titled *Illustrations of Madness: Exhibiting a Singular Case of Insanity, and a No Less Remarkable Difference in Medical Opinion: Developing the Nature of Assailment, and the Manner of Working Events; With a Description of the Tortures Experienced by Bomb-Bursting, Lobster-Cracking, and Lengthening the Brain*, Matthews remained in shackles, and his case became known as the "the earliest clear description of schizophrenia in British psychiatric writing."[64]

What the Matthews case also provides, I suggest, is a prophetic metaphor for the psychological burdens of a surveillance culture in which individual autonomy is continually disrespected and increasingly eroded. Matthews may have been mad, but he was also on to something.

What Haslam mocked as "maniacal hallucinations" leading to a "deranged state of intellect" rendering the patient "wholly unfit to be at large," Matthews experienced as "atrocities practiced upon him by the workers of this infernal machine." Providing elaborate drawings and descriptions, Matthews explained that the Air Loom was designed to control his behavior through "magnetic impregnations" and "pneumatic chemistry" that could even penetrate walls to assail body and mind. What was the nature of this "assailment"? Like a paranoid protagonist from a Philip K. Dick novel, Matthews described a "gang" of spies with dramatic names, including an ancient doctor and the mysterious Glove Woman, who were hiding in the walls of old London. With the Air Loom directed at Matthews and other political figures, no one could retain their normal sense of self. No longer autonomous, human beings could be reduced to mere puppets, each of whom might fight against the hijacking of their minds and bodies but could never prevail. Once hijacked, a body could be made to do anything, often through baroque processes that Matthews described in vivid detail. Ideas were floated into a subject's mind through a process called "kiteing," the stress of being manipulated from afar was known as "lobster-cracking," while "lengthening the brain" produced "distortions" that could make someone a pawn in a political game rather than a self-governing subject. These were not the only ways in which spies altered his mind with their surveillance apparatus: "Cutting Soul from Sense" caused "his feelings to be severed from his thoughts," and "the extraction by suction of one train of thought and its replacement with another" was a torturous process he called "thought-making."[65]

Maddeningly, such surveillance was often half-detected. Even if he knew spies were nearby, Matthews could never quite see them. "On some occasions Mr. M. has been able to discern them," Haslam reports, "but whenever he has been watching their maneuvers, and endeavoring to ascertain their persons minutely, they have appeared to *step back*, and eluded his search, so that a transient glimpse could only be obtained."[66] Like the main character in J. G. Ballard's unnerving short story from 1962, "The Watch-towers," Matthews seems driven mad by his sense of being watched and an inability to see who is watching. Only at a moment of what seems like true insanity can the surveillance agents be seen. For Ballard's protagonist, it comes at the end of an Orwellian tale of ominous surveillance towers that may or may not exist in reality, even if he seems to see them clearly in the final paragraphs of the story. For Matthews, observing his torturers occurs during a similar revelation: a burst of magical telepathy in which he travels "magnetically" to their secret lair, and is finally able to glimpse the entire operation, an early vision of the NSA. If Matthews couldn't literally see them, at least he could hallucinate them quite vividly.[67]

"Even paranoids have real enemies," as the poet Delmore Schwartz famously said, yet surveillance alarmism is often seen as a sign of mental illness. Popular culture has been unkind to those who fret about being watched: crazy Mel Gibson as a crackpot taxi driver in *Conspiracy Theory* (1997), Dale Gribble reaching for his tinfoil hat in *King of the Hill*, paranoia as a sign of madness in *Shutter Island* (2010). At least Keanu Reeves losing his mind in *A Scanner Darkly* (2006) is the result of an actual conspiracy. For me, Matthews offers a powerful metaphor for a mind cracking under surveillance, one to which I am sympathetic today, even if he also offers more bizarre formulations that were either evidence of Haslam's bias against him or legitimate suggestions of a schizophrenic mind (or both). "In order to ascertain whether a person be impregnated," he allegedly told Haslam, "imitate the act of swallowing, and if he should perceive a grating noise in the ears, somewhat resembling the compression of a new wicker-basket, he is certainly attained." More indelicately, he swore that the spies could drain vital fluids from his body in a "very dexterous manner," extracting it "from the anus of the person assailed, by the suction of the air loom." "This process," we learn, "is performed in a very gradual way, bubble by bubble."[68] Schizophrenia may have been the real agent of his demise, not the Air Loom gang, but in either case, he suffered in body and spirit, with all signs of a body violated, an autonomous self in shatters.

Bringing surveillance inside our bodies is more than a metaphor or a matter of schizophrenic fantasy. As we blur the line between human and machine, with a bone-resonating sound system in our Google Glass headset and data being transmitting from our RFID-tagged heart valves, we will have embodied surveillance in strange new ways that we can hardly imagine. Its impact on our mental and emotional health is unknown, yet it is barely considered. No doubt, many people are struggling with unfamiliar feelings that new systems and practices bring into the most intimate quarters of their lives. And some people have been enduring aggressive forms of surveillance for a long time, and often for the ugliest of reasons, having to do with racial, gender, or class biases. With the indignities of the TSA scanner and the watchful eye of drones overhead, middle-class white men are finally getting a taste of what women, poor people, and racial and sexual minorities have long known about the burden of living under supervision.

At the very least we need to understand that *feeling surveillance* is a complex experience with real implications for individual emotional lives as well as our collective political lives. We need to consider the possibility that it feels worse to some people than others, and for very good reasons. And we need to consider the possibility that by embracing certain feelings that help us endure the airport, the gang-proofed school, or the suspicious boss, we may be doing more than just surviving the unforgiving institutions in which we find ourselves — we may be unconsciously signing the terms of our surrender to the status quo. Instead of rendering ourselves frozen with fear, apathetic, or hyper-alert in response to the scrutiny of the powerful, we could think about the alternatives, the other ways of being in our bodies in this country right now. We could even seek out an emotional space for autonomy, resistance, outrage, or utopian yearning, creating a space for saying "no" to the demands of surveillance systems, "no" to the generalized sense of fear and loathing that has haunted American life since 9/11, "no" to the bad vibes of fortress America and its obsession with monitoring and archiving our every move. It's possible for the country to feel different, better, freer.

CHAPTER TWO

Welcome to the Funopticon

It sometimes feels like a damp, Orwellian blanket has been draped over American life in the anxious years since 9/11. During this period of almost constant war and painful economic upheaval, ordinary Americans have witnessed the rapid expansion of a mysterious infrastructure of national security, the stunning proliferation of drones and CCTV cameras in public spaces, and Big Data's creeping omniscience about our innermost desires. Surveillance, it would seem, is an inherently serious business.

Yet surveillance has another register, a lighter side that can be seen with wonderful clarity in a commercial that Coca-Cola released in 2012. A bold celebration of CCTV as a tool of global grooviness, it was quickly enshrined as an "ad worth sharing" by the influential nonprofit known as TED as part of their "initiative to recognize and reward innovation, ingenuity and intelligence in advertising."[1] What was worth sharing, according to TED, was the way in which "security cameras around the world capture some of the lowest moments in human behavior—but they also capture some of the most beautiful."[2]

I agree that the spot is worth sharing, but not for the same reason. At first glance, the commercial seems like nothing more than a well-produced collection of the usual surveillance tropes: urban chaos, traffic accidents, random street hustles, all seen through the flat and impersonal gaze of CCTV. Yet even from the first frames, these otherwise ordinary security cameras seem weirdly alive with curiosity and feeling. Moving like gentle, thoughtful cyborgs out of the *WALL-E* universe, the cameras capture not the customary terrors and traumas of the nightly news, but unexpectedly harmless, even joyful moments of public life: "people stealing . . . kisses," "attacks of friendship and kindness," "friendly gangs," and "peaceful warriors," as the on-screen text explains during a montage of actual CCTV videos with surprisingly happy endings. The upbeat music of Supertramp's "Give a Little Bit" is the only sound we hear for the duration of the commercial, which presents itself with the smug superiority of a public service ad. Interestingly, we don't hear the first verse of the song—"There's so much that we need to share"—perhaps because it could remind sensitive viewers that we live in a post-Snowden age in which data "sharing" is quietly compulsory. Instead, we hear Supertramp's joyous refrain of "Give a little bit of your love to me," while we see sweet and playful scenes playing out on screen. After a minute and a half of small triumphs, most of them seemingly in the Middle East or on the Indian subcontinent, the final title declares, "Let's look at the world a little differently," while dozens of CCTV-camera images transform themselves into the familiar shape of a Coke bottle. It's a startling association—the surveillance camera as happy, trusting, and humane—and it elicited some online guffaws alongside the praise of the TED brigade. Not long after the commercial's release, an anonymous parody appeared on Vimeo under the title "Real 'Security Cameras.'" Featuring a series of gruesome murders and beatings caught on video, with some of the horrific Columbine footage thrown in for good measure, all set to the same Supertramp song that Coke employed, the video hints at the hollowness of the original. Whoever posted this little-seen parody (perhaps its un-named producer?) added this useful advice in their description of the video: "Welcome to the real world, bitches."[3]

This cynical, unnamed satirist is onto something: the seductiveness of what we might call "playful surveillance," a seemingly lighter mode of engagement with the tools and practices of surveillance culture that is becoming increasingly widespread, from Disneyland to our own backyards.[4] Although the enchantments, possibilities, and pleasures are real enough, we might still wonder about the implications of surveillance cameras hidden within children's toys, bird feeders, and consumer drones; the glorification of the surveillance aesthetic in film, television, and videogames; the fusion of gaming and surveillance technologies and techniques; the social-media apps that help us find friends if we share our data with unseen marketers; and many other surveillance products that blur the line between entertainment and something less savory. As surveillance and entertainment become increasingly intertwined, it seems that we are entering a new moment in which everyone's watching, everyone's playing, everyone's enchanted with seeing and being seen, sorting and being sorted. *Here I am. There you are. Isn't this fun?*

Welcome to the "Funopticon," a new metaphor that I want to suggest for the increasingly playful surveillance culture of the twenty-first century. Even as surveillance wraps itself around our bodies in ways that might strike some people as humiliating and exploitative, it is doing something else as well: it is operating in a way that doesn't always feel oppressive or heavy, but rather feels like pleasure, convenience, choice, and community. In other words, personal debasement increasingly exists in a dialectic with new modes of enchantment, connection, and entertainment that challenge the grim logic of the Panopticon, which Jeremy Bentham proposed for penal reform more than two centuries ago.[5] Of course, I'm not the first to chip away at the gray façade of the Panopticon.⁶ More than a decade ago, literary scholar Vincent Pecora joined what was then a small number of social scientists interested in tracing the underappreciated pleasures of surveillance culture. Looking at the rise of social media, which asks us to share intimate details of our lives with friends and strangers, Pecora suggested that "the possibility arises that, for a growing number of people in contemporary Western society, surveillance has become less a regulative mechanism of authority (either feared as tyrannous or welcomed as protection) than a populist path to self-affirmation and a ready-made source of insight into the current norms of group behavior."⁷

But even now, what has not been fully understood is how much pleasure is driving the expansion of surveillance in our daily lives—and how this playful surveillance creates a paradoxical space in which the cold mechanisms of control, monitoring, and social sorting are increasingly experienced as entertainment and pleasure, with billions of dollars at stake. While governments are willing to operate in this playful mode of information-gathering, the Funopticon is primarily the product of corporations looking to expand markets, create demand, and harvest consumer data to an unprecedented degree. It is also where ordinary people find themselves encouraged to play along with surveillance technology and practices, and most are happy to oblige in the name of convenience, connection, or simple fun. Yet we might ask: *What are the hidden costs of entertaining ourselves with surveillance tools and techniques?* In helping to market surveillance, sometimes quite literally, as something pleasant and entertaining, the Funopticon might serve a pedagogical function by teaching us how to think and feel about surveillance in ways that conform to the expectations of corporate Big Data and the NSA alike, not to mention those who sell its wares. As the Funopticon *softens* and *normalizes* surveillance, converting a source of fear and anxiety into a fountain of pleasure, it may encourage the raucous carnivalization of surveillance for reasons both hopeful and grim. In other words, the fun is real—but so are the trade-offs.

Ultimately, the Funopticon may provide a useful metaphor for life in what Nigel Thrift has dubbed "the security-entertainment complex."[8] Moving beyond the contours of the traditional military-industrial complex, it is, as economic geographer Ash Amin puts it, a new system that trades on "extreme sports, video games, theatrical citizenship, virtual war simulations, consumer spectacle, speculative behavior, and other forms of energetic ways of being in the world that involve extreme emotions." It is "engineering the gladiatorial consumer habituated to the idea of the future as permanently risky but also apprehended through enthusiastic forms of dwelling."[9] I think we are now being invited to "dwell enthusiastically" in a strange new place where surveillance becomes entertainment and entertainment becomes surveillance in surprising and sometimes disturbing ways. Before giving some representative examples of playful surveillance in action, intended to illuminate the Funopticon in its many forms, I want to explore the limitations of the existing paradigms for understanding surveillance and the possibilities in a new metaphor that emphasizes pleasure and participation. Finally, I will end with a discussion of David Fincher's 1997 film *The Game*, in which we see that the playfulness of the Funopticon is a complex pleasure indeed.

Dark Masters

Nothing looms larger over our understanding of surveillance than the somber faces of three European intellectuals whose lives span almost 250 years: Jeremy Bentham, George Orwell, and Michel Foucault. Their insights, metaphors, and even moods endure to the present day in both popular and academic conversations about surveillance, so much so that it is almost impossible to speak about the subject without reference to Big Brother or the Panopticon. Yet in the pages ahead I want to point to the historical particularity of these three wise men of surveillance studies; the ways in which they lived in a world whose specifications are quite different from those of our own; and the ways in which we might expand our sense of surveillance to incorporate fun, pleasure, and laughter, seldom a part of their dour visions of control, while still being aware of how many of the underlying mechanisms of the Panopticon or *1984* might remain in place. Although we need these three writers to remain in the conversation about surveillance and its implications in the twenty-first century, we also need new ways to account for the love, joy, pleasure, and warmth in our seemingly cold systems of social sorting and networking, and how those positive feelings are created, experienced, and even exploited. Doing so requires us to shift the tone of surveillance studies and to push beyond the grim contours of our foundational metaphors, beginning with Bentham's famous Panopticon.

Few worthies of the Enlightenment get a worse rap than Jeremy Bentham, the early-nineteenth-century reformer best known for his controversial designs for English penitentiaries. Eager to create a more humane alternative to the shackling of convicts in pre-Dickensian hellholes, Bentham tried to imagine a scheme in which mental constraints would replace physical ones. By locating a nearly invisible warden at the center of a specially designed circular prison, Bentham proposed "a new mode of obtaining power, power of mind over mind, in a quantity hitherto without example."[10] Because prisoners would never know when they were being watched in this so-called Panopticon, they would have to assume that they were under constant surveillance and act accordingly. Although the design was not widely implemented in English penitentiaries,

the concept of the Panopticon has become fundamental to surveillance studies in the age of all-seeing drones, omnivorous
dataveillance, and the sort of NSA activities to which Edward
Snowden has alerted the world. Yet scholars have long pointed
to blind spots in the Panopticon model in its original formulation or, as I'll discuss later, in Michel Foucault's expansion of
the concept in the 1970s. For instance, in an excellent article
about class and gender in the surveillance of young people in
northern English schools, two scholars have noted that "totalizing visions of 'panoptic' power also tell us very little about
how people situated in different 'social positions' respond to
monitoring by 'new surveillance' technologies."[11] With such
limitations in mind, the sociologist David Lyon has complained that the "mere mention of the Panopticon elicits exacerbated groans" among surveillance scholars who feel overwhelmed by its ubiquity.[12]

For this reason, scholars have been moving toward a less
totalizing model that takes pleasure, care, and desire into account. Following in the footsteps of sociologist Gary Marx, two
European scholars, Anders Albrechtslund and Lynsey Dubbeld, published a brief but provocative article in 2005 in which
they described the need for researchers to imagine surveillance
"not just as positively protective, but even as a comical, playful, amusing, enjoyable practice."[13] Lyon has also been opening up surveillance studies to such ways of thinking throughout his long and influential career. As he put it in one lecture,
surveillance culture is more than the sinister stuff that often
comes to mind—it's also a "fun" activity that we experience in
the "routines of everyday life," often with a guileless belief that
"we have nothing to hide."[14] For these reasons and many more,
surveillance scholars have been picking at obsolete paradigms
for more than a decade, looking for ways to account for the
brighter shades of surveillance experience.[15]

If the old paradigms seem a bit long in the tooth, it is not surprising. After all, Bentham, along with the equally influential Orwell and Foucault, are dead white men who never saw the twenty-first century's soft despotism in its full glory. They never saw the narcotic effect of electronic media on teenagers with iPhones and Xboxes and Facebook accounts, and never witnessed the real diversity of human experience in a way that wasn't inescapably bound up in their own privilege—racial, gender, colonial, or otherwise. What could the three wise men of surveillance studies know about the potential pleasures of social sorting in the age of social media and ubiquitous CCTV? What could they know about surveillance-based video games and blockbuster movies that celebrate the power of drones and other spy gadgetry? What could they know about miniature wearable health monitors that beam our vitals into the Cloud in the name of longevity, or granny-cams that help us take care of our aging loved ones? Not much, though we can't fault them for not living long enough. After all, Bentham made a valiant taxidermic grab for immortality in the halls of University College London, where his somewhat ragged corpse remains on display for the benefit of students and assorted visitors.

Corpse or no corpse, Bentham might have faded from view if not for Michel Foucault, who revived the Panopticon with a combination of theoretical genius and theatrical flair in the mid-1970s. His great insight in *Discipline and Punish* (1975) was that, beginning sometime in the nineteenth century, the power of the sovereign underwent a profound shift whose nature is fundamental to the inner workings of modern society— and the workings of surveillance as a technology of social control. Where once a criminal was beaten in a public spectacle that would wreak vengeance on his person and shock bystanders into submission (e.g., poor Robert-François Damiens, the failed regicide in 1750s Paris), by the nineteenth century we had entered a more insidious regime of internalized punishment that wore away minds and souls in ways that are disturbingly familiar. Using Bentham's Panopticon as his central metaphor, Foucault argued that overt brutality was no longer needed because we had learned to see ourselves through the gaze of an unseen "warden." The subsequent portrait of surveillance that emerges in Foucault's work and that of his followers is of a joyless regime of self-monitoring in which our authentic selves (if such a thing can be imagined) wither away, supplanted by institutionally prescribed visions of the normal, healthy, and sane. Despite the brilliance and originality of Foucault's analysis, it brought with it an emotional limitation that made it better suited to moments of anxiety and obligation than of laughter and communion. Heavy with Gallic gloom and post-1960s frustration, Foucault painted a gray and totalizing vision straight out of science fiction—not to mention a particular historical moment in modern France. As his biographer James Miller has suggested, Foucault was a privileged revolutionary whose vision of an all-controlling Panopticon was shaped by his experiences during the student revolts of 1968. A product of that chaotic and frustrating moment for the European left, *Discipline and Punish* has woven a melancholy spell over academic and journalistic discussions of surveillance ever since its publication in 1975.[16] As the book became a founding document of surveillance studies in sociology and allied fields—if not one of the most influential works of scholarship ever published—Foucault had an intellectual as well as a tonal impact on most academic conversations about surveillance, shifting the mood toward the somber, heavy, gray, and dark in ways that have both deepened and narrowed our understanding of the phenomenon.

Such emotional narrowing runs through much of *Discipline and Punish*. His chapter on the Panopticon begins with a typically dramatic scene in which a plague-infested seventeenth-century town tries to contain the disease through the utmost vigilance: "The gaze is alert everywhere," he writes darkly, as "inspection functions ceaselessly" throughout a village stricken with fear.[17] As he does with his earlier example of Damiens the regicide, Foucault is spinning an artful fable of oppression, a dramatic allegory in which the "penetration of regulation into even the smallest details of life" is made vivid and memorable far beyond the scholarly norm. In an extreme case of a forgotten old village overcome with a deadly infestation, Foucault finds a dramatic expression of a modern disciplinary society then just emerging. Lepers, plagues, madness, prisons—his examples are often vivid, dramatic, and extreme, even a touch melodramatic. Nowhere is this more evident than in his ultimate evocation of our own oppression in a newly fleshed-out metaphor of the Panopticon. More than Bentham's penological innovation, it is now a generalizable condition of internalized surveillance, a "state of conscious and permanent visibility that assumes the automatic functioning of power."[18] This is the "generalizable model" for "defining power relations in terms of the everyday life" that Foucault proposes for contexts far beyond anything Bentham imagined for certain prisoners. Like characters in *The Matrix* or some other dystopian sci-fi tale, Foucault's children are subjected to a "permanent, exhaustive, omnipresent surveillance" in a "cruel, ingenious cage."[19] We are all in the prison, whether we know it or not—that was the implication of his work.

The drama and force of his case against benign modernity is unmistakable. Rhetorically and emotionally, *Discipline and Punish* electrifies its readers due in no small measure to its author's handling of striking visual metaphors. One might question, however, as few have paused to do, whether some readers are seduced by Foucault's images more than his ideas. In other words, does his dramatic artistry overwhelm one's historical or sociological imagination? Though some later historians have rolled their eyes at his occasionally haphazard methods and penchant for exaggeration, he's not wrong about surveillance: he's just monochromatic in ways that we need to reconsider.[20]

Yet I understand why he was seduced by the Panopticon — and why it has weighed so heavily on our understanding of surveillance. In the back of the 1791 edition that I examined in the British Library, a reader can find two enormous foldout illustrations of the Panopticon that Bentham envisioned. So vividly is his model rendered, in word and image, that it is extraordinarily tempting to fall into its embrace, to be seduced by its contours, and to imagine it as a constant companion in the "matrix" of twenty-first-century securitization, which is far different from the conditions that produced Bentham or Foucault. Something so striking is difficult to leave behind, which has also been the blessing and the curse of the novelist George Orwell for surveillance studies: his monolithic vision of surveillance in *1984* has had an enduring, and sometimes distorting, influence on our understanding of the subject.

Because of Orwell's power as a novelist with a gift for striking visual images, *1984* rightfully became one of the central novels of the twentieth century, sometimes blocking out the sun, conceptually speaking. Indeed, it has sometimes proven difficult for scholars to imagine surveillance without Big Brother's brushy mustache popping into view, pulling the emotional register toward the heavy and grim. As a consequence, *1984* looms so large that it is sometimes difficult to think an original thought about surveillance without its outsized influence pressing on us. Yet his great book was very much the product of living in the unique time and place of Europe in the 1940s, in which the fate of the world was seemingly being decided in the battle between fascism, communism, and democracy. As if that wasn't enough to raise the stakes for Orwell's literary production, the author was also struggling with a precipitous decline in health that led to his early death in 1949,

not long after the publication of his bleak novel. While the
novel retains its universal relevance in many ways and is no
doubt one of the crowning glories of twentieth-century Anglo-
phone literature, I worry that it is getting in the way of seeing
the lighter side of surveillance that is emerging in the twenty-
first century. We're simply in a very different spot than was
the protagonist Winston Smith, in many ways (or so we like
to imagine). For instance, when Winston conspires to meet
his lover in Victory Square, he must take great pains to conceal his true purposes from the telescreens around the base of
Oliver Cromwell's statue. Now we bring our own telescreens
wherever we go: iPads, smartphones, digital cameras, and
the rest of the accouterments of electronic connectivity. Big
Brother is still at work, of course, but now a million smiling
Little Brothers share the burden of surveillance. What Orwell
imagined as misery—to live in a "place where there is no darkness"—has become a goal that we are eager to achieve through
social media and other forms of participatory surveillance.

These writers made the functioning of surveillance into
something simple to visualize, emotionally arresting, and dramatically powerful. Their metaphors set the stage on which we
now act in ways that are useful and inspirational—but also dis-
tracting and distorting at times. What Orwell, Bentham, and
Foucault couldn't foresee are the pleasant and banal qualities of contemporary surveillance culture, which often seems
far removed from the threatening and oppressive culture that
their work suggested. What we need, I suspect, is an updating
of their models to account for this strange new turn of events
toward the entertaining and glib.

A recent novel from the United Kingdom provides a useful re-
vision of the old surveillance paradigms. Jenni Fagan's *Panopticon* suggests that securitization will arrive with a whisper,

not a bang. The implication of her book is that melodramatic metaphors might obscure the incremental nature of the real changes currently under way, dulling our awareness of the slow slide into something undesirable. Liberties are seeping away drop by drop, not drained all at once. Fagan, a young Scottish writer, has created a fierce fifteen-year-old protagonist, Anais Hendricks, a troubled "client" sentenced to a residential care facility called "the Panopticon." Violent, orphaned, drug-addled, and abused, Anais may feel tortured, but the facility is not heinous—her social worker is less Nurse Ratched than harried grad student collecting data for a social work PhD. Indeed, what we see in this surveillance-themed novel is a world that doesn't look like *The Matrix* or some other sci-fi dungeon of gloom. Orwell's Room 101 is nowhere in sight. The new and improved Panopticon is less obviously authoritarian, less overtly oppressive. The implication is fascinating: the world won't get a radical makeover when surveillance becomes omnipresent, woven deep into our buildings and bodies, but instead it will look reassuringly familiar to us. The new Panopticon will have Wi-Fi, cappuccino, and vegetarian options. It will utilize the language of choice, freedom, and pleasure. It will speak casually about freedom and dignity. It will make us laugh and feel connected, with a lightness of spirit that seems, at least on its bright, shiny surface, very far from the world of Bentham, Orwell, and Foucault. It will make surveillance seem cool.

Softening Surveillance

The entertaining side of surveillance culture should not come as a surprise. Hollywood films love to celebrate the seductive glamour of surveillance systems, as well as the valiant attempts to thwart them. Popular videogames present CCTV as an exciting part of the action hero's arsenal, so much so that editorials fulminate about games that make us "too comfortable with the modern surveillance state."[21] Facebook and other popular social media are infused with the logic of surveillance culture, which creates systems for endless monitoring, sorting, and archiving of other people's behavior, not to mention our own, that we use to share funny videos and keep ourselves in the loop with friends, family, and former lovers.[22] Even traditional news programs now serve up endless CCTV footage as low-cost infotainment, often with the implicit suggestion that something hilariously or horribly real is going to happen: a child disappears; a bomb goes off; a celebrity melts down. With its implied promise of unmediated observation, CCTV footage is often presented, quite cynically, as the ultimate documentary pleasure in an era of insatiable reality hunger, a moment in which the most magical words are "Live—Caught on Camera!" To cite just one example: the ubiquitous Russian dashcam footage of traffic accidents, which has garnered a huge online audience for its jaunty presentation of death and destruction. Even mundane CCTV footage has found a new entertainment niche: popular apps now invite us to peep via ordinary security video feeds from around the world—parking lots in Japan, restaurants in France, beaches in Florida. One app promises "10,000 real time CCTV surveillance cameras," along with the ability to customize our "cam collection" and even vote for "favorite cams." Another app lets us shake our phone to change the CCTV feed whenever we become bored, a common occurrence with cameras so often trained on desolate roads and closed shops from Taiwan to Finland.[23]

And as they say in the infomercial business: *But wait . . . there's more!* If we grow bored with watching anonymous CCTV, we can purchase our own cameras for purely recreational purposes. The online auction site eBay provides a buyers' guide, titled "Cool Surveillance Gadgets That Make Fun and Unique

Gifts for Kids." One section ("Fun with Surveillance Gadgets") suggests that "properly placed surveillance gadgets might even help find Bigfoot or the truth about UFOs."[24] Of course, eBay is hardly the only vendor of such devices: most any medium-sized city will have a brick-and-mortar spy shop that specializes in hidden microphones, night-vision goggles, and other "cool spy gadgets," including "CCTV novelty gifts" such as "bird feeders that take bird watching to a whole new level." Of course, the Internet remains the best place to purchase gear for *recreational surveillance*. For a few hundred dollars, anyone can deploy a small UAV and create "stunning drone videos" that attract thousands of viewers.[25] "I love flying in the mountains and zooming down mountainsides," one amateur drone photographer explains. "It allows me to experience all the thrills of flight in spectacular locations with my body never leaving the ground."[26] We can also use Periscope or other popular apps to live-stream from our smartphones to the world, where millions of people are surprisingly interested in watching a lot of nothing in the lives of random strangers, all in the name of aimless voyeuristic pleasure.

Even when surveillance technology is being used for its original purpose, it is often imbued with a new spirit of whimsy and fun. A *Wired* magazine article ("DISNEY MEETS ORWELL WITH THESE SUPER CUTE SURVEILLANCE CAMERAS") discussed charmingly designed but fully functional monitoring devices.[27] (Such security cameras might have special appeal to those who grew up watching the Disney Junior cable network: one episode featured tiny roving ladybugs with spy cameras atop their heads, adding to the "cutification" of surveillance technology.)[28] Even the TV set is shifting its function within our living rooms. Perhaps not surprisingly, as surveillance and entertainment become interwoven, a new-generation television is more than an appliance for watching *Dancing with the Stars*; it's also a remote-sensing device that tracks our viewing habits better than the NSA. Not long ago, Samsung released a smart TV that uses facial-recognition software to confirm our identity, detect our movements, and even record what we are saying—all of which is automatically shared with marketers and other interested companies. Hidden in Samsung's 50-page privacy statement is a notice that "if your spoken words include personal or other sensitive information, that information will be among the data captured and transmitted to a third party."[29] In a similar vein, gaming hardware is being repurposed for the security industry, along with the associated skill set of the gamer. Using Kinect, a hands-free motion-control system developed for gamers, today's security professional can zoom their CCTV cameras with the same hand gestures they learned for an Xbox bowling simulator.[30] Meanwhile, other companies are literally turning gaming consoles into home surveillance systems: a gamer who leaves home can even get automated texts when motion is detected somewhere near their beloved Xbox.

The interpenetration of entertainment and surveillance practices is also happening in commercial settings devoted to recreation. To ensure a controlled good time, biometrics have started to appear in the physical spaces of entertainment, from Disneyland's pioneering use of finger scans to identify ticket-holders, to a Spanish comedy club's use of facial recognition to calculate a patron's total number of chuckles, which allows them to charge more for each additional laugh during a given performance.[31] (No word on whether customers get a discount for mirthless glowering.)

Playful surveillance also has a central role within a complex phenomenon known as *gamification*, a buzzword that corporations use to describe the "playful" acquisition of marketing data. With its stated goals of increasing brand loyalty and "customer engagement," corporate gamification is actually financial surveillance on an epic scale—after all, its primary purpose is to find out more about us, usually more than we would be willing to divulge were it not for the three-card Monte of marketing surveys masquerading as free games on a phone or laptop. Big Data doesn't have a complete stranglehold on the gamification of surveillance and gamification can work for privacy advocates in some contexts; Camover, for instance, is a German game in which players score points for disabling real-life security cameras. But such acts of gamified resistance strike me as ultimately marginal pursuits on the edge of surveillance culture.[32]

In all the examples above, corporations are the driving force behind the fusion of surveillance and entertainment, but the US government wants private citizens to "play" with surveillance as well. In 2005, the NSA launched a website filled with wacky cartoon characters designed to put the "fun" into the process of "learning" about its activities.[33] The agency even invests in in-house games to help its analysts become more comfortable with new spy software; the more an analyst "plays" with a new system, the more points she can earn toward an unspecified prize.[34] In other contexts, NSA analysts have gotten into trouble for being too interested in so-called loveint (intel about one's love life), which involves the misuse of NSA systems to scope out former romantic partners.[35] The same is true of bored male TSA workers, for whom securitization breeds gross forms of sexual objectification, down to the development of code words for attractive women approaching the full-body scanners.[36] Something is wrong in the creepy basement of the Funopticon, where some twisted pleasures are emerging from the dark fusion of security and entertainment.

The libidinal energies in surveillance culture are hiding everywhere in plain sight, often in problematic ways. For instance, it is difficult for women to escape high-tech ogling and other forms of "perveillance" that provide a sadistic form of pleasure for some male CCTV operators. In the 1990s, researchers found that security cameras were used more often for ogling than for actual security, by a 5-to-1 margin.[37] Caesars Atlantic City Hotel Casino was fined $80,000 because its employees had used CCTV cameras to ogle women in 2000 and 2001.[38] A few years later, a CCTV operator in Belfast, Ireland, was convicted of using public cameras to watch a particular young woman over an eight-month period entirely for "sexual gratification."[39] And as surveillance becomes pornified, actual porn looks more like surveillance. Geographer David Bell describes an emerging "surveillance aesthetic" that is proliferating in visual media in general but especially in porn, "where the technologies of surveillance structure the narrative, the action and most importantly the 'look' of porn."[40] In some ways this is an unsurprising outcome of surveillance culture. "The surveillance state is intrinsically omnipresent," architecture professor Dana Cuff has written. "There is no escape except perhaps to exhibitionism."[41] No doubt, surveillance is sometimes sexy, perhaps even liberatingly so. Bell has even written about "eroticization as a way of resisting or hijacking surveillance," but it sounds like something that would work better in the realm of performance art than real life.[42]

Not everything in this new wave of playful surveillance is as light and liberating as it might appear. In addition to being a zone for genuine pleasure and connection, the Funopticon is also a place where the securitarian impulse can find a new market, a way of domesticating the tools and techniques of the war on terror by turning them into ostensible playthings, and a way of engaging us in a potentially dark game that I explore later in this chapter. Certainly, we should wonder if we give away more of ourselves in moments of fun than in moments of fear—that through pleasure, laughter, and desire, we are turning over the keys to our inner kingdom to strangers with long memories and endless data storage. What we glimpse on Snapchat, what we watch on YouPorn, what we read on Kindle, what we post on Facebook, and what we tweet to our followers reveal a great deal about who we are (or who we want to be), but we are often having too much fun to notice how much we are revealing — or how much we are being altered. Sociologist Ariane Eller-brok has claimed that biometric video-gaming "sets the stage for pleasurable identification with practices of state surveillance."[43] She writes that TV shows, games, and even spy-store gizmos invite the user to fetishize biometrics and other surveillance gadgetry, encouraging us "to suspend critical judgment regarding the social role of biometrics, placing questions of 'why' and 'for whom' on the back burner to the more enjoyable question of 'how.'" Her fear, it seems, is that we might end up like the young readers of Dick Tracy comics in the 1940s, enthralled by the gadgets of spycraft but blind to the ethical considerations surrounding their use. I think this is plausible, but I would go further in highlighting the dangers of playful surveillance in general. By presenting the tools and techniques of surveillance culture as nonthreatening forms of entertainment, the Funopticon serves a crucial pedagogical function: it teaches one how to think and even feel about surveillance in ways that conform to the expectations of Big Data and the NSA alike. Like Winston Smith, people are learning that it is not enough to obey Big Brother: we must also love him — and laugh at his jokes.

The Dark Pleasures of The Game

The film character Nicholas Van Orton is a man for our times. A depressed billionaire with monogrammed shirts and nervous underlings, Nicholas can't even enjoy his forty-eighth birthday party at an exclusive private club — he just sits in annoyance while the servants sing "Happy Birthday" to him. Friendless, heartless, and haunted like a twenty-first-century

Scrooge, Nicholas is hardly present—instead, he keeps flash-
ing back to a horrific scene from his childhood: his father's
suicidal jump off the rooftop of their San Francisco mansion.
Forty years later, unable to shake the pain of seeing and being
seen, Nicholas begins a long journey toward his own rooftop
suicide—as well as a surprising resurrection from an artfully
simulated death. In the midst of his "game," whose real nature
I will describe shortly, he learns to appreciate the pain of exposure as well as its surprising pleasures. Ultimately, he discovers the re-enchantment that had been drained from his life
of joyless accumulation and privileged seclusion at the pinnacle of capitalism. Rather than hiding from the sharp edge of
visibility, Nicholas learns to play with it in a way that restores
his will to live—and even to love. What he learns, in an underappreciated film from 1997 titled *The Game*, is how to live inside the Funopticon.

Often lost in the buzz about *Fight Club* and *Seven*, better-
known films from the same director that bookended it in the
1990s, *The Game* remains the least appreciated and most
interesting movie from David Fincher, who went on to compile
a celebrated but uneven body of work that includes *Zodiac*, *The
Social Network*, *The Girl with the Dragon Tattoo*, *Gone Girl*, and
The Curious Case of Benjamin Button. Whatever the limitations of Fincher's work may be, *The Game* remains fascinating
for reasons I want to explore here, hoping to illustrate the ways
in which playful surveillance might be experienced in greater
detail. With superb performances from Michael Douglas, Sean
Penn, Deborah Kara Unger, and others, *The Game* is a perverse
parable of enlightenment in the age of electronic surveillance,
a pulpy yet elegant look at paranoia and privilege, and a mo-
rose thriller about depression, isolation, and redemption. Aes-
thetically, tonally, and psychologically, it is a masterpiece in
almost every frame, thanks to Harris Savides's bravura cinematography and Howard Shore's evocative score, as well as

seamless performances, direction, and production design. As the commentator David Sirota wrote in *Salon*:

> *The Game* is the enduring classic, standing out not only for its abiding story, but also for its dim ray of hope during these seeming end times. Amid its darkness, Fincher's film proffers an alluring solution: Human connection, it suggests, will inherently evoke enlightenment and morality, even among those previously insulated in a lawyer-protected cocoon of luxury sedans, mahogany-paneled offices and cutthroat financial transactions.[44]

The engine of this enlightenment, I believe, is the roller-coaster experience of playful surveillance that keeps *The Game* rushing forward. As my reading of this film will suggest, life in the Funopticon is joyful and thrilling, filled with twists and turns, tension and release, and a bracing sense of unpredictability and possibility. In some sense it is a noir life, providing a jolt of excitement to our quotidian existence and a way of charging the landscape with a new layer of meaning, a new network of possibility that feels exciting and hopeful. Such is the parable of Nicholas Van Orton.

As the expressions of sour displeasure on his face make clear, the experience of playful surveillance does not begin well for Nicholas (portrayed by Michael Douglas). In the first moments of the film, he sees his life thrown into disarray by a birthday present from his younger brother Connie (Sean Penn). The present is a mysterious "game" that is tailored to each customer to provide "whatever is missing," an elaborate process that is orchestrated by a secretive company known as Consumer Recreation Services (CRS). Once the customized game begins, somewhat against his will, Nicholas is tracked, tricked, tormented, poisoned, seduced, kidnapped, and bank-rupted by CRS agents who know his every move, hear his every word, and unearth his every secret through various forms of surveillance and subterfuge. Neither anguished pleas nor legal threats can stop their creative assault on Nicholas's highly de-veloped sense of security and control. Although he is a man who has invested heavily in security in every sense of the word, CRS drops him into a game that makes him feel naked, inse-cure, and existentially exposed.

The real carnival of visibility begins, appropriately enough, with a clown—a creepy, nearly life-size mannequin that Nicholas finds in his circular driveway on the eve of his joy-less forty-eighth birthday. Bringing it into the sumptuous den inside his gated mansion, he discovers that hidden in its eye socket is a surveillance camera that allows CRS to spy on him, something that becomes apparent when his television starts addressing him personally. "There's a tiny camera looking at you right now," a newscaster explains through a hijacked tele-vision signal, ostensibly to introduce him to an experience that has been specially designed for Nicholas in ways he cannot yet fathom. "That's impossible," Nicholas scoffs to the figure on the TV, played by the real-life journalist Daniel Schorr, who in turn replies, "You're right, *impossible*. You're having a conversation with your television." For the first time in the film, Nicholas seems not merely annoyed or depressed but truly rattled—he is not accustomed to being exposed to the light of day, as it were, a fact that CRS exploits to destabilize him further. "You want to know how a camera got into your home?" the newscaster taunts him, making one of many references to the invasiveness of surveillance throughout the film. The answer, of course, is worse than the question: Nicholas is to blame. Although CRS planted the clown in the exact spot where Nicholas's father died on the driveway, Nicholas himself has created the real opening for surveillance in his life: he dragged the thing inside his home out of curiosity, just as he had divulged his full psychological profile to CRS when he first received his present.

As is already evident in the clown scene that serves as his introduction to the "game," Nicholas is not so sure about playing. With the "NVO" monogram on his shirt vaguely suggesting "no video," Nicholas seems increasingly reluctant to continue his uncontrolled descent into anarchical exposure, but once the game begins he has little choice. Increasingly against his will, he is pulled out of his wood-paneled isolation into a state of nakedness in which his body, his business, and his assets are all exposed to the world—or *seemingly* exposed, since that is a key word in this neo-Hitchcockian thriller in which nothing is what it appears.

The question of visibility—of *what is really being seen*— lurks at the heart of *The Game.* When he meets a waitress who might be working for CRS, she nods at cameras hidden inside a smoke detector and whispers, *"They're watching. Not here. They can see."* Later, as the game becomes stranger and even criminal in nature, he receives blackmail photos depicting a cocaine-fueled tryst that he cannot recall, leaving him dazed and wondering: *Who has taken these? Who has seen them? Are they real?* No longer sequestered behind the walls of private clubs and blacked-out limos, Nicholas is constantly looking over his shoulder, trying to make sense of his sudden visibility and vulnerability. "You're afraid someone is going to see!" his brother shouts at him in a tense exchange about the real nature of the "game." Even the Bible is brought to bear on this theme when a fellow CRS client, who turns out to be a CRS agent, describes the power of illumination with a religious allusion: "John 9:25," he intones with a messianic stare, before spelling out the quotation to Nicholas: "Where once I was blind, now I can see." Not even halfway into *The Game*, the film is beginning to suggest that surveillance can wound and overwhelm us. But there's something else at play: surveillance can add magic and mystery in addition to predictability and control. This is the dual nature of the strange and costly gift that Nicholas receives from his brother, who, we learn at the end, is hoping to jolt his brother's humanity back to life.

Despite its unusual premise, *The Game* mines some familiar terrain, for those with an interest in film history. To find naked blackmail photos of yourself that you don't remember; to have unfamiliar people know your name; to hear *they are watching*—these unnerving elements of the game are straight out of the classic paranoid thrillers of the 1970s and 1980s: *The Parallax View, Three Days of the Condor, The Conversation,* and *Blow Out.* Similarly, the classics of postwar film noir were stocked with allusions to surveillance: private dicks rummaging through garbage cans for telltale signs, tough dames peeking through venetian blinds, crooked cops on a stakeout with coffee in one hand and binoculars in the other. Although Fincher plays up these generic expectations with his customary panache, ultimately *The Game* transcends them to reach an unexpected point with interesting implications for surveillance studies. By the end of the film, our battered protagonist finds himself reaching a rapturous point of re-enchantment and rebirth, almost literally. By the time a mischievous Jefferson Airplane riff ushers in the closing credits, Nicholas has been buried alive in a Mexican cemetery and tricked into jumping from the roof of a skyscraper, only to be "reborn" as someone who can see, love, and connect—and to do so, significantly, through the machinery of playful surveillance. He is so transformed by the experience that he is eager to dive deeper into the Funopticon, even to the point of joining the CRS team as it heads out to play its surveillance games with its next unsuspecting client. Having endured the various stages of what one critic has called "perverse exposure therapy," in which the walls of his corporate castle have been knocked down, Nicholas has learned to experience visibility, insecurity, and unpredictability not simply as trauma but as salvation.[45]

In this manner, *The Game* suggests that surveillance is something more than a grim agent of control and oppression that produces *disenchantment*, Max Weber's great term for the alienated manner in which modern people find themselves rationalized almost to death, either in soul or body, to fit the needs of state and capital. As one of Weber's best critics puts it, disenchantment is the condition of living in a bureaucratic world in which "everything becomes understandable and tameable, even if not, for the moment, understood and tamed." As science, capitalism, and state bureaucracies grabbed the reins of power in modern Europe, a new emphasis on order, illumination, and predictability snuffed out the premodern wilds of enchantment that had long dominated human experience.[46] Surveillance had an important role in this historical transformation. After all, it reduces our bodies to data points for bureaucratic purposes, rationalizes our behavior for state and corporate needs, and seems to put us in Weber's infamous "iron cage" of social control with ever-greater precision.[47] At least in theory, it brings order to the streets, efficiency to the idle, illumination to the dark—and leaves little room for awe, wonder, and laughter.

But what if surveillance is experienced as oppressive *and* fun? What if people find both pleasure and pain in it? What if it provides disenchantment as well as re-enchantment? Such both/and propositions are nothing new to the scholars working to update Weber's insights. For instance, the sociologist Richard Jenkins has encouraged Weberians to push beyond the dyad of enchantment and disenchantment to imagine ways in which something hopeful can reemerge even in the most rationalized modern spaces. Fascinatingly, he suggests that sterile modernity carries within it the seeds of its own liberation: "formal-rational logics and processes can themselves be (re)enchanted from within, or become the vehicles of (re)enchantment."[48] With this in mind, even someone who shares the skeptical views of Edward Snowden might ponder the upside of surveillance culture and wonder if a technological system designed to capture our buying habits and to assess our terroristic potential, to control our borders and to monitor our parking lots, might serve more humane and hopeful purposes. We might even wonder if something unaccountably beautiful lurks inside the networks, sensors, archives, and apps of the Funopticon. What if surveillance not only maps a place for control and predictability but also enlivens that place, charging it with social energy and the potential for new connections between friends, collaborators, lovers? What if it schools us in the pleasures of seeing and being seen, the satisfaction of leaving a trace in a vast network of data collection and social sorting in ways that are nurturing and joyful? Then, perhaps, we might discover a strange kind of *surveillance enchantment* in this mysterious system of sorting and knowing that is almost God-like in its omniscience about our lives. Suddenly, surveillance systems might seem like something other than an iron cage—they could be imagined as a beautiful connective tissue that brings us together in new and exciting ways (an apparent fact that social media has already begun to exploit). Feeling lost in front of a screen or alone on a street, we could always remember that surveillance is there to catch us in an endless web of social potential—it always pulls us in, always marks our presence, always offers its peculiar embrace. Whether it takes the form of a CCTV camera, a Facebook page, or a Visa statement, surveillance is the one place where we know that our lives will register and resonate, the one place where we can say with utter certainty: *We made a mark. We were here. We mattered. Just check the file.*

Unless, of course, there's a twist. Could playful surveillance

be a cynical form of "disenchanted enchantment," a bogus return to magic and awe that uses pleasure, excitement, and joy
against us?[49] As Richard Jenkins puts it, "Domination is often,
perhaps even always, underwritten by at least a modicum of
enchantment, charisma is utterly enchanted, and power has
always cast its own spell."[50] Perhaps this is the ultimate secret
of the Funopticon (and perhaps *The Game* as well): it lets you
think you've won, that you've found a pleasurable way out, that
you've transcended your fears of being watched, tracked, and
archived, when in reality you've been ensnared more artfully
than you could ever imagine. Even more worrisome is the fact
that we're far more vulnerable than Nicholas Van Orton, who
ultimately is in control of his surveillance experience. After all,
his brother is paying for it, his friends and associates are playing along, and CRS wants a satisfied client, even if it torments
him on the way to profound customer satisfaction. What we
see in *The Game* is, in fact, a very privileged exchange among
plutocrats, an outlandish executive service rendered to the
high-end dead souls of late capitalism whose lives are increasingly distant from those of ordinary Americans. Of course, not
many people have the luxury of engaging such a service. Even
if we are able to find real pleasure and amusement in the Funopticon, we will never have the level of control and customiza-
tion that someone like Nicholas Van Orton can afford, nor will
we ever have the satisfying denouement in which Facebook,
Google, and the NSA pull back the curtain on their operations
and explain that it was all lovingly designed for our well-being.
More likely, we will remain unconscious pawns in someone
else's lucrative "game," whether it's Big Data or national security, and, like eager young tourists at Disneyland, we'll come to
know the bright surfaces and considerable enticements of the
Funopticon, but almost nothing of its deeper purpose or meaning—unless, that is, we seek out a path of playful resistance.

Pleasurable Implications

In a book written in 1973 but not published until almost forty years later, the French Marxist Henri Lefebvre looked with disdain at the rationalized spaces of postwar Europe, seeing not the order and progress of a mature civilization but rather a "destructive and reductive capability" that needed to be "curtailed" with the best means at our disposal: an "economy of enjoyment."[51] In his quasi-utopian vision of radical playfulness, Lefebvre describes how ordinary citizens might rework the spaces that surround them, regarding them in new ways that are liberating and subversive. Interestingly, the theorist (and fellow Frenchman) Michel de Certeau came to a similar conclusion around the same time. Writing in *The Practice of Everyday Life* (1980), de Certeau hinted at the pleasures in little games of concealment, such as when we disguise the fact that we are penning a love letter at work without the boss's permission. Well before the era of Big Data and ubiquitous CCTV, de Certeau advised us to "make use of the cracks that particular conjunctions open in the surveillance of the proprietary powers. It poaches in them. It creates surprises in them. It can be where it is least expected. It is a guileful ruse."[52]

Lefebvre and de Certeau were on to something about the subversive implications of playing with surveillance. After all, most surveillance technologies are not inherently oppressive; the suffering stems from their use, which is often oppressive and asymmetrical in nature. Looking at how geocachers "creatively misuse" the serious business of GPS and other tracking technologies, Jason Farman has argued that playful reworkings of surveillance technologies are valuable "acts of resistance to the dominant modes of spatial production."[53] Similarly, McKenzie Wark has claimed that the playful use of GPS turns "the whole surface of the earth into a board game."[54] Other scholars have celebrated the spirit of the "playable city" that artists have instilled in Bristol, in the United Kingdom, hoping to bring a new spirit of lively participation to the mundane experience of commuting.[55] And when people circulate urban legends about missing persons found by Google Earth's satellite on mysterious islands that seem straight out of the TV fantasy drama *Lost*, the machinery of surveillance begins to seem almost magical in its capabilities.

Likewise, joyful opposition to surveillance culture is often a delight to behold. Artists have been known to "bedazzle" security cameras with gaudy rhinestones or adorn them with shiny party hats.[56] One even came up with the CCTV-thwarting cosmetic called CV Dazzle, which one wearer described as "joyful" as well as apocalyptic in feel (although it made him look like a part-time Juggalo).[57] Or consider the playful resistance of the Surveillance Camera Players, with their public performances of Shakespeare directed toward CCTV operators, or the artist-activist playing chess with a CCTV operator in a subway station by holding up a sign ("YOUR MOVE") before providing a number to call to make the play.[58] Or the creepy pleasures of Spacewurm, the artist who stealth-recorded cell phone conversations in the 1990s and turned them into poignant little dramas on the pages of a book.[59] Or the British kids who enjoy video sniffing, which is "like going on safari to look for wireless CCTV signals," according to one British artist who self-describes as an avid "sniffer." "Groups of kids typically walk down a street watching as a signal becomes stronger," he says, "and then it becomes an art to judge from your surroundings what sort of buildings are being surveyed."[60] These are joyful hackers sticking it to the man: they romp with their mates. Roll their eyes at Big Brother. Laugh at the Matrix.[61] It's one of the great feelings of our era: the feeling of freedom and subversive possibility that one gets when being on top of surveillance, not underneath it.

Of course, a cynic might not be impressed by playful resistance. After all, what looks like joyful participation might be little more than a decorator's touch being applied to the grey old interior of the Panopticon, a chance for prisoners to add some color and whimsy within their cells—not to bust open their walls and escape to a better place. The playful, rather than being something that helps us change the nature of surveillance and the ways we experience it, might be simply another way, often an insidiously pleasurable one, for surveillance to expand into our private lives without a hint of protest. The Funopticon may even be training us to blithely internalize its logic, to gawk and strut in the glare of nonstop publicity as our highest aspiration, and to never stop performing for the pleasure of others who never stop performing for us. If this is the case, we should consider ourselves checkmated on the issue of privacy: we've given up personal autonomy and freedom in the name of connectivity, pleasure, and convenience.

But the despair that this might cause can mask a failure of imagination, at least when it comes to the quickly shifting landscape of surveillance culture and what might be in store in years ahead. For this reason, we can be cautiously hopeful about the subversive pleasures of the Funopticon and where it might lead. After all, whenever ordinary people are laughing, connecting, creating, and talking more intimately—as these playful forms of surveillance often encourage us to do—new forms of freedom, new kinds of community, and new modes of resistance are within reach.

CHAPTER THREE

Growing up Observed

Long before his many years on stage and screen, Alan Cumming was the survivor of a rough childhood on the Scottish moors. In his recent memoir, *Not My Father's Son*, the actor recounts the years in which he was on a constant lookout for his volatile father, the head forester on a once-grand estate in eastern Scotland. A former military man with a taste for drink and ill-disguised extramarital affairs, his father lorded over his wife and sons with an unpredictable rage that required perpetual vigilance from a boy hoping to avoid a beating, a cursing, or the bloody application of sheep's shears on his young head. As a young boy, Cumming learned that anything could set off the "pure violent rage" born of alcohol, depression, and anger. Like a prisoner in a domestic Panopticon, Cumming lived with a permanent awareness that his father might be watching him, an awareness that was often accompanied by vicious self-scrutiny. In a sudden "flash," when he knew he was being monitored, Cumming could feel the "myriad of anxieties about my flaws and failures [whirring] across my mind." The only relief was escape from his father's gaze. Even during a family meal, Cumming remembered, "all I could think of was getting to the end of this meal and upstairs to my homework, or better yet far into the woods with my dog to hide."[1]

Notice how the young actor learned to watch the watch-

man: *Was his father home? On the phone? In a foul mood?*
Had he been drinking? How had his day been? At the same
time, Cumming learned to watch himself with equal precision:
"I prayed that my hair was combed the way he liked it, my
school bag was hanging on my shoulder at the right angle, and
my shoes were shiny enough." Scrutiny was damnation, but
also a salvation of sorts—if only he could gauge his father's
moods, predict his responses, present just the right face, the
young boy could short-circuit his father's obsessive need to
control. "I had learned from a very young age to interpret the
tone of every word he uttered, his body language, the energy he
brought into a room," Cumming recalls, before musing about
the long-term impact of living with this never-ending inspection of his behavior and appearance. "It has not been pleasant
as an adult to realize that dealing with my father's violence
was the beginning of my studies of acting."[2] In other words, he
took his experience with constant monitoring, his urgent need
to control his effect on an unpredictable authority figure, and
channeled it into the delicate art of impression management
that we call acting.

If his grim experiences with domestic surveillance don't
seem to have tainted his sense of the world in general or left
him with crippling self-consciousness, anxiety, or other mala-
dies, Cumming does not seem entirely unscathed—even his
positive childhood memories are now inseparable from his experience of brutal parental monitoring. "We remember happy
times with our mum. Safe, quiet times," he writes, before
noting that "honestly there is not one memory from our childhoods that is not clouded by fear or humiliation or pain."[3] That
is the insidious nature of surveillance in its subtler forms: it
does soft-tissue damage that is easy to overlook in discussions
that focus on Big Data and the NSA to the exclusion of all else.
Nowhere is this more apparent, to my mind, than in childhood
and adolescence, where we have our first experiences with sur-

veillance, often in formative ways. Surveillance, it turns out, can be a very intimate business.

Broadening our sense of what counts as "surveillance"—and how we get our first taste of it—is essential to understanding the subtle flows of surveillance culture in the contemporary world. Indeed, going beyond the state and corporate modes of surveillance to something like a family dinner table makes particular sense on an emotional level. After all, no one entity has exclusive control over the emotional landscape of surveillance, no matter how much the Department of Homeland Security, the NSA, or the hidden architects of Big Data might want to mold our experience of the world, and no matter how much someone wants us to feel compliant, covetous, relaxed, anxious, or alert at a particular moment of citizenship or consumption. While governments and corporations are acknowledged as the dominant forces in the realm of security and insecurity, they are rarely acting in isolation—our feelings about various kinds of monitoring are shaped much earlier in life, in far more intimate settings. Surveillance begins at home, in our first exposure to the culture of invasive monitoring that can color our relationships to our parents, teachers, and other authority figures, something that we can see in certain memoirs.[4] In ways that have been generally underappreciated, childhood might be a crucial time in the formation of "surveillance consciousness," which we bring into our adult roles as citizens and consumers, parents and neighbors, friends and lovers.[5]

In order to visualize the biographical roots of surveillance consciousness—the awareness of and occasional wariness about being monitored at home as much as in the public sphere—I am blending psychology, sociology, and memoir in this chapter. The stories are about childhood, social class, anxiety and depression, immigration, shame, and anger—and most of all, feelings of security and insecurity, watching and being watched. Nothing here would surprise someone who has internalized the lessons of modern therapeutic culture: when it comes to our lived experience of securitization, so much depends on our family of origin.

In the 1960s, the social critic Paul Goodman struck a nerve when he published *Growing Up Absurd: Problems of Youth in the Organized Society*, a bleak look at the homogenous mass culture, with little space for rebels and dreamers that grew up during the Eisenhower years. Now our children are reared with an additional layer of absurdity: the controlling gaze of the parent, school, and state are fused into a culture of almost constant monitoring. Rather than growing up absurd, we are *growing up observed*, with an unprecedented level of precision and permanence. And this constant emphasis on control, predictability, and security can have a perverse byproduct: the more we press for a deep and lasting sense of security, the more we are miserably insecure. Childhood surveillance has its own paradoxes: what often begins with love, care, and protectiveness thrives equally well on judgment, uncertainty, and apprehension. In early 2015, the British government asked preschool teachers to report on toddlers who seemed like future terrorists. "Turning our teachers and childminders into an army of involuntary spies will not stop the terrorist threat," said one disgusted human rights worker. "Far from bringing those at the margins back into mainstream society, it will sow seeds of mistrust, division and alienation from an early age."[6] Whether the seeds are sown at home, at school, or in the highest levels of government, their eventual development is what is important here. Do these early experiences help to form a lifelong pattern of acceptance or resistance, nonchalance or irritation, in the face of CCTV, dataveillance, drones, and other aspects of the surveillance infrastructure?

Yet we know relatively little about surveillance and the young.[7] As sociologists have lamented, the child's experience of surveillance has been the subject of very few studies, even as surveillance technologies and practices have increasingly colonized previously unmonitored aspects of childhood. Imagining the modern child as a potential "victim who must be placed under surveillance for protection" or "an anti-social threat who must be placed under surveillance to protect society" is limiting, if not distorting. "From either perspective," scholars have argued, "the richness of the child's lived experience is lost."[8] I want to hint at something of that "lost" lived experience in the pages ahead.

Watching Children

Let me start with two quick sketches. First, imagine a calm and loving home where being watched feels like nurturance. Even wearing an RFID-chipped jacket while sleeping under a CCTV-equipped Elf on the Shelf seems like a form of loving protection that swaddles the child in a network of concern.[9] Feeling incorporated into a system of interconnected care that seems nonthreatening and rational, the child might look at her parents, teachers, and even local police and think: *thanks for watching!*

But imagine a different sort of childhood, one vibrating with emotional volatility of the sort Alan Cumming describes, one in which the child is a cringing vassal subjected to the feudalism of a domineering parent. "*Everyone* in a walking-on-eggshells family loses some degree of dignity and autonomy," writes one psychologist. "It seems that you become unable to decide your own thoughts, feelings, and behavior, because you are living in a defensive-reactive pattern that runs largely on automatic pilot." As we might imagine from the brief account of Cumming's childhood above, surveillance simply *feels bad* to children struggling against parental domination at home. Indeed, for someone growing up in a dysfunctional family obsessed with monitoring, controlling, and judging its young, external surveillance might even feel like a form of emotional abuse. ("Emotional abuse is an assault on the child's psyche, just as physical abuse is an assault on the child's body.")[10] In this context, the child might look at her domineering parents and other authority figures and recoil from the experience of being watched and judged in any form. From their earliest years, such children endure the humiliation of parental surveillance in ways that surely bleed into a dark view of educational, consumer, and state monitoring practices as an adult.

No doubt, surveillance is an essential aspect of childhood. "In a sense, to be a child is to be under surveillance," Valerie Steeves and Owain Jones have written in a special issue of *Surveillance and Society* devoted to the subject, one of the few academic publications to focus on childhood experiences of surveillance.[11] When familial life appears in discussions of surveillance, parents, not children, often take center stage. For instance, scholars have argued that media depictions of unrealistically idealized families have turned motherhood into a "psychological police state" that requires constant scrutiny of self, child, and peer to make sure that one is measuring up— but what about the kids who are also trying to "measure up"?[12]

Strangely enough, this absence also exists among creative writers and filmmakers who have spent so much energy exploring the dramas of surveillance culture. Consider the best-known films devoted to surveillance: *Caché, Rear Window, Blow Up, Blow Out, Parallax View, The Conversation, Enemy of the State, Eagle Eye, Nineteen Eighty-Four, Red Road, Brazil, The Lives of Others, A Scanner Darkly*, and *Minority Report*. All of these movies focus on adults struggling with surveillance, while children barely register as minor characters.

Perhaps this exclusion is less surprising if we recall that our grim surveillance paradigms, the essential texts of surveillance studies, are built around the brutalization of adults, not kids. Bentham imagined recalcitrant adult prisoners in his eighteenth-century Panopticon, while middle-aged Orwell's *1984* gave us the decrepitly middle-aged Winston Smith at war with a vigorously middle-aged O'Brien, not to mention a middle-aged Big Brother at odds with a middle-aged Goldstein. Orwell did provide some chilling glimpses of children in a surveillance culture in his brief but significant depiction of the Parsons kids keeping tabs on Winston from next door. Orwell writes about these monstrous beings who from birth have been subsumed into the machinery of surveillance. "Nearly all children nowadays were horrible," Orwell writes, before explaining:

> What was worst of all was that by means of such organizations as the Spies they were systematically turned into ungovernable little savages, and yet this produced in them no tendency whatever to rebel against the discipline of the Party. On the contrary, they adored the Party and everything connected with it.... All their ferocity was turned outwards, against the enemies of the State, against foreigners, traitors, saboteurs, thought-criminals. It was almost normal for people over thirty to be frightened of their own children.[13]

Such exceptional moments stand out in a vast surveillance literature devoted to adult experience—and most tend to be quite recent. The teenage hackers in Cory Doctorow's 2008 novel *Little Brother* are another exception, even if the seventeen-year-old protagonist is on the verge of adulthood. The same could be said of sixteen-year-old Katniss Everdeen's experience on a homicidal reality program in *The Hunger Games* (even though she's depicted by twenty-year-old Jennifer Lawrence in the film adaptation).[14]

The fifteen-year-old protagonist of Jenni Fagan's 2013 debut novel *The Panopticon* provides another rare glimpse of

the youthful burden of surveillance. Having endured the Scottish foster-care system for most of her girlhood, Fagan sets her
first novel in a literal Panopticon that has been converted into
a residential care facility for troubled children.[15] The pain of
being monitored overwhelms her main character, a working-
class Scottish girl who has had serious run-ins with the law and
sexual abuse at home. "They watch me," the narrator explains
about growing up under surveillance both literal and symbolic,

> not just in school or social-work reviews, court or police
> cells—they watch everywhere. . . . They watch me sing, and
> joyride, and start riots with only the smallest of sparks; they
> even watch me in the bath. . . . They watch me not cry. They
> watch me lie like an angel, hiding my dirty feet. They watch
> me, I know it, and I can't find anywhere anymore—where they
> can't see.[16]

Fagan is touching upon something crucial to the youthful experience of surveillance, when the literal and figurative bump up against one another in unsettling ways. If most
of us avoid the literal experience of a Panopticon during our
childhood, we still endure its abstract pressures enough to appreciate the metaphor for constant scrutiny. Even if we don't
literally witness the NSA recording our text messages or the
marketing firm squirreling away our data, even if we don't see
a cop on the corner or a snooping neighbor in our window, we
can have a gnawing sense that it is happening just the same.
For this reason, one of the subplots of this chapter on early surveillance dramas is the way in which surveillance operates on a
symbolic level as much as a literal one: it is mythic and imagined as much as it is real and observable. In some ways this
mythic quality is more damaging: we can debate the reality of
the technological and social processes that invade our privacy,
but it may not hit us with the visceral force of the symbolism

involved. In other words, the *mere idea of surveillance* can affect us, most especially the surveillance-averse, as much as the practice. The sheer notion that someone or something might be watching, might feel the need to watch, or might have the right to judge, is enough to unhinge some people, while others remain blissfully unconcerned, perhaps feeling protected by the magical words "I have nothing to hide."

Perhaps these feelings are acquired early in life, long before we are brought to account by advertisers and governments invested in the endless scrutiny of human possibility. Perhaps they begin, like so much else, with our early experiences of parental monitoring, which is itself shaped by the constant pressures of race, class, capital, nation, gender, and sexuality. Because a "surveillance memoir" (mine or anyone else's) cannot make sense if it doesn't take into account the sociological realities in which we are raised, I want to look first at the fusion of class, memoir, and gender that marks the work of Richard Hoggart, Carolyn Steedman, and other scholars who might not seem to take up surveillance, at first glance.

Working-Class Surveillance

The writing world lost a giant with the death of Richard Hoggart in 2014. One of the first scholars to take popular culture seriously, Hoggart was a self-described "scholarship boy" whose fusion of literary and sociological analysis made him an intellectual star in postwar Britain. His most influential book, *The Uses of Literacy* (1957), explored the impact of mass media on English working-class life, using many of his own experiences as fodder for an innovative and sensitive reckoning with the impacts of tabloids, pulp fiction, and popular songs on the organic folk culture of ordinary Brits. In order to allow readers to grasp the world that produced him, Hoggart crafted a two-part text that remains vividly appealing. Alongside what anthropologist Richard Handler has called "a beautifully evocative, generalizing portrayal of working class neighborhood life" was a thoughtful consideration of how external forces were reshaping older ways of being and feeling, something that translates quite well to the rise of contemporary surveillance culture.[17] As a child, Hoggart learned the need to keep up appearances, to placate the controlling gaze of authority figures visiting the family flat, even if this meant hiding a decent teapot so a social worker wouldn't think the family was wasting public support on inessentials.

Remaining impressively free of bitterness, Hoggart details how he sprang from circumstances both meager and mean. An impoverished child, he grew up in the grimness and want of northern England between the wars, a monochromatic time of privation if ever there was one. His humble upbringing might seem an unlikely beginning for a founding figure in the establishment of cultural studies—he was the first director of the influential Centre for Contemporary Cultural Studies at the University of Birmingham in 1964—but it was an ideal preparation for understanding the intersection of class, culture, and mass media that would transform postwar Britain. Until his death in 2014 at the age of ninety-five, he was that rare organic intellectual, an endless autodidact, a poetic sociologist, and a person for whom the personal was indelibly, inevitably political—an autobiographical fact that he never set forth clumsily. His was a more subtle form of cultural critique, one that appeals to me through and through. Well known in England and Australia to this day, Hoggart is out of fashion in the American academy beyond particular qualitative sociology circles. While he is acknowledged as an early influence in the development of cultural studies, he often receives little more than a quick nod from scholars who have moved on to other enthusiasms. I'm not ready to move on—we still have much to learn from Hoggart's infusion of the personal into the academic.

Others have made a similar case in recent years, especially about his radical unwillingness to maintain an unscalable wall between scholarship and personal writing. In an essay on Hoggart's empathetic mode of writing, the Australian scholar Melissa Gregg defends the use of personal recollection as a tool for cultural studies. "That experience or memory may be used as a means to base an argument is assumed to be troublesome due to its inevitable bias, its rose-coloured lens," she writes. "Cultural studies' development has been characterized, however, precisely by this kind of writing of the self, the voicing of one's formative environment to provide the material for pressing critical inquiry."[18] Hoggart's other explicators have suggested that his autobiographical writing "constructs his experience as a critical resource, rather than as an impediment to 'objective' analysis." In this sense, Hoggart's best work "demonstrates that social analysis is not just a matter of collecting, sifting, and interpreting a safely distanced body of material using a neutral, accepted set of techniques but is a more active, engaged, essentially political process."[19]

I admire that blurring of professional and personal ways of knowing, in part because it honors the vast swath of personal experience that is roped off as "unprofessional." And, like Hoggart, I want to respect the distinctive qualities of the world that made me, in no small measure because the world of 1970s blue-collar striving often goes unnoticed and unappreciated in contemporary scholarship. Hoggart's gift was his ability to look back at his own life *without* anger, placing his memories in a larger expanse of cultural transformation, toggling between the personal and the sociological. To his credit, he wrestled with the question of how to accomplish this task well into later

life. "How do I find a tone of voice which is neither too distant
nor too close?" he wondered in his memoirs, in 1994. "How
to avoid self-justification—or that kind of admission of weak-
ness which is really only another form of self-praise?" And perhaps trickiest of all, he realized with novelistic insight, is the
question of what is emblematic in an individual life. "Is this
incident really 'representative' or merely a quaint happening I
am hung up on, but one without 'resonance' beyond itself?"[20]
These are good questions for us all, but especially for me as I
pull at the roots of my own surveillance consciousness.[21]

So the uses of Hoggart are threefold for me. First, he combined memoir and traditional scholarship in a manner that I
want to emulate here. Second, his work has a deep personal
resonance for me: he wrote about the precise places and cultural attitudes that shaped and scarred my own path in this
world. Third, although he did not write about security per se,
he wrote about childhood, class, place, technology, culture, and
consciousness in a literary manner that remains an inspiration
to those of us wrestling with the subtleties of surveillance culture. I suspect he would understand the inegalitarian application of surveillance in class terms, as well as its awkward intru-
sions into human consciousness, its uncomfortable shaping of
our sense of place, and its imposition onto an older way of being
in the world. In short, his way of thinking is worth trying on.

Surveillance often felt like something that "they" did to "us,"
a fact that Hoggart writes about at great length. The Uses of
Literacy describes a basic worldview of "us" versus "them," the
latter of which is regarded more with "mistrust" than fear.[22]
The local policeman, for instance, was understood "primarily
as someone who is watching them, who represents the authority which has its eye on them, rather than as a member of
the public services whose job it is to help and protect them."[23]
For working-class people, and even those who fled to a differ-

ent life but retained an older sense of the world, surveillance often aggravates the hidden wounds of class, the sense that the authorities don't trust us and we don't trust them.

What Hoggart helps us realize is how much the class-infused experience of surveillance is emotional in nature: *it often makes the world feel bad.* Especially when you are young, surveillance is something that happens to you, something that reminds you that you are a small cog in someone else's machine, something that intrudes on your life. For this reason, it undermines the intimacy and dignity of working-class life, which was already under threat in the mid–twentieth-century world that Hoggart describes. Surveillance, I would argue from this Hoggartian perspective, undermines the pride of "Ah keep meself to meself," the autonomous sense of "live yer own life," the "insistence on the privacy of the home" that Hoggart found under threat from mass media and commercial culture in midcentury northern England.[24] Later research has added to what Hoggart was discovering.

In a study of surveillance and social class in a northern English high school, two scholars identified the "chilling effect" that working-class students felt in response to being monitored—which "led them to change 'legitimate' forms of behaviour or activities due to a concern that their actions could be misinterpreted by the 'surveyors.'" Some boys were "nervy" in response to the gaze of the school security system, while others were burdened by its presence (and its disproportionate focus on working-class bodies). Fearing that CCTV operators would misinterpret even harmless behaviors, students sometimes altered their behavior to appear more docile on screen.[25]

The literary scholar Rita Felski has described the culture of shaming in the working class, using the work of academic memoirists such as Carolyn Steedman to explore "how class-based attitudes of fatalism, resentment, envy, and shame are inexorably transmitted from the working-class mother to her child."[26] Steedman's book *Landscape for a Good Woman* is an essential counterpart to Hoggart's *The Uses of Literacy*. In her account of her mother's life in midcentury England, Steedman writes about how class-consciousness is acquired in a maelstrom of shame, envy, isolation, and uncertainty during childhood. It is a look at the "bits and pieces" of which "psychological selfhood" is made in our earliest years, one that filled a gap in the literature on class, gender, and childhood: "people's history and working-class autobiography are relatively innocent of psychological theory," she lamented, "and there has been little space within them to discuss the development of class-consciousness (as opposed to its expression), nor for understanding of it as a learned position, learned in childhood, and often through the exigencies of difficult and lonely lives."[27] With its vividly anguished portrait of growing up poor and exposed to the cruelties of English society, the book helped some readers understand why they felt the way they felt about the world. "Reading *Landscape for a Good Woman* let me see that my story, too, had slipped through the net of other people's interpretations," wrote one admirer.[28] Such autobiographical stories that have "slipped through the net" may help us understand surveillance culture in a new light, broadening our sense of what counts as surveillance and what might shape our experience of it. None of these stories—mine included—represents some universal experience of childhood surveillance. My point is quite the opposite: I'm interested in particular kinds of early experiences that might increase adult sensitivity to CCTV, drones, Snowden, cyberstalking, Big Data, TSA scanners, and facial recognition software.

Not everyone has these sensitivities, of course, and some of them may be generational in nature. Is it different for young people today, growing up immersed in social media and other forms of monitoring? Will they experience surveillance more positively, more naturally, than a transitional generation like mine, which came of age long before drones, smartphones, and GPS were commonplace? We don't really know yet (researchers are working on that question). But I suspect that young people today, just like previous generations, will experience surveillance in ways that are profoundly colored by parenting styles, class and racial identity, immigration status, gender, and other biographical factors that I explore in the pages ahead. Indeed, the following surveillance memoir is primarily an invitation for readers to think about the autobiographical roots of their own surveillance sensitivities, or lack thereof, and to wonder how their own attitudes about monitoring, insecurity, and connectivity were shaped in their earliest years. Looking at these early experiences, I suggest, is one way of understanding why some people are so aggrieved, some are blasé, and some are quite enthusiastic about the latest manifestations of surveillance culture. Are you comfortable with a home security drone hovering over your house? Do you want your child's school to monitor her social media posts? Do you mind if Yahoo! is scanning all of your personal emails for keywords provided by the NSA or FBI?[29] Do you bristle at the idea of someone looking down at you from a CCTV camera? The answer may lie in your biography, particularly in aspects of your identity that make you *feel* empowered or not, autonomous or not, respected or not, vulnerable or not.

A Surveillance Memoir

That won't do at all. You must remember your place.

—ANTON CHEKOV

Perhaps it would be no surprise if the black seeds of insecurity could grow into something unhealthy in an adult, or if the youthful experience of surveillance could breed certain kinds of mental and emotional distress. I wouldn't be surprised in the least, but I would prefer to have some hard evidence in academic journals. Unfortunately, very little work has been done on the psychological impact of living under surveillance in its contemporary form.[30] To start a conversation about the ways in which youthful experiences of surveillance remain with us, often problematically so, as we grow older and encounter new modes of monitoring, I want to look through the same lens I've used elsewhere in this chapter: personal experience combined with cultural analysis.

No doubt, some of my own sense of being watched was utterly normal for a boy of my time and place, a fact simply woven into the fabric of 1970s America, where paranoia was an understandable response to the strange times in which we lived as well as a sometimes overblown reaction to bits of nothing that somehow seemed like something.[31] One writer has described her own Cold War childhood as filled with needless paranoia and spy games. "My anti-surveillance measures were all out of proportion to any threat I was likely to encounter," she recalls sheepishly. "A quiet middle class girl, in a boring Maryland suburb? I was never on any kind of Russian superspy watch-list, even if my father did work for the government."[32] With such sentiments in mind, I'm open to the possibility that I may be confused about what was really happening in my childhood, that memory is often fraudulent, that feelings surge in inexplicable ways that we can never quite comprehend. Yet I think a personal approach can help us to get at the strange tonality of surveillance culture, its shifting moods and textures, its long roots and tendrils, which seem to reach into unexpected parts of our lives far beyond what normally counts as surveillance.

Certainly, I felt it long before I started worrying about Google and the NSA, long before I had read Orwell, and even before I got suspended from school for unaccountable wildness (looking back it seems more like mildness) that wasn't so uncommon in my place and time. I grew up on the Jersey shore in the 1970s, during those prehistoric days before reality TV stars J-Wow, Paulie, and Snookie arrived with Jell-O shots and string bikinis. Back then the shore wasn't much of anything except a punch line ("You from Jersey? What exit?")—just a sleepy place to ride out stagflation, disco, and Catholic school on the way to somewhere else. Ninety minutes from Manhattan on the train, it was somehow as provincial and lonesome as a Midwestern farm town, if not quite as repressive as the small hamlets in East Texas where my mother's family was stuck. Back then the locals on the shore prided themselves on looking and thinking alike, and even small differences could cause serious problems. I remember the ubiquitous insult of *faggot* echoing in the hallways as boys monitored one another's sexuality with a perverse vigilance. I remember the FBI arresting an eighth-grade classmate who unsuccessfully pipe-bombed our only Jewish teacher's car. I remember the utter absence of black or brown faces in a town filled with flag-waving European Americans who loved sports and beer and, to a lesser extent, church.

We were not the dignified and interwoven working class of Richard Hoggart's youth: we were something else, something far less cinematically intriguing, something more awkward. Working-class culture had a different face here than in pre-hipster Brooklyn where I was born, but it was still all around us, morphing into something lonely, cheap, and disconnected, just as Hoggart had feared. I saw it on the walls of my pleasant little house, where bullfighter paintings hung over simulated tinfoil wallpaper. I saw it on my dinner table, where canned peas rolled around chopped steak on Pathmark plates. I saw it outside our bay window, as I looked up and down a short street bookended by a funeral parlor and a cemetery. Next door was a tiny weeping bartender, who performed a midnight exorcism on his dying infant (did I hallucinate that? No, I didn't), and a grown woman who sat by herself in a kiddie pool on summer days with a ceaseless grin that made us wonder about her sanity. Across the street was a pipe-smoking car mechanic, the father of my best friend. A bow-hunting factory worker was two doors down, his tiny house flanked by retirees and used-car salesmen, and finally, in the simplest house, a little rectangle the size of a mobile home, the person with the most education: a historian who commuted to the city three days a week. At the other end of the street were two sullen poster boys for blue-collar lethargy: a pair of scabby brothers obsessed with stockcar racing. Their open-air garage was a grimy temple to speed in which they roared their engines, much to the despair of everyone else. A few retirees in their eighties rounded out the scene in a dull and disjointed neighborhood where no one *really* knew anyone else, though it still managed to feel strangely coercive. As children, we felt the weight of social expectation, of being monitored and judged, even if we were unable to name it.

Like most teens, I was watchful at home as well. While I was lucky to have a home with loving parents, I was unlucky to have experienced certain kinds of humiliation that continue to shape my experience of surveillance. I know there are many ways to learn the power of watching and being watched, many of them far more degrading than what I'm detailing here. But small-town living exacts its own psychological price. The fathers we knew ran their houses like mercurial wardens, alternately jocular and menacing, exerting influence over the smallest detail. If these working-class men couldn't control life outside the house, they often made up for it in their own private Panopticons.

I say this with the realization that I came of age before the most insidious surveillance technologies were ready for parental deployment. I learned to drive decades before the Drive

Pulse dongle could plug a parent's gaze into my car, automatically texting them whenever I drove over a certain speed or into a predetermined "bad neighborhood."[33] My Catholic high school didn't have biometric access control to keep out *maleficia*; the all-knowing, all-seeing Brother Andrew was more than adequate to secure the perimeter. But surveillance can thrive without the latest technology; it can move in subtle ways. What I have been calling "surveillance consciousness" is not simply a matter of CCTV and TSA scanners. It also has mundane sources in our schools, churches, and homes. It's about parenting styles, all-seeing teachers, and nosy neighbors as much as it's about homeland security and law enforcement.

Every day, in a million tiny ways, we learned that invisibility was freedom (it was a perfect childhood for surveillance studies). You learned to conceal and dissemble. You learned to separate the surface from the depths. You learned to watch for authority figures (parent, teacher, coach, priest, cop). Like most of my teenage friends (and perhaps teenagers just about everywhere), I waged a passive-aggressive guerrilla war against parental rule. We hid our forbidden orange soda in brown bags at the bottom of the fridge, slid Hydrox cookies into the nether regions of the lazy Susan, concealed the spots that Wiffle Ball wore into the lawn where we had been warned not to play. A few years later we were hiding bottles of crème de menthe pinched from liquor cabinets and illicit magazines fished out of the convenience-store dumpster. More important, we hid our opinions, tastes, and desires from the adults who monitored everything from our posture to our attitude. We hid our feelings, our dreams, even our hatred of being watched, second-guessed, scrutinized, corrected. On the list of things subject to constant monitoring: *how we ate, how we stood, what we said, where we went, what we wore, what we thought.* It was the same in many other houses, I'm sure.

The impact on social capital, that sense of the world as a

trustworthy place, was profound—and it shaped my under
standing of surveillance in pretty much any form. At every
turn, we were taught that our small towns were conformist
enclaves, big cities were sewers of danger, neighbors were voyeurs, strangers were perverts, charity was for suckers, and
no one could help you except yourself. Maybe this is why, in
my impressionable young mind, I identified with the mythic
criminals who adopted a noir sense of life as violent and un-
knowable. My friends and I learned to escape into masculine
fantasies of control from 1970s and 1980s cinema: *Magnum
Force*, *The Dogs of War*, *The Wild Geese*, each a tale of an out-
sider who survived to break a corrupt, authoritarian system.
Above all my brother and I worshiped at the altar of the original *Mad Max*, that dark Aussie fable of a cop driven into a
stylish rampage against the world that had hunted down his
family and caged his soul. My friends and I embraced the paranoid scripts of these films because they resonated with what
we already knew as boys staggering into puberty with low
self-esteem and alcoholic tendencies. We loved macho fantasies that were the opposite of our reality: ultimately, we were
soft boys, pawns without dignity, constantly pushed one way
or another by parents, teachers, coaches, and clergy, the aspi-
rational white-collar children of blue-collar parents. Some of
this is particular, some universal. Grubby New Jersey in the
late 1970s had the unique texture of the Carter administration,
though in some ways its challenges were not unusual. To be a
child is to be watched and controlled, often with a mixture of
love and anger, hope and hostility.

Where this often leads is the therapist's couch, the pharma-
cist's bottle, the liquor cabinet, the self-help manual, the lone-
liness of exodus, or an academic career. It's no worse than any
other battle with anxiety and depression that the agony of self-
consciousness invites. ("In my experience of treating nearly
6,000 family members who walk on eggshells," writes one psy-

chologist, "no fewer than half suffer from clinical anxiety and/ or depression.")[34] And it's no worse than any other childhood, each of which has its own raw spots. I certainly don't have a new chapter to contribute to the "misery lit" shelf, because my upbringing was a festival of privilege compared to many childhoods. Able-bodied, straight, white, and male, I didn't have to deal with the gawking and gendered power games that the young women around me on my street were enduring, or the structural racism that marred the experiences of people of color. Mine was simply a tense childhood on the blurry line between blue-collar America and lower-middle-class strivers in a time of big ugly cars and itchy polyester shirts. In short, I was just another well-meaning white kid getting his feelings bent out of shape while much more painful forms of immiseration churned in the distance. Yet whatever happened in my formative years was stressful enough to instill a lifelong sensitivity to surveillance, an enduring sense that watching and being watched is an anxiety-producing labor required of the weak and vulnerable in the presence of the strong, that the rituals of Homeland Security evoke a kind of bodily trauma (paradoxically in the name of bodily safety). That watching can be an act of domination. That being watched can be humiliating. That surveillance sucks.

Surveillance was woven into our family life, a symptom of collective dysfunction and immigrant fears. Tell lies, put up walls, bar the door—anything to keep out the inquisitive gaze of strangers who might judge us before we could judge them. My Scottish grandmother, the daughter of Irish diaspora from Glasgow, spent half my childhood peering out her window, wondering if the authorities were coming to deport her to the old country. Meanwhile, one of my uncles, a sociopath with a banana-yellow Eldorado and a bad perm, installed a special water meter to make sure his wife and kids didn't shower too long. (This was just before the divorce. And just before a car-

nie punched his teeth out for mouthing off at a cut-rate circus.)
The underlying lesson to all this: *always watch out* (especially
for carnies).

What gave this monitoring its real teeth was violence.
These working-class men made no secret of their potential for
it: they had suffered and inflicted pain in equal measure, and
they told stories that were designed to intimidate and impress.
From an early age I knew my grandfather had fought on the
Brooklyn docks with a razor blade snapped into the brim of
his cap, pulling other men's faces into it with his longshore-
man's biceps. I knew he was found in the street, drunk and
bloodied, with a loading hook protruding from his backside.
And I knew my other grandfather, an illiterate rancher with
missing fingers, had killed a man while fighting in the East
Texas logging woods. I knew someone else in my family kept
a ball-peen hammer under the front seat of his car and used
it to chase kids who threw snowballs at him. I knew an uncle
had bribed someone to get a drug-dealing cousin out of jail
in the middle of the night, when his son was held as an acces-
sory to murder. I knew family members had threatened to kill
other family members, and for very good reason. I knew all of
these stories by the time I was twelve, and it was part of the
regime of enforcement in which we operated: we knew there
were rules and we knew there were penalties—and we knew
people were watching us closely.

Rage, anxiety, insecurity, self-consciousness—these are the
gendered underpinnings of surveillance culture as I knew it.
The hardness of working-class New York masculinity in the
1970s had the sweat and feel of Scorsese: *Raging Bull* wife-
beaters, *Mean Streets* swagger, *Taxi Driver* resentments. Some
of this was unique to families such as mine: the uncles had all
come out of the rougher parts of midcentury New York City
and strutted like Bowery Boys well into their middle age. As
small-town boys in the 1970s, we certainly wondered how they

could have spawned us. After all, we were a transitional generation with a very different trajectory. We didn't grow up in
the city, we didn't get shot at, we never went hungry—and as a
result we were lost somewhere between old and new, hard and
soft, clarity and fuzziness. The hard face we put on for one another (and for our dads) was always an awkward performance,
marked by hollow aggression, a guilty sense of our shortcomings, and constant confusion for boys more suited to video
games than the aggression of the mythic street. We felt our
existential softness but couldn't put a name to it: it was as forbidden as another softness, that queer masculinity with which
we had more in common than we could admit back then. That
would have required real bravery, a real freedom from crippling
self-consciousness about our status and identity, a liberating
sense that we could tune out the constant policing of our masculinity and our very essence. None of my friends knew how to
do that back then. The weight of surveillance was too much.

If the small-town culture of monitoring was toxic for me,
it was generally harder on the women around me. As scholars such as Hille Koskela have demonstrated, surveillance
is tougher on women than on men—from CCTV in parking
garages to ogling security guards, it is something that men do
to women, often in a sexualized and demeaning manner.[35] I'm
sure it was worse, but I only saw hints, such as maternal relationships infused with crippling self-consciousness that inspired its own form of surveillance vigilance. Working-class
women, especially immigrants from rural poverty like my
mother, often found themselves overwhelmed by shame and
uncertainty in the strange new world of TV dinners, plastic
plates, and gleaming shopping malls of the postwar United
States. Recent arrivals to the American dream in some modest form, these women often modeled a fearful trepidation
about the outside world, a sense that the institutions of modern life were designed and run for people very different than

themselves, that school systems and insurance companies and government agencies and law offices were places where they were not welcome, where they could not understand the language being spoken. It is a narrow mind-set of anxious skepticism and uncertainty about how the world works and how it's set against them. And in this sense, surveillance compounded the ways in which we were socially and emotionally fragile: we couldn't afford mistakes because the shame hurt so much. We couldn't stand the constant monitoring of our shortcomings that we felt at the mall, at school, at work, when the people in control looked our way.

Even a regular childhood as *just another white boy* made me allergic to the culture of invasive monitoring that has intensified around me in the past fifty years. How much more sensitive would I be if had I grown up with a different skin color or sexual orientation? Even as a big sullen teenager in a hoodie, my white privilege meant that no one followed me in department stores, that I didn't get much attention from the police, that I didn't activate the "see something, say something" imperative of the New York City subway signs. I didn't know very much about the "prison" of homophobia that José Esteban Muñoz describes in *Cruising Utopia*.[36] I didn't know anything about the burden of what sociologist Tina P. Patel calls "browning," the racialized social sorting in which "terror-related surveillance over-focuses on all those of middle Eastern appearance, or of South Asian or Arabic heritage and of the Muslim faith," color-coding these brown bodies as suspicious "despite the lack of any actual evidence of criminal wrongdoing."[37] I didn't experience the "enhanced, discriminatory and unnecessary surveillance" to which American Muslims have been subjected since 9/11.[38] Consequently, I also didn't feel the elevated anxiety levels in response to state surveillance that they have reported, resulting in "longstanding emotional and behavioral consequences."[39] I had a different sort of monitoring to endure, yet it was still damaging to my sense of the social. That is to say, even if we escape the worst slights of history and sociology that befall certain categories of human beings at certain times, we can still grow up raw about surveillance, we can still chafe under its pressure. I still experienced it as a kind of abjection, a disquieting force in my life, a simmering misery that always threatened to get much worse. As Alan Cumming points out in his memoir of growing up with an unpredictable parent, things were not always "that bad," but the threat was always lurking. At any second, things could go wrong if he was seen taking the wrong step, making the wrong face, sitting in the wrong chair. Only constant vigilance could save him from his father's volatility. Perhaps in this sense, scholars need to look more closely at the overlapping terrains of memoir and psychology to get at the experiences and recollections of everyday life, especially among children, who have often escaped their attention.

Even now, some forty years later, I sometimes shift my expression, my posture, my path, to conform to the expectations of some real or imagined observer. I still bristle when I spot a security camera, a supervisor, a cop. I'm even allergic to the abstract idea of surveillance, and even if I don't see it in my surroundings, I always know it's deep in the machinery of the world. I can hear it grinding away, like an old-fashioned tape recorder hidden inside a desk, and I feel myself subtly deferring to its powers of observation. I suspect I'm not alone in this response to a vast technological system in our lives, even in a "nation of rebels" that has enshrined rugged individualism and personal autonomy as its guiding myth. Surveillance is inscribed on our bodies whether we register its presence or not.[40]

Status offers some protection from constant monitoring. During my seemingly interminable years of teenage grubbiness, I aspired to the professional middle class not simply because people went on proper vacations and ate better food, but because it seemed like a paradise of autonomous living where a person could roam free from observation (I was naïve). I wanted to get somewhere I wouldn't be watched, where I would be free from the weight of surveillance, where I might be implicitly trusted. If that youthful fantasy seemed plausible in 1982 as I pondered the life ahead of me, it seems absurd in 2017 as I look back on the times in which I've lived. After a very long slog, I did make it into the comforts of the professional middle class, but the old surveillance anxieties have come along to the present day, taking on new forms. Even in the relative safety of adulthood, I know these childhood sensations have followed me into an academic career now approaching the two-decade mark.

Like most people, I suspect, I still carry my childhood resentments into other realms. I wince when I see CCTV on the wall or hear about the latest Facebook privacy breach; I feel an ache, a sense of disappointment and anger and imprisonment when I hear about Edward Snowden's revelations. I don't even like the sense that someone in a café is watching these words being composed. And to this day I still experience surveillance in class terms, as if the CCTV camera is asking me to go hat in hand, like an orphan in a poorhouse. In other words, my response to the implicit deference of surveillance culture is weirdly visceral and perhaps irrational; it surges through me with an overwhelming heaviness, flooding my body with an external force that I can't wait to shake off. It's a kind of violence to the spirit that I want to minimize in my life—and in public life generally. I know that such intense reactions are not simply the product of mature conversations about security, privacy, and autonomy. As much as those are very real factors, the template for my response to surveillance was set much earlier, in ways that are unique to me but that are shared by many other people with similar stories (and probably not shared by people with different childhood experiences). What I feel about the NSA and Big Data was what I felt about priests and parents several decades ago. That's why it behooves us to wonder about the psychological impact of surveillance that starts early and never quite leaves us—even if that is something we can only address anecdotally at this point. I started with an artist in Alan Cumming, so I'll end with another artist.

Torment Saint

"My childhood made me feel like I didn't exist," the musician Elliot Smith said near the end of his life. "I was nothing." A gifted songwriter and mesmerizing performer who pulled together disparate elements of punk and folk, Smith is often cast as a tragic hero from the alternative culture of the Pacific Northwest, a disheveled young singer-guitarist who committed suicide at the apex of his success—in other words, another mythic modern who lived and died like Kurt Cobain, the central figure of the early 1990s grunge movement. But Smith's story really begins in sunny Texas, in the conservative Dallas suburbs where he was born and spent his early years in simmering conflict with a controlling stepfather. Smith's biographer hints at the likelihood of sexual and emotional abuse, but the musician was reticent about the subject, only making vague allusions in his song lyrics to the pains of his youth. What his biographer pieces together is a childhood in which "any imperfection, trivial or not, was noticed and commented on," resulting in a sensitive boy driven to distraction by the obsessive monitoring of his behavior. His biography suggests that the pressures of living with a controlling, raging parent resulted in bitter self-loathing, endless paranoia, and epic drug abuse. Eventually becoming "intensely fearful of imaginary spying" and toting around books on sexual abuse alongside

Kafka, Dostoevsky, and other works that fed his suspicions, Smith grew into a hypersensitive human being whom his biographer dubbed a "torment saint."[41]

What is the linkage between a controlling parent and a tormented adult with a driving fear of surveillance? Perhaps Smith was paranoid because he was taking too many drugs, prescription and otherwise—or perhaps his relationship with his stepfather set him on this course toward feeling ill at ease in the world, feeling wracked with uncertainty about what was being said and who was taking note. No one knows what was in the thirty-four-year-old's mind when he plunged a knife into his own chest in 2003. But I wonder if his painful self-consciousness, even paranoia, reflects something more than his individual psychology—if he provides, even anecdotally, one small reflection of the psychic cost of growing up in the crosshairs of surveillance.

If anything, the real burden of childhood surveillance is only beginning to be felt. New surveillance technologies are monitoring children with an unprecedented intensity and thoroughness. Beginning with webcams and CCTV cameras in the home and school, one researcher has listed "tracking devices including GPS locators fitted in a range of children's accessories such as clothing items, backpacks and mobile phones; biometric ID and fingerprinting systems for school roll-calls and borrowing library books; online 'spyware'; drug testing kits for parents; and an expanding range of other devices and database tools that provide new ways to track, monitor and control children's activities."[42] *Horton Hears a You, Charlotte's Webcam, Where the Wild Things Are Under Surveillance*, even *Everybody Snoops*—parodists have had a field day in recent years with the NSA's books and websites aimed at teaching kids about the joys of spying.[43] If nothing else, such spoofs are a welcome distraction from a sobering fact: we are all children of surveillance now.

Of course, these various monitoring technologies are not in-herently oppressive for either children or adults. They become problematic when they are employed in relationships based on hierarchy, control, intimidation, and secrecy, whether between parent and child, school and student, corporation and con-sumer, or government and citizen. Yet even when surveillance practices are well-intentioned and thoughtfully administered, they can still feel unpleasant and invasive to those of us with heightened sensitivities caused by early wounds in a culture of monitoring. For reasons that may stem from our childhoods in ways that I have outlined in the preceding pages, some of us feel the implicit distrust inherent in being watched in a way that is difficult to endure. While people with happier child-hood experiences might feel safe and pleased with the latest surveillance technology, we resent having to check ourselves, to wonder once again, as we did in our youth, "Is this space pri-vate? Am I under scrutiny? Am I measuring up?" Years later, we might loathe the nauseating sense of being sorted, judged, and archived for unknown reasons related to the institutions in which we live: school, family, corporation, nation. "Grow-ing up observed" in ways that were psychologically and emo-tionally draining, we resent living that way as adults. No mat-ter how much we are told that it is for our own good, that the seamless functioning of nations, businesses, and schools de-pends on careful monitoring of our behavior, we know, often from painful experience, that the truth is more complicated.

CHAPTER FOUR

Watching Walden

Imagine that you've parked your Subaru at a trailhead and hiked into a remote corner of the Rockies. Even in the middle of July, long drifts of snow remain on the untouched mountainside. Winded but exultant as you near the summit, you take a second to marvel at the cloudless sky. Not a building, road, or human being in sight—in fact, nothing is stirring except a single gray fox trotting toward the horizon at 14,000 feet. Such glorious isolation is exactly what you sought when you moved west to Colorado, exactly what you sought when you veered off trail just a few hours ago for a taste of radical solitude. Then and now, you headed into the proverbial wild, entering a mythologized space that has long captivated artists, environmentalists, and even political theorists interested in the relationships among democracy, individualism, and nature in the United States. Somehow America has always needed "the wild" as part of its self-conception, and somehow you've always needed it as well.

In your knapsack you stroke the cover of your paperback Thoreau and feel a rush of satisfaction. Even if *The Maine Woods* is not your favorite book, you brought it along because its narrative has a terrifyingly wild mountain at its core and because, *hey, it's Thoreau.* For your bookmark you've inserted another happily symbolic item, a postcard of Caspar David Friedrich's

Wanderer Above the Sea of Fog, a celebrated nineteenth-century painting that throws the European Romantic conception of nature into stark relief—or so you hope, because you teach the painting every autumn to teenagers in your AP European history course in the Denver suburbs. It's not the American West, but the image captures something about the glory of the wild that seems vital and necessary. Lungs still straining, you peek at the postcard for the umpteenth time, studying the lone figure posed on a mountaintop above churning clouds, neither commanding nor recoiling from the wilds below. Like the figure in Friedrich's painting—at least as you imagine it—you regard the uninhabited landscape as a force of regeneration and mystery, a sublime power to contemplate and internalize for the good of the soul. You want to feel the immensity of the mountains, their ability to blot out civilization's traces until nothing is left but rock, water, sky, and trees, with their promise of unbreachable privacy and seclusion. As your entire being fills with something that feels like spiritual renewal, you unzip your jacket and dance an awkward jig, delirious to have found refuge from the traffic jams, subdivisions, and fast food that dominate your everyday living. Here in the middle of nowhere, you've attained a special kind of a freedom, a kind of deep autonomy, that often eludes you at home in the suburbs. Arcadian bliss is yours at last.

But then: *bzzzzzzzzzzzzzzzzzzzz*.

What a strange bird, you think at first. Blinking, you decide it's a very small plane ... *but that's not quite it.* ... Suddenly, you realize it's one of those drones, a flying machine the size of a condor, purposefully circling your otherwise private mountaintop. At this elevation you are practically eye-to-eye with the thing, which you later discover is the county sheriff's prized purchase. Soon thereafter you'll read up on drones in the rural West, not to mention specially equipped planes and satellites with ultra-high resolution imaging capacities, learning enough that you feel embarrassed to have danced your celebratory jig in front of unseen spectators. Already you feel a little bit foolish, a little bit exposed. You want to ignore the drone circling the valley in front of you, but its presence gnaws at something in you. It seems wrong, out of place, weirdly *unnatural*. Something about it just chaps your hide. Walking the Maine backcountry in the 1840s, Thoreau described the endless challenges of "the grim, untrodden wilderness, whose tangled labyrinth of living, fallen, and decaying trees only the deer and moose, the bear and wolf, can easily penetrate." Now the sheriff of some pissant county, not to mention the secretive overlords at Google and the NSA, can penetrate such "untrodden" land with high-tech ease—silently, efficiently, continually.[1] A queasy feeling descends upon you as you wonder: *Who else is watching?*

You zip up your Gore-Tex in annoyance and head down the mountain, studying the landscape in a harsh new light. You run into some hikers taking photos on their iPhones and you wonder what their GPS reveals about their whereabouts. Further downhill you spot a "critter cam" and wonder if it's broadcasting your face to the world, or at least to a classroom of curious school kids somewhere.[2] Back at the trailhead, you notice a security camera with a National Park Service sticker that you strolled right past before. These cameras remind you about something you read about—something called Google Trekker, a way of capturing the natural landscape with an unprecedented level of detail. Back in your car, you find a headline on your phone that announces, "GOOGLE IS CALLING ON TREKKERS TO HELP CREATE STREET VIEWS OF HIDDEN CORNERS OF THE WORLD," and you shake your head in wonderment.[3] Once you start looking for surveillance in the wild, it feels like it's everywhere—everywhere "the wild" used to be.

Surveillance Gone Wild

What we generally imagine as surveillance technologies seem as far from our ideal of wilderness as Diet Coke and video games. UAVs, ultra-sensitive microphones, spy cameras, thermal sensors—what is this high-tech stuff doing in *nature*? Indeed, the whole infrastructure of watching, tracking, and sorting seems like something for nervous cities and suburbs worried about car thieves and pedophiles, not the quiet calm of the tallgrass prairie of Oklahoma, the blinding white desolation of Utah's salt flats, or the barren stretches of the Texas Gulf Coast, where normally nothing is in the air apart from a few whooping cranes. The idea that electronic surveillance is proliferating in such natural locations, many miles from obvious signs of human activity, is perplexing and maybe a little disheartening to imagine. Yet it is real: something big is happening out there in the places where surveillance technology and wilderness have begun to intersect. The surveillance is creating a new ecological crisis, one in which a new form of technology is intruding upon the landscape and quietly adding a new layer of "anthropogenic stress" on the integrity of ecosystems, without anyone seeming to notice.[4]

Some people might shrug at the prospect of CCTV in the wild, noting that the intrusion of surveillance into the natural world is a very old story. After all, what we think of as the wild has never been completely free from monitoring and tracking. Migrants have always traversed the toughest deserts with maps in hand; hunters have always followed their prey into the deepest underbrush; presidents have sent surveyors into distant landscapes in the name of empire and enterprise; and eventually ordinary people brought cameras, notebooks, GPS, and other tracking devices on camping trips and hunting expeditions. Yet there is a new level of intensity to this wild surveillance. With every passing year drones and satellites are coming in for a closer view of the treetops, arroyos, and scrub-brush critters, sometimes in ways that seem straight out of science fiction. To my mind, these UAVs, night-vision goggles, wireless CCTV cameras, and other forms of remote sensing are challenging long-held conceptions of untouched nature as a refuge from connectivity, a place where we can leave behind the feeling of being watched by governments, corporations, and our fellow citizens. Emerging surveillance technologies are altering our idea of the wild, perhaps even taming it, in ways that strike me as worrisome, if not depressing. The result is a wilderness that is increasingly under the watchful eye of the governments, corporations, and individuals who are asserting spatial dominion over places that once seemed free from obvious signs of human control. Even if *seeming free* was an illusion that grew sketchier with every passing generation, it was a potent illusion that spoke to a deep need in many people.

A natural landscape in which *everything is illuminated*, everything is instantly observable, everyone is on stage everywhere is a problematic thing. As surveillance expands into seemingly pristine environments, we will have to struggle a little harder to find an unobserved spot. Not to put too fine a point on it, this will represent an extraordinary transition in human consciousness: the end of rural solitude. Computer scientists describe an approaching moment in which computers attain self-awareness as "the singularity," but I wonder if the term is equally suited to the time when the surveillance infrastructure completes its global embrace, finally wrapping its arms around city and country alike. Right now the system is incomplete, still lacking coherence and integration in significant ways (its many parts are often separated by national or commercial interests, for the time being). Yet someday soon, the singularity will change this, signaling the end of wilder-

ness as we have generally imagined it. Even if no one will com-
memorate the surveillance singularity with a golden spike, as
they did the transcontinental railroad, we should take note of
this equally historic occasion in the history of technology: a
significant new infrastructure will have engulfed the planet,
as meaningful and transformative as railroads, power grids,
and interstate highways. Even a humanless void in the Mojave
will be subject to extraordinarily precise forms of monitoring,
if it isn't already. The most desolate wasteland will be incorporated into a vast system of knowing and remembering in the
surveillance infrastructure. To those with the power to scrutinize, those fortunate owners of the means of surveillance production, this moment of singularity will bring an unforeseen
level of control and illumination to landscapes near and far. As
seemingly raw nature is incorporated into a rapacious machinery of knowing, a bright new light will shine on the small details of human and nonhuman life that now escape detection:
the morning stroll of a lone Tibetan farmer; the relaxed goat-
herding of a Ugandan villager; the morning trawl of a Haitian
fisherman; the lighting of a match around an Alaskan campfire
(which can already be spotted by a small sensor more than 12
miles away). Even those who are not political refugees, angry
libertarians, or criminals on the lam might mourn the loss of
hidden spots on the planet: escaping into the mountains or
jungles or densest forests will have no plausibility outside of
a Hollywood movie. Fleeing to the natural world for sanctuary and solitude will become a fantasy of the highest order,
one that will require the suspension of our critical faculties.
Listening to birds squawking and streams flowing, we might
still pause on an isolated ridge and tell ourselves, *At last, I'm
truly alone.* We might take a deep breath, or a sip of bour-
bon, to really complete the illusion of the world at bay, out of
sight, out of mind. But more than ever before, that feeling will

be a Class A delusion, a cruel joke on the technologically Ill-informed who don't realize what is occurring in the seemingly quiet skies above their head. For humans as much as any other creatures, electronic supervision will be as inescapable in the wilderness as in a the neighborhood shopping center.

What is the psychic price of this development? The philosopher Mark Kingwell has written about the importance of buildings to the cities in which we live: "the logic of inside to outside," he writes, "structures consciousness itself."[5] But what happens when these two qualities collapse, when outside and inside start to blur, even in places that appear to be manifestly outside of the built environment? What does "outside" or "outdoors" mean if surveillance technologies have brought nature inside the web of constant scrutiny and urban knowing? How might the rapid expansion of surveillance into the wild structure our consciousness in new ways? All of the qualities we associate with a control society, for good and ill, are creeping into what was understood as uncharted, untouched, and uncontrolled. If by wilderness we mean a seemingly unmapped, uncontrolled, unobserved stretch of land or sea, will we have to shift our definitions and expectations?[6] In other words, how will we reimagine (or cease to imagine) wilderness in the age of surveillance?

The reality of this predicament has been slow to seep into human consciousness, perhaps because the global embrace of the surveillance infrastructure is not quite complete. For now a few dedicated *isolatos* (Melville's great term for the wanderers of the world), pot farmers in the Bible Belt, or stressed-out survivalists might still find a small gap in the information grid. If someone sits very still beneath a rock overhang in the desert near Moab, Utah, crouching into a small ball of undetectability, they might still enjoy a brief moment of uncompromised solitude, the thrill of human existence unregistered on any sensor whatsoever, whether a gauge hidden in the ground or a satellite camera hurtling through space. But it's getting harder every day.

If it is still technically possible to hide somewhere between cell-phone towers and wireless sensors, the gaps are closing fast. When a white-collar criminal hid for almost a year in a makeshift tent in the piney woods of East Texas, locals were astonished that he was able to elude detection for so long, even though Nacogdoches County is home to some of the thickest, darkest underbrush on the continent.[7] If nature has not been subdued—and out-of-control climate change attests to that humbling fact—it's coming under supervision to an unprecedented degree. Theodore Kaczynski, the homicidal hermit known as the Unibomber, railed against such domination of the natural world in his manifesto, "Industrial Society and Its Future." In this screed he predicted that "whatever may be left of wild nature will be reduced to remnants preserved for scientific study and kept under the supervision and management of scientists (hence it will no longer be truly wild)."[8] Even nonpsychopaths will agree with the bushy-haired mathematician: with a diminishing number of exceptions, the landscape and its animal inhabitants have been mapped, watched, sorted, and fenced for quite some time. It's not a secret: Americans began fretting as far back as 1893, when Frederick Jackson Turner announced the so-called closing of the frontier. "There is no question that wilderness, *as we have understood it*, has vanished," writes political scientist Paul Wapner. "A world that is pristine, uninhabited, and unaltered by humanity is nowhere to be found anymore."[9]

In some ways surveillance technology merely adds a strange new twist to an old story of wilderness in peril. Yet I want to ask what this new twist might mean. With satellite cameras, drones, iPhones, and Trekker looking over our shoulders even on the highest mountain peak, will we continue to look to

the regenerative power of wilderness as a tonic to the enerva-
tion of postindustrial life in the suburbs?[10] Will the prospect
of desert solitude in the American Southwest be reduced to a
quaint historical fiction? By putting the new surveillance into
dialogue with concepts such as wilderness, individualism, and
autonomy, I hope to weigh the implications of wild surveillance for the United States and for eco-consciousness generally. Much of this will happen in conversation with an unlikely
theorist of surveillance, the nineteenth-century naturalist and
writer Henry David Thoreau. But first, treading carefully, I will
take on the wilderness as an idea, often a highly problematic
one, to understand where surveillance is going next.

Wild Ideas

The arrival of modern surveillance systems is hardly the first
wrinkle in the story of North American wilderness. In the fif-
teenth and sixteenth centuries, Europeans approached the so-
called wilderness of the New World with more fear than celebration, regarding it with a suspicion that indigenous peoples
could scarcely fathom. In his classic *The Invasion of America*
(1975), historian Francis Jennings describes a natural landscape in which two dubious concepts—"civilization" and "savagery"—struggled for control. Jennings beautifully sketched
out the contours of this essential American myth, one that
continues to shape the conception of nature in America. Civilization, we are led to believe,

> was required by divine sanction or the imperatives of progress
> to conquer the wilderness and make it a garden; that the sav-
> age creatures of the wilderness, being unable to adapt to any
> environment other than the wild, stubbornly and viciously re-
> sisted God or fate, and thereby incurred their suicidal exter-

mination; that civilization and its bearers were refined and ennobled in their contest with the dark powers of the wilderness; and that it was all inevitable.[11]

For much of the seventeenth and eighteenth centuries, European colonists retained their wariness of the natural landscape, even imagining wilderness as a vile place filled with physical and spiritual dangers that would thwart any attempts to exploit its seemingly boundless resources.

Something shifted, however, in the early Republic, and by 1800 the wild seemed to have secured a vaunted place in US nationalist mythology.[12] Increasingly, this mysterious place of "resisting control" and wild "unknownness"—two qualities antithetical to the very idea of surveillance—became central to European Americans' conception of themselves and the western territory to which they laid claim. As European Americans poured into the "maw of the unknown" throughout the nineteenth century, they fulfilled their "manifest destiny" to extend settler colonialism from coast to coast.[13] No longer a place of demons and heathens, as seventeenth-century Puritans had feared, wilderness was fast becoming an aesthetic, moral, and national resource of the highest order, a sacred place for a regenerative experience that was not possible in the burgeoning cities of the East Coast and upper Midwest. By the time Rudyard Kipling visited Chicago in the 1890s, the American city was already too wretched for his taste. "Having seen it, I urgently desire never to see it again," the English writer and poet complained. "I had never seen so many white people together, and never such a collection of miserables. There was no color in the street and no beauty—only a maze of wire ropes overhead and dirty stone flagging under foot."[14] As American cities grew into vast monstrosities that prompted similar alarm among progressive reformers, including nascent environmentalists, the wilderness was held up as the nation's saving grace,

a virgin land of problematically gendered possibility and renewal that the nation could not live without.

Yet wilderness was always a fishy proposition. In a famous
essay in the 1990s, the eminent historian William Cronon un-
masked the wild as "more a state of mind than a fact of nature,"
a projection of a civilization looking for its antithesis.[15] Even
earlier generations had a sense that going off the grid required
some wishful thinking. "It is in vain to dream of a wildness
distant from ourselves," warned Henry David Thoreau. "There
is none such."[16] Similarly, Native American people must have
been surprised by the idea of roping off a part of the world as
wild and untouched. As an example of how native languages
often lacked a word for "wilderness" as a distinct category of
the natural landscape somehow separate from humanity, the
contemporary Navajo poet Luci Tapahonso has said that in her
tribe: "You can speak of places that are far away or places where
there are few people, but that's all."[17] Yet European Americans
had a word—and a powerful appetite—for this idea and the
real estate it designated. What literary scholar Michael Johnson calls a "hunger for the wild" has often been a problematic
enterprise in the United States, where it often resulted in violence against Native Americans and the land they had long
occupied. Indeed, the European American idea of wilderness
has often been disastrous for native peoples, whose footsteps
had long shaped what was wrongly perceived as untrammeled
land in need of new forms of ownership and productivity. To
the extent that we lose this problematic notion of the wild, we
have lost very little of use to the present. But to the extent that
we lose something that inspires and consoles us—the idea of
the wild—we have lost something dear.

For all its problematic ideological shadings, the wild is still
something that many people feel in their bones is meaningful
and worth preserving. The mythic wilderness may be a cultural
construction, but it feels very real indeed when we are stand-

ing in the middle of it. At the very least, it is this *feeling* that is in jeopardy at the present moment. We will continue to feel the enormity of nature long after the global population hits 10 billion and endures whatever ravages that inflicts upon the planet. But the sentiments that we have attached to that vast natural world may be altered, if not damaged, by the spread of new forms of surveillance into the hidden recesses of the planet.

The Googleization of Nature

Let me now concede the obvious: the introduction of new surveillance technologies into the wild is sometimes a marvelous thing. We should fawn over the scientific applications of CCTV, UAVs, and other forms of remote sensing that have tangible benefits for wildlife ecosystems—it is not for nothing that entire organizations have devoted themselves to spreading the gospel of UAVs in the environmental community.[18] Although I wince at their choice of metaphor, I share the optimism of the ecowarrior website for "Real-Time Video Interactive Systems for Sustainability," which celebrates *Big Brother finally going green*, as they put it, in order to protect the earth from harm.[19] Without question, scientists are making good use of new technological opportunities to measure, watch, and record the natural landscape from great distances. For instance, California's San Jacinto Mountains are strewn with "devices known as motes [that] measure light, wind, rainfall, temperature, humidity, and barometric pressure to detect the presence of a warm body."[20]

From Iceland to Costa Rica, so-called eco-drones are going where no human pilot could safely navigate, bringing back essential data about climate change, volcanic activity, and other scientific matters.[21] Scientists are gathering important data on hurricanes in the Atlantic with what National Public Radio insists on calling "spy drones."[22] Drones with thermal imaging cameras are following sandhill cranes into wetlands, while Predator drones are providing the intel needed to battle forest fires in Yosemite.[23] One South African farmer owns thirty drones to protect rhinos from poachers, while the Indian government is doing the same for its beleaguered tiger population.[24] Similarly, the Brazilian government is putting the Amazon under "permanent surveillance" to fight illegal deforestation.[25]

Meanwhile, in Appalachia, drones are visiting ordinary gardeners to help them monitor soil moisture and invasive insects. "Usually, I'm just out there in sweat pants," one local said, "but if this thing is coming around taking pictures, I'm going to think twice about what I wear to the garden."[26] The federal government even has blimps with surveillance capabilities roaming the skies from Lake Erie to North Carolina.[27]

Government agencies are also investing in wilderness surveillance for nonscientific reasons. An Oregon man was busted in 2013 when his hidden marijuana fields were revealed on Google Earth satellite images. Such stories are not unusual in the United States and elsewhere, with the Swiss government pulling in more than a ton of weed through satellite images as early as 2009.[28] The US Air Force drones equipped with the so-called Gorgon Stare can bring an extraordinary level of illumination to any landscape, using "an array of five electro-optical and four infrared cameras to capture day and night images from different angles, which are stitched together in a single mosaic scene much broader than what any single lens could deliver."[29] Even if Gorgon Stare has not been used in the United States, the astonishing optical powers of these machines are not entirely unknown here. We know, for instance, that drones belonging to the border patrol have been used to track and arrest US citizens in rural areas. In one case, a drone spotted a North

Dakota farmer accused of stealing a few cows, resulting in a three-year sentence.[30] If multimillion-dollar quasi-military drones chasing part-time cattle rustlers seem too absurd to contemplate, I would point out again that Google has gotten into the game as well, using its Google Earth program to pinpoint the location of marijuana fields for law enforcement not just in Oregon, but in Wisconsin and elsewhere.[31]

But as the infomercials used to remind us on late-night TV: *But wait ... there's more!* Backpackers can blithely stride past motion-activated remote cameras that can be squirreled away in a bush or crevice to send images wirelessly to their owners. These covert cameras are sold, according to the marketing materials, "exclusively for law enforcement, military, and corporate security to monitor marijuana fields, border security, graffiti, illegal dumping, and much more!"[32] (In other words, anyone can buy them.) In 2009, the state of Texas set up a "virtual border watch program" to monitor the scrubland along the southern border of the Lone Star State, and suddenly thousands of "virtual deputies" were logging on to monitor empty stretches of the Rio Grande.[33] Ironically, the same people who were joining the online posse to round up "illegal aliens" might reject a similar form of surveillance in the wild: *Field and Stream* magazine complained that animal-rights activists were selling small drones to anyone who wants to keep an eye on local hunters. The magazine quoted the sales pitch, presumably with gritted teeth: "Using your hobby drone, you can collect instant to-your-phone video footage of hunters engaging in illegal activity, such as drinking while in possession of a firearm, injuring animals and failing to pursue them, and illegally using spotlights, feed lures, and other nasty but common hunting tricks. Your amateur footage can be used to alert game wardens and other authorities to who is doing what to animals."[34]

Apparently, everybody is watching everybody in the new

American wild. A Canadian video-game developer wants to scan the entire globe to "reproduce accurately, at scale, the whole planet and its different ecosystems, environments, countries and cities using small civilian drones" to create a virtual world that replicates the actual world, like something out of a Borges short story.[35] The giants of Silicon Valley have already devoted themselves to this project of global illumination. While Facebook's Mark Zuckerberg dreams of an Open Planet of total transparency in which all movements are tracked for the benefit of Facebook users (well, at least for Facebook's advertisers), Google is also playing a part in taming the wild, and it has plenty of help. Hikers may now wear Google Glass on their favorite trails, recording the flowers as much as strangers wandering into shot. And going beyond that, Google is bringing its controversial Street View concept to nature with Trekker, a backpack-mounted data collection apparatus that can capture images of the natural landscape in stunning detail. With fifteen specially designed lenses mounted on a forty-pound device that pokes out of a backpack, Trekker has begun to pierce the mysteries of Mount Everest, the Galapagos Islands, Antarctica, and the Great Barrier Reef.[36] "Since 2005, Google has mapped 28 million miles of road in 194 countries," one report noted in summer 2013. "And it won't rest until the whole planet is on its servers."[37] By harnessing the power of what Google dubs "citizen cartographers" (more than 40,000 worldwide as of 2014), Google Trekker will allow the company to tackle something that would have been impossible until just a few years ago: "Our goal is to put together a sort of digital mirror of the world," says one Google exec.[38]

The pushback against this project, perhaps the greatest cartographic undertaking in world history, has been almost nil. One British newspaper wondered if Google Trekker would dull "the experience of traveling" by removing mystery and surprise from the landscape.[39] I would add some other uncomfortable questions before we rush into Google's perfect future. Do we really want a world in which everything is mapped, monitored, and accessible from any digital device? Do we really want a world in which the wild is forced to shed its secrets? Why does this transformation of the wild feel like a fait accompli rather than something for the public to debate? Such questions seem strangely absent from the broader discussions of Google's project.[40] This is something that geographer Jason Farman explores in an article on Google's "digital empire." Describing the shadow of colonialism that haunts the information giant's quest for totalizing spatial knowledge, Farman writes: "The technological gaze of aerial and satellite imagery—the essence of the interactive maps presented in Google Earth—has a long history with war and imperialism and subsequently has a historical relationship in the ways maps delineate 'us' versus 'them' as well as defining 'our territory.'"[41]

Even beyond the political economy and subtle colonialism of what I am calling "wild surveillance," we might consider the emotional burden that these new technologies and practices are adding to the natural world. One scholar has written about the shifts that occur at the emotional level that might push against logic, intention, or explicit meaning: for instance, watching news broadcasts or game shows have an impact on us "not so much in their ideological effects, but in their ability to create affective resonances independent of content or meaning."[42] In other words, something in the room is setting the tone, but it's not always the thing in the foreground. To my mind, Google's website might trumpet the excitement of Trekker as a new way to connect with remote landscapes and natural wonders, thereby putting the grandeur of nature in the center of the frame, as it were, but something might still feel *off*. A person might even feel a sense of quiet desperation, a kind of sadness or intimidation, as he realizes just how much Google knows about his secret spots in the woods.

The taming of the wild simply *feels bad* to many people. For those who like their nature without a side order of scrutiny, surveillance technology is anxiety-producing in almost any context, even in the calmest corners of the woods or prairies. For others, wild surveillance touches on thorny political questions. I'm thinking, for instance, of Senator Rand Paul and other conservative libertarians who patently reject the prospect of Big Brother in the great outdoors: "My privacy's only inside my house and not in open spaces?" Senator Paul, of Kentucky, asked incredulously on the floor of the Senate during his 2013 antisurveillance filibuster. "I disagree with that."[43] Even if our political sensibilities are not offended, some of us have an aesthetic beef: the ugliness of UAVs, CCTVs, and their ilk corrupts the beauty of nature as we would prefer to experience it. For aesthetic and sentimental reasons, keeping nature pristine is often its own reward. As ecologist Paul Wapner puts it, "*People get pleasure out of protecting the nonhuman world.*"[44] It is a quaint sentiment that would have appealed to a canonical figure in American letters, someone whose voice has not been heard on the subject of surveillance, who might even seem an improbable commentator on technologies of control emerging in the twenty-first-century wilderness. Yet Henry David Thoreau is always more than we assume, and I think he can take us where we need to go.

What Would Henry Do?

"I wish to speak a word for Nature, for absolute freedom and wildness." So begins an essay titled "Walking," published in *Atlantic Monthly* one month after the death of its author, Henry David Thoreau, in 1862.[45] Obviously, a mid-nineteenth-century writer will have nothing to say on the topic of electronic surveillance as we know it today. However, it is not unreasonable to imagine what he might have said if we had strolled alongside him as he mused, prodded, critiqued, and scoffed at the follies of his own age. As a political theorist, essayist, and cultural critic, Thoreau wrote eloquently about the role of individualism in a democratic republic, the necessity of privacy to the development of moral character, and the encroachment of technology on his beloved landscape. Perhaps because he is so indelibly linked to nature, we seem not to have noticed how much he offers to discussions of contemporary surveillance culture, especially as it intersects with the natural world in new and surprising ways. In his own peculiar and often beautiful manner, Thoreau may be an untapped theorist of surveillance. Given his profound attachment to autonomous living and other gently libertarian virtues, I suspect he would have recoiled from surveillance's subtle claims on our lives— its implicit demand for social conformity and adherence to the law, its insatiable desire to pry into our personal affairs for commercial or bureaucratic reasons, its implicit threat to our mobility. In short, I think he would lament our contemporary surveillance culture for systematically stifling freedom, independence of mind and movement, and the dignity of solitude that, for him at least, thrived best in nature. Surely he would mourn for an America in which rugged individualism and pastoral regeneration had become dusty relics trotted out on special occasions, appearing in presidential speeches and advertisements for SUVs as mere fantasies for a citizenry huddled together nervously, wired up for endless infotainment and in a constant state of anxious self-defense in an increasingly urbanized nation. Most pointedly, I suspect that he would find the ruthless securitization of the natural world demeaning in the extreme. To put it mildly, it would cramp his style.

To those who imagine him as turning his back on civilization and its advances, Thoreau might seem like a strange commentator on the subject of electronic surveillance or any other emerging technology. Wasn't he more interested in rivers than people, more attached to pastures than machines? Not quite. Contrary to stereotype, Thoreau was no Luddite. "Whatever he thought of the results of mechanization," writes his finest biographer, "he clearly had a flair for machines and contrivances themselves."[46] In this regard, Thoreau was more sensitive to the benefits of new technologies than one might assume about the hermit of Walden.[47] Even as he lamented the arrival of the railroad, he would also concede that its "sounds ... and even its smoke as seen from a distance could add interest to a landscape."[48] And his appreciation went far beyond aesthetics. Perhaps the best surveyor in New England, an inventor who revolutionized the pencil for a few lucrative years, and a small-factory owner with a keen eye for the details of manufacturing, Thoreau was as skilled with new technology as he was in the woods around Concord, Massachusetts. Indeed, he brilliantly combined science and poetry in his later years, bringing together biology, statistics, and botany into a naturalist project of unprecedented depth and care.

Thoreau possessed a rare blend of relevant interests, an uncanny skill set. How often do we find someone whose scientific know-how is counterpoised by the perceptions of a cultural critic and the talents of a literary artist? (Let me know if you find others.) While he could be appreciative of the latest technology from an engineering point of view and could implement scientific methods of observing natural processes that foreshadowed contemporary eco-surveillance, he was still exquisitely attuned to the ways in which technological advances could create more trouble than they were worth. For instance, he famously fretted about devices that were "but improved means to an unimproved end," and he lampooned the great breakthrough in communication technology of his adulthood. "We are in great haste to construct a magnetic telegraph from Maine to Texas," he quipped in *Walden*, "but Maine and Texas, it may be, have nothing important to communicate." Given his blend of technological know-how and skepticism, Thoreau is perfectly positioned to speak about the impact of new technologies on the natural landscape.

Students of technology may have overlooked the relevance of Thoreau's work on some occasions, but environmentalists, naturalists, and eco-critics have always been closely attuned to his writing. Indeed, the philosopher Philip Cafaro puts him at the heart of American eco-criticism and environmentalism: "All the key American thinkers, from John Muir to Aldo Leopold to Rachel Carson, show Thoreau's clear influence."[49] Few would doubt that *Walden* is an essential text in the ecological tradition, a book that informs so much of the American conception of nature. For this reason alone I am naturally curious about what Thoreau might offer on the relationship of surveillance technologies and the natural world. Would he relate to our dilemma as an intensification of one he knew in a simpler form? Would his practical side intercede, telling us to go about our business in the *seemingly* wild, calmly accepting the expansion of transparent society to the land and water at the extremes of the earth? Or would he rage against the machinery of knowing? Would he shake his head and rebuke us for spoiling a natural paradise with anxious gadgetry? Would he suggest that the ancient encounter with the ragged edges of the natural world is undercut by the mere knowledge that someone could be watching our every step, recording our every movement? Would he lament the fact that going off the grid is an increasingly quixotic enterprise in a world in which every location, every movement, can be tracked and plotted? Would he grit his teeth to see that *everything*, even the farthest reaches of the Rockies or the sandiest stretches of Death Valley, is now illuminated with an unprecedented intensity and accuracy? Surely he would wonder about this new level of scrutiny and control in "the wild" and whether it still makes sense to use that phrase for anything but a recurring cultural fantasy.

Such questions are the natural extension of his work as I imagine it. His writing was a poetic lament against collective pressures; his life was a very civilized protest against containment and accountability, two of surveillance culture's defining qualities. Hoping to preserve the ideals of democratic autonomy, untrammeled mobility, and personal liberty, unrealized though they might seem, Thoreau thought hard about how civilization weighs upon us in subtle ways—and how it was weighing upon nature with increasing force as the industrial revolution gathered steam in the mid–nineteenth century. In making his quiet protest, he wasn't positioning himself outside society, turning his back on neighbors, friends, and strangers. Instead, he stood in the doorway between two worlds, wild and tame, raw and cooked, natural and cultural, gazing in both directions with a wistful, defiant poetry. Ironically, the wild didn't come naturally to him: he had lived a middle-class life in the comfortable home of a businessman who sent him to Harvard for a classical education. Yet, after college, he spent his life in pursuit of something wilder than he had known in Boston: he hungered for an unfettered life of radical autonomy, of dignified individualism, of passionate engagement with the natural world, whether in the gentle hills around Concord or the harsh granite peak of Mount Katahdin in Maine.[50] He urged us to "separate . . . from the multitude" and to scrutinize ourselves internally, something that the surveillance regime, with its surface attentions, cannot fathom.[51] Instead of allowing oneself to become lodged in a web of social expectation and tacit intimidation (such that drones and CCTV might suggest), he counseled a thoughtful retreat into unsurveilled seclusion. "There are times when we have had enough even of our Friends, when we begin inevitably to withdraw religiously into solitude and silence, the better to prepare ourselves for a loftier intimacy," he wrote.[52] These are not the sentiments of a misanthrope, but rather someone who prizes a deeper form of engagement that begins, somewhat paradoxically perhaps, with the care of the self. Privacy, distance, quiet, beauty, calm, solitude, trust, naturalness—these are his organic virtues, none of which are enhanced by plugging into a vast network of monitoring and sorting.

For reasons related to his political inclinations and personal ethics, Thoreau would never want us to be intimidated into higher purposes; he would not want pressure coming from an external force (the implied threat of the state's camera, for instance) when we should be relying on our own inner lights as we make decisions about right and wrong. Thoreau lived in a time of bourgeois ascendancy, a period in which an emphasis on fashionable appearance was becoming more widespread and in which the open possibilities of the revolutionary era were being shunted aside by "constraints and contradictions."[53] I suspect that he would have viewed electronic surveillance as one more constraint closing tight around the throat of individualism, one more sign of the superficial attention to surfaces over depths. Control, order, expectations, social and legal norms—the virtues of surveillance culture are antithetical to living life as Thoreau proposed. After all, surveillance is always pulling us inside a system of accountability like a teacher watching wayward children in a classroom, while Thoreau wanted to live outside, sauntering amid his beloved wild apples and huckleberries. To one so inclined, surveillance is another affront to individual liberty, one more attempt to tame the human spirit, one more way in which the collective bears down on the individual.

Thoreau might even wonder if being monitored, whether in nature or in the city, would have a corrosive effect on our capacity for moral judgments. After all, his goal in going to Walden Pond was "to transact some private business with the fewest possible obstacles"; by obstacles he meant the gaze of the state, commercial interests, and bustling townspeople. I suspect that modern surveillance culture would intrude on his ideal of "private business" with an insidiousness that he would find abhorrent, even maddening. Because he loved the idea of having "a little world all to [him]self," he appreciated fishermen who were thoughtful enough to leave him undisturbed when they sought his pond for night fishing. He was grateful when they "soon retreated, usually with light baskets, and left 'the world to darkness and to me,' and the black kernel of night was never profaned by any human neighborhood."

While surveillance culture asks for more and more information and interaction between strangers, Thoreau recommended firm boundaries, even "a considerable neutral ground," between people. We were already too close, he complained:

> We meet at the post-office, and at the sociable, and about the fireside every night; we live thick and are in each other's way, and stumble over one another, and I think that we thus lose some respect for one another. Certainly less frequency would suffice for all important and hearty communications. Consider the girls in a factory—never alone, hardly in their dreams.[54]

In a similar vein, he gently mocked the ills of "spectatordom," the worthless gawking that might have felt especially painful to a man who considered himself homely. None of this sounds like the making of a surveillance apologist, especially in the context of the woods where he spent his most vital years largely on his own. In some ways he anticipates Hannah Arendt's *On Revolution*, in which she describes the external scrutinizing that I associate with surveillance:

The search for motives, the demand that everybody display in public his innermost motivation, since it actually demands the impossible, transforms all actors into hypocrites; the moment the display of motives begins, hypocrisy begins to poison all human relations.... It is, unfortunately, in the essence of these things that every effort to make goodness manifest in public ends with the appearance of crime and criminality on the political scene. In politics, more than anywhere else, we have no possibility of distinguishing between being and appearance. In the realm of human affairs, being and appearance are indeed one and the same.[55]

Despite her admiration for his civil disobedience, Arendt didn't appreciate Thoreau as a political theorist, rejecting him as irresponsibly solipsistic.[56] I see him as neither.

If we recalculate our sense of Thoreau, shaking off the thick layers of stereotype and myth about a canonical writer, we can see someone with a wealth of insight about the relationship of technology and nature, something that can then be applied to our current predicament. We can see someone who is far more than a Transcendentalist mystic and weather-beaten naturalist; we can discern a shrewd critic of civilization's expansion and an underappreciated political theorist of the democratic condition. We can see someone with a libertarian heart, who "heartily accepted" the motto that "that government is best which governs least," an idea that the modern NSA and FBI have forgotten to preserve in their endless files. Widely admired if seldom imitated for his civil disobedience against the federal government, Thoreau was willing to use his body in opposition to an unjust American war with Mexico, preferring to meet the government only once a year on tax day. He would be appalled, I suspect, to see how many "meetings" we have with the government in the contemporary United States, where various state agencies track our license plates automatically; archive our online activity; and request the titles of the books we check out from the library. "Must the citizen . . . resign his conscience to the legislator?" he wondered, 150 years ago.[57] His ideal America was a place where citizens were ruled by their own consciences, not by state coercion or corporate seduction, a place very unlike the world in which we live—indeed, a world very unlike the actual world in which *he* lived. For this reason he wrote against the grain of America, pushing it in more hopeful directions that were rarely taken.

I wish he were here to give advice. As a card-carrying member of the "What Would Henry Do?" brigade, I am acutely aware that no one speaks for him (and few speak as well as him). Yet we can draw from his words and spirit to glean something we might otherwise miss. He wouldn't be an antisurveillance zealot—his thinking was too nuanced for easy certainties, and he would have appreciated the scientific possibilities of wild surveillance. But I think he would be a surveillance skeptic in general, willing to pose some uncomfortable questions about our endless craving for security at the expense of beauty, dignity, autonomy, and liberty, all of which would strike him as equally necessary to a robust and meaningful life. To those who might wonder how beauty or dignity could rival security as a national interest, Thoreau would likely ask another question in return: What are we securing with our surveillance regime if not the higher virtues of our kind? Are we keeping out the dangers or fencing in our true natures? Thoreau had a genius for reversing the prevailing wisdom, something that would help us understand the latest outrage in the Panopticon.

He would also raise spiritual and aesthetic questions that are rarely asked about surveillance culture. For someone with a devotional approach to the natural world, someone with a vision of the wild that was simultaneously poetic and immensely practical, the encroachment of technology must have seemed like a desecration of what he loved best in the *out-*

side, not to mention all that he held necessary to the development of character and creativity on the *inside*. As Jane Bennett puts it in describing Thoreau's techniques for developing the self, "One goes to the desert to escape the order imposed by the They"—the chattering, judging mass of men and women who dictate fashion, custom, and law at the expense of true individualism, as Thoreau perceived it. I imagine he would have resented surveillance in the wild as an intrusive presence breathing down his neck. He would resent the bright light of publicity shining on his private reverie in the woods. He would rue a world in which cameras and sensors could trespass on every river and stream; after all, he never wanted to "profane" an older "sacred" way of being.[58] He might even view surveillance as a form of pollution, another of society's "dirty institutions," pursuing and pawing at us no matter how far we flee from its grasp. A child of European Romanticism, he would surely resent the taming of the wild, the measuring and monitoring of the sublime, the arrogant desire to dominate the natural world in the name of science, security, or profit ("defiant gestures of isolation and retreat are familiar to any student of Romanticism," one historian has reminded us).[59] In a society that celebrated fashionable trends and currying favor with tastemakers, Thoreau prized autonomy and a way of living in which we were the sole overseers of ourselves, living free and uncommitted. He wanted us to find the truly *respectable* in ourselves, rather than accepting what was merely *respected* in society. In *Walden* he asked us to live on trust, to eschew anxiety, to live on faith in ways that seem incompatible with our high-tech culture of suspicion. Nearly two centuries after he began writing, the bane of his existence—anxious conformity and needless scrutiny—has infused our lives in ways that would have astonished him.

What does all this mean for students of Thoreau's politics? By looking beyond the usual stopping points for scholars of his

politics, namely his essay "Resistance to Civil Government,"
political scientist Shannon L. Mariotti helps us to see the
deeper significance of Thoreau's obsessions with autonomy,
liberty, and privacy, three elements that come together in what
she calls his practices of "democratic withdrawal." Far from the
self-indulgent retreat from civic obligation that is sometimes
attributed to him, Thoreau's "withdrawal" takes on a positive
new light in Mariotti's work, in ways that might help us to
imagine Thoreau's response to modern surveillance culture.
For Mariotti, Thoreau offered a critique of a society in which it
is maddeningly difficult to think and act with real autonomy,
but his position was discounted, along with any other form of
critique or negation. Here is where Mariotti makes her most
interesting move: she puts the sage of Walden Pond into an unexpected conversation with Theodor Adorno. By pairing these
two writers—two intellectuals who wrote on opposite sides
of the American continent almost a hundred years apart—
she examines their shared belief that an unfettered "critical
self" was the essential wellspring of democratic culture. Opt-
ing out of the system, whether nineteenth-century taxation,
the twentieth-century culture industry, or twenty-first century
surveillance, is not running away from democratic responsibility to some private island of individual privilege. It is not a
solipsistic retreat from the social accountability that society in
general, and that system in particular, demands of us. Rather,
this unplugging from society's watchful mechanisms is a way
of nurturing the solitary way of being that democracy requires
as much as it does social engagement.[60] Some care of the self,
some preservation of the personal, is required for democratic
culture to thrive. In using Thoreau as a political theorist who
celebrates idiosyncrasy as much as solidarity, boundaries as
much as belonging, Mariotti argues that civic engagement is
much more than citizenship, and that "the democratic politics
of withdrawal ... need not necessarily be equated with apoliti-

cal apathy."[61] It makes running from surveillance seem quite reasonable.

Thoreau must have been aware of his friend Ralph Waldo Emerson's vision of turning into an "invisible eyeball" while walking in the woods. His neighbor, friend, and sometimes employer was crafting a metaphor for the individual's capacity to see beyond the mundane to the mystical, to feel the ineffable power of experience surging through the human body. Emerson could be a little more mawkish, a little more goofy, than his more practical protégé, but Thoreau was no stranger to this feeling of intoxication in the wild: it is what drove him to Walden Pond, the mountain peaks of Maine, and even into the upper Midwest for a spell to restore his health. After all, he lived in Concord at a time of rapid population growth that one scholar has called the "urbanization of Massachusetts," a demographic fact that may partially account for his passion for solitude.[62]

Perhaps we can adapt Emerson's famous metaphor for surveillance culture. A new set of invisible eyeballs is ascendant in the twenty-first century security state, the endlessly varied ways of seeing and sorting our actions online, on the street, and even in the woods where the Transcendentalists hoped to experience nonrational bursts of beauty and energy that flowed like a unifying force in the universe. Thoreau would have chafed at these hidden watchmen, perhaps running farther off the grid than the outskirts of Concord permitted, perhaps as far "into the wild" as the young romantic who died on the Alaskan tundra in the 1990s before being eulogized in a book and film of that name. But would that be far enough to avoid leaving tracks, to avoid being seen by these new invisible eyeballs in a version of nature that Emerson could hardly have imagined? Probably not. In an age of sharp-eyed satellites and UAVs, the wilderness no longer holds its secrets.

The View from the Cabin

Not much has changed since 1850 for the visitor reaching the edge of Walden Pond today, at least not at first glance. The large pond is still bucolic to contemplate, its waters calm on the August morning when I wander its shoreline. As I move uphill and into the trees, the sun still pierces the canopy in a few places, while most of the forest floor remains in shadow. Animals and insects still move, seemingly undetected, in the stillness of the woods. Thoreau built his cabin not far from the water's edge, just a short walk up the hill in an idyllic clearing. Now it is a shrine to the mythic past of the continent, the disappearing wildness of North America. It is a place where we come to ponder our relationship to the natural world, just as Thoreau did, though we tend to remain for an afternoon, not two years. What strikes me is how the land here is ordinary and extraordinary at the same time, a common New England landscape that has been made sacred by a thoughtful conspiracy of bibliophiles and naturalists. For a nation as fraught with violence and delusion as the United States, Walden is as close as we get to an American Eden.

Yet something has changed. The original cabin is only a memory, a shrine to the pristine wild marked only with rocks and signs and, at least for today, a woman in an orange leotard practicing transcendental meditation. The cabin itself has long since disappeared, with only a replica near the parking lot to help us remember something of its old form while we pause for a photo, twenty feet from families unloading their minivans. Even at the old cabin site, the sublime calm of the woods is punctuated, sometimes quite abrasively, by the sound of helicopters overhead, cars on the nearby road, and visitors such as myself. A squad of runners tears through the woods while gossiping at high volume. Morning hikers consult their iPhones to keep up with the demands of social media. I certainly don't judge them—I'm using mine to send a photo to my young daughter, a few ironic megabytes of "Look, dad is in nature!" I don't mention the empty can of Bud Light and the plastic lid from a Big Gulp that I find where Thoreau famously grew beans. I don't mention the not-so-subtle hints of the control society: official signs warn visitors to remain on trails marked with barbed wire in places (barbed wire at Walden Pond?), and tan-suited rangers prowl the grounds to ensure compliance, which is probably necessary when teenage knuckleheads are toting coolers of beer into the holy water of the American Renaissance. Even Walden has become part of the surveillance regime, and I fear that the Romantic "drama of the self's engagement with nature" is subtly but decisively altered by the reality, or mere sensation, of being watched.[63]

I don't mean to make too much of the changes, to buy into the decline-and-fall narrative that speaks to my inner Iron Eyes Cody (fake TV Indian extraordinaire, famous for crying over a spoiled landscape in 1970s commercials). I don't mean to suggest that we're dealing with forces that Thoreau and his contemporaries could never have fathomed. (Temporal hubris is one of the many pitfalls of the historical imagination.) Yet the interplay of what we might problematically envision as distinct entities—nature and civilization—is no more dramatic to us than it was to Thoreau in 1850. He was keenly aware of the advance of technology into "his" woods, and would most likely see our predicament as different in degree, not kind. Even if we permit ourselves a momentary feeling of separation from the thrumming machine of civilization when we head into nature, it is an illusion, just as it was for Thoreau in his recycled hut on the outskirts of the most intellectual town in antebellum America. The ants still bite, the "no-see-ums" are still an invisible nuisance, just as they were to Thoreau—yet something is shifting with the arrival of new technologies in the wild. Something is afoot.

Today on the banks of Walden Pond, my iPhone not only tells me where I am, ensuring that I will never become truly lost, but it tells the world where I am, where I've been, and, most ironically, where I've paused to think about being alone. My cell phone company may keep my secret, but more likely it will divulge my information to the NSA and other unnamed parties. Even something as innocuous as sending a message to my daughter from Walden Pond or stopping for a moment to play Angry Birds (an old game the NSA surreptitiously mines for clues about its millions of users) is registered somewhere, a matter of quasi-public record for those with the right security clearance to peek at my woeful video-gaming results.[64] Of course I could turn off the phone or leave it at home, but that only helps me enact the fantasy of natural solitude with greater verisimilitude. Like some sort of Gore-Tex Garbo with a backpack stuffed with trail mix, I can shout "Leave me alone!" in the make-believe wilderness, but the invisible technologies of tracking and sensing will not honor my political, aesthetic, or psychological need for the dignity of solitude. In this sense, surveillance technologies are the new "no-see-ums," always buzzing around us, a nuisance to those who crave a moment's peace, a frustration to those who prize a sense of emotional liberty, of at least *feeling free* from the pokes and prods of the modern world.

The ubiquity of monitoring technologies would surely grate on Thoreau's nerves. We imagine him as a cranky hermit with nothing but bile for others, but he could be surprisingly sociable, and we should not overlook his humor, compassion, and radiance (even in the face of death). Still, he often went to great lengths to avoid detection as he hiked around Concord. When he was sauntering through the woods, indulging his passion for unconstrained mobility, he made it plain that he wasn't interested in seeing neighboring houses or other "cultivated parts" that would press upon his consciousness.[65] Of course, walking is never simply walking in Thoreau's mind: it's a sacred enterprise for individual and nation alike. More than a pleasurable diversion, it instills a democratic way of being within the souls of Americans, preparing them for a more autonomous future when the government will not govern so much, "when the state will not form citizens into obliging wooden men."[66] As Shannon Mariotti puts it, "The experiential, adventurous nature of his daily walks oppose the modern convention for what we think and how we should behave," putting him at odds with social convention and even property rights.[67] Unfettered mobility in the public sphere allowed him to "work against becoming like a machine," resisting the sort of scrutiny that the machinery of surveillance expects: these systems are waging war on unpredictability, the unknown, the wild. Being watched would violate the liberating spirit of his walks, so essential to his creative practice and political sensibility alike.[68] Simply on a visceral or poetic level, Thoreau would have shuddered at the thought of a gaze other than God's peering down at him while he roamed along the rivers of Massachusetts.

"Walking is a path to freedom, an organic activity that redirects humankind's attention to the natural, organic, or essential," writes Max Oelschlaager in his valuable study of the idea of wilderness, but surveillance is often an inorganic mechanism of control and containment—*don't walk here, don't linger there!*—that seems highly un-Thoreauvian.[69] Deploying a revealingly military metaphor in the pages of *Walden*, Thoreau describes how he crawled through a swamp under bushes "to screen us from a house forty rods off whose windows completely commanded the open ground." When he and his friend "emerged into the grass ground," he notes how "some apple trees beautifully screened us."[70] The emphasis on *screening* is significant: it is the language of privacy, concealment, and modesty. It is precisely what surveillance seeks to penetrate: it seeks to look over our privacy screens in the wild or at home. It is at odds with "the tonic of wildness," "the indefinitely wild," the "brand new" land that Thoreau found essential to a life well lived: "We can never have enough of nature," he proclaimed. "The most alive is the wildest."[71]

Yet even Thoreau was part of the subtle dewilding of America in one sense: he was a surveyor by profession for long stretches of his adult life, and as such he was engaged in bringing order, boundaries, and measurements to the chaotic, unbounded, and unmeasured wild. If the surveillance of the natural landscape can be understood as a form of surveying—for it likewise establishes boundaries—then Thoreau was complicit in the surveillance of the wild in his lifetime. Perhaps his work as a surveyor is why he was so sensitive to the power of wilderness, which was disappearing even in his times— he saw and studied the changes in the landscape with much more range and precision than most of his contemporaries. As ecologist David R. Foster reminds us, "As Thoreau observed on his walks, the imprint of human activity was so great across New England that it seemed as if all the land was confined and bounded by stone walls, wooden fences, and ownership boundaries that had been surveyed many times over."[72] Surveillance, even as an extension of the surveyor's art that he practiced, would thus be another insult to the Arcadian tradition to which he belonged. Lest his duties with a transit seem very different from those of a CCTV operator, I would note that the words *surveillance* and *surveyor* share a similar etymology. While Thoreau's profession took its name from the Anglo-French *surveiour* ("guard, overseer") and the Old French verb *sorveoir* ("to survey"), "surveillance" comes from the French *surveiller* ("oversee, watch") and *sur-* ("over").[73] To very different degrees, both surveillance and surveyors are uninvited guests in the wild and, when connected to the government's demands of its citizens, subtly authoritarian. Modern surveillance is the surveyor's art on steroids: it maps, delineates, and records the soil, rocks, fields, rivers, and woods with a level of detail that Thoreau could scarcely have imagined. More than simply marking the lines of property ownership in the manner of a nineteenth-century surveyor, who measured the land and then departed, the modern "surveyor" is actively watching the wilds with GPS and high-res cameras, constantly alert to potential threats to ecological, political, or commercial interests, to which it can summon a police or military response.

Such scrutiny of the wild may stop poachers in their tracks; it may prevent forest fires; it may even provide data that saves the world from the ecological ravages of climate change. But it will also shift something in one's experience of the wild, altering something more akin to poetry than science. The German poet Ludwig Tieck and other European Romantics of the nineteenth century enthused about the feeling of being alone in the woods, or *Waldeinsamkeit*, describing it as a rapture that we will soon not know.[74] Some aspect of inscrutability and impenetrability is necessary to the Romantic conception of the wild, but the architects of modern surveillance are building a world in which everything, everywhere is readable, known, sensed, mapped, and archived in the most grimly un-Romantic manner imaginable. I'm not just talking about the surface of things—the rustle of trees, the movement of animals, the clothes we are wearing, the messages we send, the movies we watch, the payments we miss. I'm talking about the depths as well—the feelings one cannot hide from corporate emotion detectors, the stress levels one cannot conceal from a wireless heart monitor, or the composite picture of one's psychology that emerges from one's Google search history, insurance claims, and Visa statements, as well as the underappreciated emotional burden of living with new forms of surveillance and new contexts for monitoring. Surveillance is entering the wilderness of people's inner landscapes as well as the actual fields and hills and streams outdoors. Surely *surveillance of the heart* is something that runs counter to Thoreau's crusty New England independence and need for privacy, not to mention is an economical poetic sensibility with little room for the ungainliness of CCTV and TSA scanners. Better yet, Thoreau might inquire: What is it that we are trying to illuminate with all of these devices and practices of knowing, sorting, and storing? What room will remain for mystery, awe, and sublime humility when the whole world is tamed by technologies of knowing and measuring? As one scholar has put it, "Nature's protection is not well served by making humans closer to it, but rather by fostering a sense of wonder and distance toward the natural world."[75] Perhaps the technocratic wild is no wild at all.

Yet Thoreau wasn't naïve about the wild, and we shouldn't be, either. He knew that even his own presence was complicating and sometimes hurting the thing that he treasured. He might have loved trees as much as people (as Emerson once joked). Thoreau loved the "nakedness" of nature, but he wasn't some delusional purist of the forest primeval.[76] Keenly aware of the ways in which nature depends on us as much as we depend on it, he would probably admire Paul Wapner's astringent suggestion that "keeping wilderness looking and acting wild is hard work."[77] Thoreau would merely want to make sure we were tending to that work of preserving the wild in the face of new challenges, rather than neglecting our duty to the world. What we learn from Thoreau, as well as contemporary ecofeminists, is the impossibility of separation, the fallacy of cleaving civilization and nature into distinct but overlapping realms. This dichotomy does not exist outside our own cultural imagination. There is no Edenic nature that must be kept free from the dirty machinery of data collection and security. Instead, nature and culture, wilderness and civilization, are interwoven in subtle ways that Thoreau recognized more readily than some of his eco-Puritan followers. From this more balanced perspective, surveillance is not the snake in the garden—but neither is it innocent. It is a complex mechanism that must be watched as carefully as it watches us.

Some scholars have rolled their eyes about Thoreau's retreat to the woods, seeing it as the privilege of a "Harvard-educated and genteelly subsidized misogynist nature lover," but one in particular, Laurence Buell, pulls us back from easy disdain to suggest the complexity of Thoreau's vision of natural refuge.[78] Thoreau was never simply playing a man's game in celebrating the pristine landscape, as Buell suggests. Moreover, Thoreau's flight from civilization resonated with many women during his lifetime and (especially) after his death. After all, women were responsible for producing the first book to emulate *Walden*, the first dissertation on his work, one of his earliest biographies, and even the first Thoreau Society.[79] The militant defense of unspoiled land may have masculinist overtones in the rhetoric of such successors as Edward Abbey, but Thoreau himself was no raging patriarch of the forest, no angry prophet of a gendered eco-consciousness: he was thoughtful, witty, mystical, ambivalent, and pained as he contemplated the encroachment of roads and trains and houses upon the deepest woods. I would like to think he would appreciate the work of the Finnish scholar Hille Koskela, who has documented the sexism of urban surveillance practices, but I'm not sure if he could quite wrap his mind around twenty-first-century feminism, given his melancholy disconnection from women in his time.[80] (He was the original 40-Year-Old Virgin.) I hope he would appreciate the holistic sensibility of modern ecofeminism, with its assertion that humans and nature should never accept "us-versus-them" thinking.[81] And he might come to appreciate the work of Carolyn Merchant, a historian who has described the conquest of the American West as "a story of male energy subduing female nature, taming the wild, plowing the land, making the land safe for capitalism and commodity production."[82] Certainly, I think he would share Rachel Carson's humility in *Silent Spring*, in which she wrote, "The 'control of nature' is a phrase conceived in arrogance, born of the Neanderthal age of biology and philosophy when it was supposed that nature exists for the convenience of man."[83]

No doubt, the desire to find true wilderness, untouched by the tentacles of society, has long resonated with ecologically minded men and women in the United States. As historian William Cronon puts it, "Wilderness serves as the unexamined foundation on which so many of the quasi-religious values of modern environmentalism rest."[84] Indeed, an ecological mind-set has often been rooted in the wild landscape that Thoreau celebrated. As Laurence Buell writes, "The myth of actual regions, even continents, as properly 'unspoiled' has helped stimulate and bolster the authority of the ecological conscience."[85] The wild is the ideal to which the environmentalist often aspires. What will it mean to this eco-consciousness if new surveillance technologies expand into the last remaining wilderness, if any such thing can be said to exist at this point? What damage to the human soul might result from losing our ancient sense of nature as sanctuary, not to mention our ability to explore and wander and lose ourselves in something uncontrollable and vast? Will the loss of wilderness exact a psychological price for those who dream of something other than roads and bridges, buildings and runways—those who find inspiration and dignity in Arcadian solitude? Is it sufficient to sit at home playing the video game of Walden—such a thing will soon exist, irony of ironies—wiggling a mouse as we commune with virtual nature?[86]

If we extend Thoreau's line of thought into the present day, as I have been trying to do, we might think twice about the further conquest of nature that electronic surveillance allows. We might think twice about further infringing on what radical ecologists call the "autonomy of nature."[87] It will pain those who seek the wild as a place of oblivion, a place where we can go to forget and be forgotten. Such oblivion will be unlikely in any natural landscape under supervision by a digital regime with an aversion to the delete key.[88] Individualists who imagine themselves in splendid isolation from the pack will also decry this development, alongside poets and philosophers of a Romantic disposition. After all, Romanticism requires some space for secrets and shadows, neither of which are permissible in a surveillance regime that has reached a critical mass. The growing surveillance of the wild will also vex the ecologically minded, who may exist quite happily without the traditional fantasy of untamed land if it means that actual land is receiving better protections, but who also may have to make certain adjustments in their thinking. As the machinery of modern surveillance reaches into the deepest forest or the hottest desert, the rhetorical opposition of "pristine nature" versus "civilization" will seem increasingly strange. After all, electronic surveillance quietly expands the reach of the city, subtly urbanizing the natural landscape even where no other structures are in sight.[89] Many fine scholars have explored the implications of surveillance technology in cities, suggesting how "practices and discourses that are uncritically placed under the banner of 'crime prevention' are actually better understood as socio-spatial ordering practices that . . . reinforce and reconstruct particular cultural sensibilities around crime, deviance and incivility."[90] What hasn't been understood is how contemporary surveillance culture is bringing urban practices and mind-sets *into* nature. Perhaps Marshall McLuhan's global village will be achieved—not with television, as the Canadian media theorist imagined, but with the complex infrastructure of contemporary surveillance culture.

It's a strange thought, but so is the idea of a world without escape. Where is our Walden, our retreat from the endless scrutiny of our age, our "island of privacy" in the era of GPS and UAVs? Where is our wilderness, our frontier, our haven? Where is the outrage over what Christina Nippert-Eng calls our "shrinking islands of privacy," which are becoming smaller, farther apart, more easily penetrated? Scholars have argued that the healthy functioning of society requires some private spaces in which we feel free from scrutiny.[91] What will happen once we can no longer know the pleasures of life undetected, when we are unable to imagine life without monitors and sensors, even in the farthest corners of the woods? By then, our remaining spheres of privacy will have faded into the realm of folklore and legend, coming to seem as "fanciful as Atlantis," as Nippert-Eng has put it.[92]

Perhaps the end of wilderness in a technical sense will have little impact on the hikers, campers, tourists, politicians, and boosters who look to the American West for the hidden spring of national essence and individual self-renewal. After all, we Americans have always had one inexhaustible natural resource: our ability to concoct comforting fantasies about who we are and what we are doing as a people. Like Winston and Julia hiding in Mr. Charrington's attic in Orwell's *1984*, blithely unaware of the watchful eye of Big Brother as they enact their dream of domesticity, we can tune out the cameras and sensors in the wild as long as we don't see them seeing us. No doubt, the deserts and mountains of the West will continue to dwarf the UAVs and other advance scouts from the mechanized control society for many years to come. For this reason, I suspect that we'll continue imagining wilderness wherever we need its services on a symbolic or material level, even if we are no more "in the wild" than Thoreau was at Walden Pond—who, after all, was almost within earshot of the Emersons' dinner bell and the other sophisticated sounds of literary Concord.

Maybe we should thank the drones for challenging the fantasy of the American wild. Scholars have hinted at the ways in which the idea of pristine nature has greased the skids for settler colonialism, environmental despoliation, and other nasty business. By fetishizing the romance of the mythic wilderness as a source of spiritual renewal and individual potency, European Americans have sometimes pursued their natural fantasies at any cost to the object of their fixation (and the people who have long inhabited the "uninhabited" land).[93] Need roads to access Pike's Peak? *Build them.* Need hotels and airports to enjoy the trails around Telluride? *Build them.* Need an escape from the real problems of American history? *Take a hike!* The wilderness offers what historian William Cronon calls "the false hope of an escape from responsibility, the illusion that we can somehow wipe clean the slate of our past and return to the tabula rasa that supposedly existed before we began to leave our marks on the world."[94] Perhaps we need to be shaken free from "the sublime's alienation psychology," the way in which we imagine the wild as something in opposition to ourselves, making it dangerously and irresponsibly outside of ourselves.[95]

Perhaps it is better to bring the sublime to our desktops, where we can admire the digital images of Google Trekker or a naturalist's webcam, rather than chasing the rustic sublime in our gas-guzzling Jeeps or ATVs? Perhaps the drones will not subject the wild to a soul-deadening form of "zooveillance" in which the whole world is in electronic captivity, but instead will thwart poaching, animal abuse, illegal development, and other crimes against nature? Perhaps the humble UAV will become nature's best ally as it provides scientists with data to combat climate change and helps keep human beings from polluting themselves into extinction?

I have hope as much as I have reservations. I know the sensation of the solitary wild has always included an element of wishful thinking. Perhaps we were never really alone in the woods, because there was always some possibility, however remote, that someone was peeking at us from along the tree line; that someone was taking note of our footprints and camp-fires; that some jilted lover, bounty hunter, or serial killer was tracking our movements in the desert outback. All of those baroque scenarios were quite possible and remain so—yet I still believe that something has shifted in the age of high-tech wilderness. What was once *unlikely but possible* is now *possible and likely*: it has become increasingly easy to follow our various tracks into the deepest wilderness. Even movements of the most innocuous sort are swept up into the vast machinery of observation and cataloging that churns away, day and night, for governments, corporations, scientists, and private individuals that we rarely glimpse ourselves, even as they are taking stock of our presence. Even far beyond the end of the longest dirt road, where we used to retreat for solace and contemplation, and where the Romantics reckoned with the sublime in glorious isolation, someone could easily be watching us on a monitor in an NSA bunker. I can't think of anything less Romantic than that.

Devoid of romance though it may be, the juggernaut of natural surveillance rolls on, moving across the continent like the great railroads of the nineteenth century. I raise the train metaphor for a reason: it still rumbles just a short walk up the hill from Thoreau's cabin site, just as it did when he was reckoning with its arrival in his woods. "The Fitchburg Railroad touches the pond about a hundred rods south of where I dwell," he wrote in *Walden*. "The whistle of the locomotive penetrates my woods summer and winter, sounding like the scream of a hawk sailing over some farmer's yard." The railroad cuts a line through his celebrated woods, but also through the suburbs and urban core of Boston, symbolically connecting one of the key nineteenth-century sites for studying the relationship of technology, landscape, and privacy to its twenty-first-century counterpart. I'm interested in following the railroad's symbolic path from Walden to downtown Boston, where an important chapter in modern surveillance culture was written in April 2013.

The pleasant shops and cafes of Boylston Street, in the heart of Boston, were the scene of one of the worst acts of domestic terrorism since 9/11. The bombings near the finish line of the Boston Marathon sparked a national conversation not simply about terrorism and immigration, but also about the proper role of surveillance in the post–9/11 United States. When the faces of the bombers were captured on the CCTV cameras at Lord & Taylor's, across from the second explosion, many commentators claimed vindication for the massive investment in CCTV in particular and surveillance technology in general. Why? Even though security cameras had failed to prevent the atrocity—an obvious fact that eluded most reporters and pundits—the cameras' role in aiding the capture of the Tsarnaev brothers was hailed with a kind of securitarian fervor: *See? This is exactly why we need surveillance!* Surveys revealed that the public's support for blanketing the nation with CCTV shot up dramatically in the weeks after this tragedy.[96] Perversely, the image of the Tsarnaev brothers wearing baseball caps and deadly backpacks was circulated around the globe as proof that CCTV works, that America needs many more cameras in its public sphere, that the machinery of surveillance needs expansion, not containment.[97] No one seemed to make the opposite point: *the Boston Marathon bombing demonstrated the abject failure of our post–9/11 surveillance state.* Consider the facts. The bombers chose one of the most monitored locations anywhere in the United States for their crime. Beyond the dense array of private and public CCTV systems one could expect in any major downtown area, Boylston Street had thousands of spectators snapping photos and shooting video of the final stretch of the celebrated race. It was into this orgy of visibility that the bombers walked confidently, seemingly eager to have their deeds recorded for the whole world to witness, seemingly unconcerned that these same cameras would be used against them. The cameras were an inducement to their crimes, not a deterrent.

I assume that Thoreau would look with disgust on the bombers, but then turn the conversation from them to us, asking us to contemplate our response to their crimes. He might suggest that surveillance weighs more heavily on the landscape than the Fitchburg Railroad ever did, yet its benefits are more elusive than the train's. What dignity, what trust, what autonomy have we forsaken in the name of security? What pathologies have we incubated in its midst? I think he would have a melancholy view of our fate. By installing a security system without end, a system of tracking and tracing with global reach, we have lost something that was dear to him. We have traded our liberty for the promise of safety, our autonomy for the pressure of authority, our wilderness for a machine. This is what I think he would see, because, if nothing else, he saw the ways in which we could deceive ourselves as a people. Thoreau had a genius for seeing cultural delusions at work, often long before his contemporaries, and he did so with a temperament that wedded poetry, philosophy, and common sense. It is a perspective sorely lacking in many contemporary discussions of surveillance culture.

This is not to say that Thoreau would be moribund with grief. After all, he warned in *Walden* that resignation to the status quo was a sign of "confirmed desperation."[98] Certainly he never surrendered to it, and for this reason I think Thoreau would counsel some degree of hope. By no means does the spread of wilderness surveillance represent "the end of nature" or "the death of the wild" with some shattering finality— except, perhaps, for those with unusually sensitive antennae, for whom any degree of oversight will poison their Arcadian raptures. For most of us, I suspect, the expansion of surveillance technologies into natural settings will simply drive us a little farther into the woods, a little farther away from the fray, where we will continue to enjoy the human fantasy of natural autonomy. Being in the high-tech woods may require a conceptual adjustment, a shift in how we think about the experience of wilderness, but I suspect that most people will quickly adapt. They'll become accustomed to nature being a little less wild. They'll get used to the idea of being *seemingly* alone while continuing to play the game of roughing it on their own — rugged individuals to the end. Few will protest. After all, as historian Frieda Knobloch once wrote, the transformation of the American West is often "understood as inevitable," whereas the possibility that the transformation of western lands is "unwanted, unnecessary, or at least susceptible to critique" is rarely explored.[99] Perhaps faux-wilderness will be good enough for most.

The situation is not entirely grim. The enormity of the challenges to the sovereignty of the individual and the poetic appreciation of the natural world might have dismayed Thoreau, but he was no defeatist. As H. Daniel Peck suggests, Walden was Thoreau's utopian project of renewal and reclamation, not some apathetic hideout from reality. Even in 1850 Thoreau was working hard to conjure up "the wild" on the outskirts of bustling Concord. He would suggest, I think, that we simply have to work a little harder today, doing whatever is necessary to preserve our wild inheritance. Could we reimagine a more trusting nation, less in thrall to fear-mongering politicians and pundits? Could we learn to prize the wild as a part of true "homeland security," poetically defined as a national resource of the highest order, somewhere above nuclear submarines and full-body scanners on the pecking order of necessities? Perhaps we could embrace the sense of technological restraint that Rachel Carson advocated with regard to pesticides — not to ditch the whole business, but to apply it sparingly and only where truly needed, not simply wherever technology leads us.

Could we mark off certain spaces as surveillance exclusion zones where we could protect the endangered species known as privacy? Or should we relearn what we mean by privacy, searching for freedom from surveillance within our minds and souls, not on our streets or prairies?

I am willing to imagine such hopeful scenarios, as long as the techno-utopians (who have a fetishistic belief that new technology will solve every problem) and securitarians are willing to consider the darker implications of surveillance in the wild that I've outlined here. With those dark shadings in mind, I would like to check in again with our imaginary hiker from Colorado, the thwarted naturalist whose quest for solitude ran afoul of a sheriff's department's UAV in the beginning passages of this chapter. Let's imagine that she is a resilient sort, that she's already hatched another plan to encounter solitude in the wild far from the prying eyes of civilization. Her quest will take her from Colorado toward the Pacific Coast. She fills up her Subaru, ignoring the fact that Visa is categorizing her gas, Cheetos, and beer purchases in the officious manner of modern banking. She ignores the CCTV in gas-station parking lots and the prospect of unseen drones buzzing overhead; she turns off social media's incessant request for her to "check in" and share her location. With nothing but natural solitude in mind, she puts the pedal to the Subaru's rusty metal and plunges into the American West with abandon. An automated license-plate reader records her passing through Elk City, Nevada, at 90 mph; she'll have a ticket in the mail when she gets home—but she has no knowledge of that yet. She passes through the endless miles of desert, land that looks like the inspiration for Edward Abbey's *Desert Solitude*, but she sees the government signs that mark this place as mapped, monitored, secured: it's a military installation, one of Trevor Paglin's

Blank Spots on the Map, even though no buildings are in sight for miles. She shakes her head ruefully: it's under wraps. She can just feel it: the Man is watching closely, but she is going somewhere the Man cannot see.

At last she arrives at a desolate stretch of the California coast and pulls a diver's bag out of her hatch. She needs it now: she needs to get away from the buzzing drones and peeping cell-phone cameras; she wants to free herself from the tentacles of the surveillance machines, the twenty-first-century equivalent of Frank Norris's *The Octopus*, that nineteenth-century indictment of capitalist overreach. Diving in the frigid ocean in her wetsuit and scuba gear, she feels free from the tentacles at last, moving into a water of real octopi, not metaphoric ones. At last she's found the sanctuary of the wild that she's been craving since her disappointment in the Rockies. Blissful silence envelops her body as she descends twenty feet, fifty feet, eighty feet into the darkness, where she rests, suspended in the blackness of the sea for a long, intoxicating moment. It's a glorious feeling, which lasts until she senses something moving. Turning on her flashlight, she spies a jellyfish moving toward her. It's abnormally large and purposeful, and as she moves away, it seems to follow her until it's inches from her mask. She studies the creature, which doesn't look quite right, before realizing the problem: it's some kind of machine, a robotic faux-jellyfish, with black wires dangling subtly from its underbelly and camera eyeballs. She pokes it and feels its hard plastic shell, on which she reads the creature's name— "CYRO"—and its description. It's a "self-powering, autonomous" machine that Virginia Tech University has developed for the US Naval Undersea Warfare Center and the Office of Naval Research.[100] Cyro is just a prototype, it turns out, but the navy hopes to deploy these robotic creatures on secret missions in oceans around the globe. *Ugh.* Unable to believe her bad luck, she lets out a furious stream of bubbles and paddles to the surface. She decides there's no point in running any longer, no point in trying to outwit surveillance machinery in the wild. So she peels off her fins and then skulks to a nearby motel that promises satellite TV and a well-maintained pool, where she reads Thoreau and thinks about the freedom and autonomy that once existed on this continent—if only for some people at certain times—in a mythic space called the American wild.

CHAPTER FIVE

A Mighty Fortress
Is Our God

At the heart of Colorado Springs are tree-lined streets with century-old houses, an unusually bucolic college campus, and droves of attractive young people who look like they alternate between snowboarding, rock-climbing, and enjoying the mind-altering edibles that can be legally obtained from local pot dispensaries. In their midst are sandal-wearing tourists who stroll along scenic streets, exploring quaint hippy boutiques that sell used crystal balls "with good energy," bits of rock candy, and homemade soaps. The city, in other words, feels like an overgrown college town, complete with the thriving alternative culture that one would expect in an eco-paradise just a few miles from Pikes Peak.

But the city center doesn't tell the whole story, which starts to change a few miles up the interstate that runs through town. None of that counterculture funkiness is evident on the northern edge of the city, where I am heading to an evangelical megachurch, the site of a security conference in summer 2014. Out here the vibe reflects the presence not only of the sprawling hilltop compound of the influential New Life Church, but also its equally conservative neighbors—the US Air Force Academy and Focus on the Family. The service academy trains young men and women for aerial combat above Afghanistan or the Middle East, whereas the latter is an influential 501(c)(3)

organization engaged in a different kind of war—a culture war
that supports prayer, teaching creationism, and corporal punishment (paddling) in American schools; the single state of
Israel; so-called ex-gay ministries; national radio programs;
and a Christian dating service. Although not as large as the
vast Air Force compound, Focus on the Family's 47-acre headquarters still has its own zip code.

Mostly because of these three organizations, northern Colorado Springs is considered by many to be the epicenter of conservative evangelicalism in the United States. It's the sort of
place where one runs into Focus on the Family staffers gossiping about Republican presidential contenders over free waffles
in a budget hotel lobby. Here, on the edge of the city, I find a
version of postwar Americana that could be anywhere, characterized by dreary gas stations, random fast-food shacks, and a
dying mall with oddball "tutoring academies" and half-empty
gift shops, all linked by a highway system that seems designed
to thwart human interaction. More than just another example
of unplanned American sprawl, this part of town has a bland
seediness that finds its counterpart in the faces of the young
men and women working on streets named Interquest Park-
way and Jet Stream Drive. Except for the length of their hair
and faded Walmart clothes, these twenty-somethings might
have stepped out of a photo of the 1930s Dust Bowl, whose
devastation almost reached this part of the state. Although the
Great Depression might seem like a thing of the past, something still haunts these parts, something that feels sad and
broken and not really worth fighting for.

It might seem like a strange spot for New Life Church,
with its sports-arena architecture and acres of blacktop parking. It is here that the influential and charismatic Reverend
Ted Haggart, long before his public fall from grace for meth-
fueled sex romps with a male prostitute, built the church into
an evangelical powerhouse more than 12,000 strong. Perhaps

Reverend Haggart and his flock embraced the starkness of their surroundings—after all, it is to the soulless and lost condition of modern America that New Life addressed itself with pious certainties and a clear vision of God's path. More than simply a place to ponder the state of one's eternal soul and form "Christ-centered relationships," this megachurch was also a place for people worried about the state of their country.[1] If the built environment offered little inspiration, the congregation could look upward, not just to their heavenly father, but also to the sublime scenery that looms over the city at almost every point. Looking from the Worship Center's oceanic parking lot to the snowy mountains on the western edge of town, even the darkest skeptic of American society might find solace and hope for renewal in a beautiful "new life"—if only the righteous could be protected from the wicked. If only evil could be kept from the door. If only the community could feel secure.

New Life was not alone in its struggle for security against the forces of darkness in modern America. In *Religion of Fear: The Politics of Horror in Conservative Evangelicalism* (2008), Jason Bivins traces the rise of this worldview since the 1960s from a fringe belief to a significant part of the American mainstream. Starting with a quote from Thomas Hobbes ("Fear of things invisible is the natural seed of that which everyone in himself calleth religion"), Bivins describes the ways in which "the forces of secularism and moral permissiveness" became the new enemies of "a previously stable and safe 'Christian America.'"[2] Often circulating violent "monster stories" to warn the faithful about the various "barbarians at the gates," conservative evangelicals closed ranks with a powerful rhetoric of fear, decline, and danger, often delivered with the verbal dexterity of a seasoned minister. Although Bivins was writing about the best-selling *Left Behind* novels, Chick comics, and Halloween "Hell Houses" for his case studies, I think his

insights can be extended to the ways in which surveillance is
bought, sold, and used in American churches. As will soon become clear, the business of what I call "sacred security" depends on these same tropes, which are wielded by men who
envision themselves as "sheepdogs" that can save the "sheep"
from the "wolves." Such rhetoric is mild for the marketing and
training related to church surveillance and security, which relies heavily on frightening anecdotes and predictions that encourage churchgoers to close ranks against the looming darkness. As Bivins puts it, "Through images of torture, death,
horror, and judgment, a specific conception of moral obligation and political authority emerges, understood both as onto-
logical truth and as rhetoric with which to denounce a political
culture thought to be hostile."[3]

In the case of New Life Church, such fears were not simply
reflections of wider cultural and religious anxieties about im-
periled Christians. Although an exaggerated rhetoric of Christian vulnerability was often at work, it was alongside something that was painfully real in the lived experience of the
congregation. On December 9, 2007, a young man named
Matthew Murray arrived at New Life Church with an automatic rifle and 1,000 rounds of ammunition. Moving from the
frozen parking lot to the interior of the church, Murray killed
three people before a volunteer security guard named Jeanne
Assam returned fire and ended his rampage. Hailed as a hero
at first, Assam later claimed that the church rejected her when
she came out as a lesbian.[4] While the church denies the charge,
one thing is certain: the shooting at New Life was a sign that
evangelical America's worst fears were coming true. The wolf
wasn't simply at the door; he was inside the church, devour-
ing the faithful. Carl Chinn, New Life's current security chief,
made this point in his 2012 book *Evil Invades Sanctuary: The
Case for Security in Faith-Based Organizations*.[5] "Faith-based
organizations are in the direct line of fire in the battle raging

between good and evil," Chinn explained. "Whether from terrorists, petty criminals, fallen leaders or hurricanes, religious
organizations must prepare for adversity." Chinn had seen such
threats in the flesh on more than one occasion, dating back to
his time in the 1990s with the neighboring evangelical organization, Focus on the Family. After the New Life shooting, he
was convinced that churches needed to prepare for the inevitable. Moving forward from the attack on New Life, Chinn and
other faith-based security experts would look for new ways to
protect their congregations from harm, even if it meant treating the church like a sports arena, airport, or any other public space that was vulnerable to violence. In the past decade,
these men—and they are overwhelmingly men—have created
companies, books, websites, conferences, and training semi-
nars like the one I'm attending at New Life in the summer of
2014, all intended to "harden" the "soft target" of the American church.

Other denominations might have had a different response
to perceived threats. Catholics, Jews, Hindus, Buddhists, and
even Muslims, who have far more reason to feel threatened
than any other religious group in the United States, have not
appeared on my radar for sacred security in the past four years
of collecting data and keeping track of relevant news stories.
Liberal and moderate Protestants have been equally invisible,
probably because they are less emphatic about their security
needs compared to evangelical conservatives. For a mix of cultural and theological reasons, it's hard to imagine Quakers or
Unitarian-Universalists investing in high-resolution surveillance cameras and security teams for their facilities, which are
often smaller and more modest than what New Life has built
on its vast campus. Such liberal Protestants tend toward the
pacifist end of the spectrum, where "turning the other cheek"
and trusting in the essential benevolence of humankind is supposed to be more than a Sunday-morning truism. Not so in

most conservative evangelical churches, which are more susceptible to a potent rhetoric of fear, vulnerability, and suspicion, for reasons both sociological and doctrinal. Evangelical congregations such as New Life and fundamentalists like Reverend Jerry Falwell's Moral Majority might have their religious differences, but they have shared important traits over the past forty years: they feel engulfed by a threatening secular tide; they lean hard to the political right; they favor free-market ideology; they are rarely critical of law enforcement or the US military; they are comfortable with guns for hunting and personal protection; and they expect men to protect their families and communities in the name of a patriarchal ideology of "family values" that they believe is under attack. All of these combine to produce a deep susceptibility to securitization. The results can be jarring to someone expecting a calm and welcoming congregation. Indeed, we have reached the point at which some strange scenarios are unfolding at the intersection of religion and surveillance.

As a result of the new emphasis on church security, I learned that, on Sunday mornings in some American towns, greeters have begun offering an ambiguous welcome to visitors at their church's door. Mixed with the smiling recognition that a fellow worshipper has arrived is something decidedly less friendly: *a professionally trained threat assessment*. It may entail nothing more than a quick scan from a church elder with a metal detector up his sleeve, but the careful policing of sacred space does not stop there.[6] Assuming that the visitor is allowed past the informal screening at the front door, she might notice a surprising number of surveillance cameras positioned inside the sanctuary, some thick-set ministerial bodyguards in the first row of pews, and even a concealed handgun on a deacon's hip. A visitor with very keen eyes might realize that the preacher is armed with a handgun of his own and perhaps even a shield of sorts: a bulletproof Bible holder, specially designed to en-

hance his in-church security. Later, when services have con-
cluded, our visitor might hear an announcement about personal safety workshops being offered on church grounds by
companies with names like Cops and Cross or Gideon Protective Services: two of the faith-based companies, mostly in the
South, that are pitching security services to fellow believers.
She even might bump into one of the church's security officers standing guard at the back of the pews, or catch a glimpse
inside an office where a security team uses high-end CCTV
monitors, not to keep watch over a stadium-size megachurch
in a high-crime neighborhood but simply a midsize congregation in a quiet suburb.

These are all aspects of sacred security, a serious business
that literally asks the question: "Is your church a sanctuary or
a target?"[7] Although secular firms are able to meet the security
needs of most religious institutions in the United States, some
churches are being courted by religiously identified security
companies that market services primarily to spiritual brethren, often in explicitly spiritual terms. These are "God's watchmen," as they call themselves, each one selling a message of
masculine guardianship and Christian vigilance along with the
typical products of the security industry. It's a hard sell, relying on emotional anecdotes, dramatic personal testimony, and
the artful wielding of shared symbols that is often difficult to
resist.

Sacred security can be found in every part of the United States,
but these religiously identified firms are most often found in
the so-called Bible Belt, where I have lived much of my adult
life. In the thousands of pages of documents that I have ana-
lyzed, including marketing brochures, websites, editorials,
training manuals, and how-to books, these companies state
neither their denomination nor their political affiliation, but

their language and other cues suggest evangelical conservatism with a southern or lower midwestern cast. Appalled by the perceived dangers of contemporary urban life and skeptical of government's ability to safeguard their well-being, these "watchmen" come across as sober, heartland Americans taking personal security into their own hands—and bringing surveillance into a new context where CCTV cameras and monitors might seem out of place. To judge from the rhetoric of the marketing materials and websites, not to mention the national training seminar I attended in Colorado Springs in 2014, sacred security's vendors are middle-aged white conservative Protestant men speaking to kindred spirits in the rural or suburban American South. Although evangelicalism includes a wide range of ideologies that can appeal to moderate women, liberal African Americans, and other groups, sacred security is not aimed at these audiences, just as it is not usually aimed at Catholics, Jews, Muslims, Hindus, or liberal Protestants. Instead, its marketing seems directed at white conservative evangelical customers, especially middle-aged men with fundamentalist leanings who either feel, or can be made to feel, a sense of masculine guardianship over the women and children of their congregation. It is in the name of those older values that conservative evangelicals appear willing to accept the high-tech fortification of church property, both inside and out.

In short, this realm of sacred security provides a microcosm of America in the age of anxiety. In particular, it provides a rich example of what Zygmunt Bauman has dubbed "the institutionalization of insecurity," which strikes me as the underlying political *problem* of our time in ways that should become apparent in the pages ahead.[8] I suspect that the drive for sacred security reflects what Bauman calls "the aggression of the powerless," "a deep and plentiful anxiety diverted from its genuine cause" in the structural misery of twenty-first-century American life.[9] In terms of security studies, I am exploring a potentially lucrative subset of the billion-dollar security industry in the United States, one that offers on-site consultations, "Church Safety Starter Kits," training sessions, and equipment purchase and installation, as well as books and DVDs. Churches may be late arrivals to surveillance culture, but they are following a path set by many other institutions in which CCTV once seemed unnecessary or counterproductive. Just as American public schools have increasingly incorporated aspects of law enforcement that range from hidden cameras to metal detectors, American churches are erecting high-tech walls to protect themselves from real and imagined threats, whose nature they describe with considerable drama and rhetorical flair.[10] Their words and actions provide a new window on American insecurity as well as on the ideological landscape of conservative evangelicalism, where I have often found a supercharged version of the general culture of fear and suspicion that has colored American life since 9/11. Theirs is the siege mentality wedded to a narrative of cultural victimization, sometimes racialized fears of urban criminality, and communitarian desires to preserve the religious and social life of a congregation that is facing existential threats from every direction. More than an occasion to circle the wagons of evangelical identity, sacred security is also an opportunity for middle-aged white men—self-styled security experts, often with dual backgrounds in law enforcement and the ministry—to assert an ideology of quasi-military, patriarchal authority and control in response to the "evil" that they fear in contemporary America. It is a complex world that I experienced firsthand, and often quite empathetically, when I attended the security conference at New Life, one of the key sites for conservative evangelicalism in America. What I found in person, and in the many documents that I analyze in the following section, helped me to explore the powerful ideological and religious undercurrents within contemporary discussions of CCTV and other security technologies.

New Life

When I first read about right-wing Christians wiring up churches for CCTV and selling bulletproof Bible holders to vulnerable pastors across the Bible Belt, I felt waves of sadness and pique, distance and familiarity. In some deep personal sense, I know these folks, from family contexts in East Texas, even if, in cultural terms, I have become a stranger to their world. How do I understand their concerns without belittling them? How do I respectfully approach something that strikes me, at least initially, as a misguided expression of anxiety and fear in a society wracked by such feelings? It is difficult to write honestly about anything without falling into unconscious patterns of belief and prejudice, but for a project that grapples with such strong feelings (theirs and mine), the challenge is even more daunting. So after reading and watching whatever I could find for several years, I headed to a church security conference to see for myself. Having paid the $200 registration fee, I walked inside a cavernous building that would rival most college basketball arenas and joined the hundred-plus men at the 10th Annual Church Security Conference in a modest training room near the main sanctuary at New Life. Run by the Dallas-based National Organization of Church Security and Safety Management (NOCSSM), the conference was being held at New Life for the first time since the 2007 shooting—as was soon made clear to us in this very room, as we prepared for two days of speakers, tours, demonstrations, networking, and prayer.

It's a relaxed event in many ways. We sit at long tables like students, with a three-ring binder in front of us, as well as coffee and Danish pastries on small, football-shaped napkins. When it comes to age, race, gender, religion, region, or politics, it's not a diverse crowd—by my quick count, roughly 96 percent are white men over forty. Another commonality is that a lot of them have brought their guns to church. A few jokes make it clear that many people are "carrying" a piece, which fits the strong law enforcement vibe—short hair, conservative clothes, quiet machismo. A show of hands reveals that fewer than 10 percent are actual cops, past or present, while the remaining men—the overwhelming majority—seem to acknowledge law enforcement veterans with subtle deference and perhaps a hint of envy.

At first the mood is surprisingly light, given the sober topics on the agenda: "Crime Stats in Churches," "Armed 'Initial Responder' Tactics," "Executive Protection in a House of Worship," and "New Life Shooting Recap." A murmur of appreciation goes through the room when the organizers announce that lunch is coming from Chick-fil-A, whose stand against marriage equality has elevated its status in conservative circles. Small acts of symbolism are important here, even down to which corporation made the waffle fries and chicken sandwiches that will be arriving at noon.

In the meantime, we have a full morning of speakers, beginning with Chuck Chadwick, a thoughtful guy around sixty who is founder and president of NOCSSM. He's also president of Gatekeepers Security Services, a company that has put "hundreds of armed Gatekeepers in churches across Texas," as he puts it in his promotional materials. Although we are in the middle of Colorado, Texans have a prominent role at the conference, as they do in the world of church security in general. Chadwick is the first of several charismatic Texans telling stories that usually keep the audience rapt with attention, far more so than any academic conference audience. Including more than a hundred security professionals from other churches and some aspiring vendors in the church security business, the audience is utterly tuned in to what is being said. No one has to tell them to pay attention.

Chadwick starts his presentation with a Fox News clip of a church shooting in Illinois, the first of many church atrocities that we will hear about. While concrete numbers about church violence are elusive, the anecdotal evidence hits hard. In case any security skeptics are in the room, Chadwick warns us that church doors can no longer remain unlocked, as in the good old days, and that we need to do more than lock the doors and buzz people into the sanctuary. In a grave, authoritative voice, he tells us that churches must steel themselves for the inevitable: murders, rapes, burglaries, scams, sexual predators, suicides, and acts of vandalism. He even warns us about al-Qaeda. Arguing that terrorists have been "targeting Christians" across the United States, he warns us about "Islamic suicide bombers" who could target churches, even in the Bible Belt. Several audience members raise their hands to echo his concern, claiming that their own churches have been cased by "Middle Eastern men" in advance of an attack that, presumably, never came. In the midst of his jeremiad against inadequate security, Chadwick throws in an important disclaimer: "Not everybody needs to get shot," he reminds us, after describing a near tragedy in which a church youth group used a fake gun for theatrical effect during a youth-minister sermon. Because the church elders were not informed in advance about the stunt, the church security team could easily have killed the teenagers on the altar of their own church. Having a well-trained security team can minimize such risks, he explains.

Next up is Carl Chinn, the security chief at New Life whose consulting work and publications have made him a central figure in church security. Quoting Nehemiah 4:9—"We prayed to our God and posted a guard day and night"—he assures us that surveillance cameras, threat assessments, and armed "life

ministries" are now essential to the American church. Law enforcement won't arrive in time to stop a Sunday morning attack, he says darkly—"they'll just be there for the body bags."
The rest of his talk tells us how to prevent those body bags from
being needed. First, he tells us that churches need to take these
matters seriously, making sure the church choir doesn't practice more hours than the church security team. Second, he tells
us to follow our instincts in spotting so-called DLRs ("Don't-
Look-Rights") as we scan the congregation for threats. Third,
he says that the plainclothes security teams should wear banners that say "DON'T SHOOT ME" to keep cops from assuming
that they are among the bad guys during an active-shooter incident. Finally, while he talks about using red, yellow, and white
alerts with his security team, depending on the severity of the
threat, he reminds us to keep things subtle. Wearing SWAT-
style clothes will freak out the worshippers for no good reason,
he reminds us before turning to his most powerful material.

Featuring photos of where people were slain in the rooms
around us, the core of his presentation is devoted to walking us
through the 2007 New Life shooting in sobering detail. On a
summer morning like this one, the New Life property seems so
sleepy and generic that it's hard to imagine such horrific events
taking place here—but that is exactly Chinn's point. Even New
Life couldn't imagine itself being attacked for years, until it
was too late. He shows a photo of his small .32-caliber pistol
next to the military-grade assault rifle that was used against
the New Life congregation. His point is clear: churches are
easily outgunned and quickly overwhelmed when "evil invades
sanctuary," as his book title puts it, unless they invest in the
training and equipment that the sacred-security firms are able
to provide.

Chinn makes it clear that the threat is not just crazed
strangers, but friends and neighbors as well, before offering
the first of several stories about men who kill wives and girl-

friends on church property. Having collected data on church-related violence for years, Chinn concedes that church violence is far more likely to involve a senior pastor killing his own wife at his own church than an al-Qaeda operative with a suitcase bomb. For a millisecond I think the conference is going to take another direction, that this information will undercut the push to install surveillance systems that are useless to protect us from a familiar face with a concealed weapon, but soon we are back on track: the threats are everywhere, Christians are in the crosshairs, tightened security is the only response. What is sociologically accurate about the targeting of Christians or the likelihood of terrorist attacks is beside the point when strong feelings are in evidence: the emotional reality here is one of vulnerability, anxiety, and exposure. No doubt, Chinn's stories—delivered in the somber tone of a man who has lived through tragic events—are legitimately terrifying, and his sincerity is evident. Church security may be a livelihood for these men, but it is clear that commercial motivations are working alongside powerful feelings of obligation, fear, vulnerability, and outrage.

Such feelings surge to a head with the next speaker, a charismatic former Dallas cop turned preacher/security professional by the name of Jimmy Meeks. "We know how evil men can be," he says with a melancholy air. Almost shouting into the microphone during his slides of church-based crimes, Meeks has the passion and intensity of a revival tent minister with an abiding faith in tough-minded security measures. Almost mocking the Christian "superstition" that the steeple will protect them from harm, Meeks exhorts his brethren to "bind evil" in the name of "Jesus, our warrior king." "Let us load our slingshots!" he roars before asserting that "80 million Christians have been killed for their faith in Jesus, including 45 million in the twentieth century alone!" We must remember that churches are "always" under threat, he says, and that

480 violent deaths have occurred in US churches since 1999 (elsewhere he puts the number at 542; other sacred-security experts put the number at 28).[11] Like his colleagues, Meeks throws around disturbing statistics with little attribution, but no one asks for footnotes when the passions are flowing and he's exhorting the crowd never to forget the fallen nature of humanity: "Trust no man, unless he has earned it!"

His long litany of atrocities, mostly taken from recent media accounts, reads like a dark epic poem of Christian victimization in the age of Obama. But it's not all darkness, all the time. If his presentation seems overwhelmingly grim, Meeks gestures to the light when he claims that "love is the driving force behind church security" and that he only wants to "prevent the heartache" that he saw in the wake of a multiple homicide in the First Baptist Church in Dangerfield, Texas, in 1980.[12] Like the 2007 New Life shooting, the Dangerfield tragedy has a mythic status here (it was even the subject of a small documentary film that is sold on sacred-security websites), and Meeks uses it as the emotional centerpiece of his presentation about the dangers churches face. With a heated barrage of anecdotal evidence, alarming statistics, and scriptural references, he presses the case we have heard throughout the morning: a day of reckoning approaches, and churches must be ready with all the tools of law enforcement.

One of the most affecting testimonials for greater security comes just before lunch. An African American pastor comes to the stage to interview David Works, a white church member who survived the 2007 New Life shooting. Works describes the agony of being shot in the parking lot and being unable to reach his daughter as she bled to death just a few steps away. With somber eloquence, he describes the unfolding horror of the shooting and his long recovery process, which included writing a book (*Gone in a Heartbeat: Our Daughters Died ... Our Faith Endures*) that, like some of the books that appeared in the wake of the Columbine High School massacre, casts the shooting in a theological light.[13] "The parking lot of your home church is not where you expect to be martyred," he says mournfully, and people nod in sympathy. He doesn't mention church security or surveillance systems per se, but he is leading us to the same conclusions as everyone else who has taken the podium: *This is the evil we feared. This is why we need to ramp up our security. This is why we need surveillance systems. This is why we are here.* Again, our location is significant. The residue of Columbine is everywhere in this part of Colorado, perhaps nowhere more than at New Life. A decade and a half may have passed since the massacre in the school outside Denver, but the references to Columbine are frequent and deeply felt throughout the day. "Christian America—this is your Columbine," the New Life killer wrote before his 2007 rampage, referring to an event to which many New Life congregants had some personal connection. As quoted (without the obscenities) on the back of Carl Chinn's book, the killer made his intentions plain: "I'm coming for EVERYONE soon, and I WILL be armed to the @#%$ teeth, and I WILL shoot and I WILL @#%$ KILL EVERYTHING." Both in his book and in person at the New Life conference, Chinn makes one fundamental point that sums up everything we are hearing at the conference about church security: "It wasn't the first time evil invaded the sanctuary. It will not be the last. Were we ready? Will you be?"[14]

It's an immense moral burden, one that the conference participants seem ready to shoulder without complaint. Yet no one asks an underlying question: Are you sure all this stuff is really necessary? Although we get plenty of heated rhetoric and the gory anecdotes that fire-and-brimstone preachers love to share, no one tries to demonstrate that churches are vulnerable to attack in a statistically meaningful way. No one can prove that churches are facing such heightened risks, that this state of emergency really exists for buildings that often seem like the sleepiest, quietest, and safest places in town. And no one demonstrates the effectiveness of installing CCTV or well-trained "life ministry" security teams in deterring crimes in churches. Instead, sacred security is operating in an emotional register, in the realm of feelings of vulnerability, fear, distrust, anger—as well as responsibility, obligation, and love for their fellow congregants. In place of the hard facts of what works, there is a strong sense of *we have to do something*. Religion and high-tech security form a powerful union in such contexts.

The conference in Colorado Springs was the embodiment of what I have been seeing and reading for several years in the marketing materials for sacred-security firms, some twenty of which I've been following online. Across most of the United States, and especially across the American South and lower Midwest, one can find self-proclaimed Christian businesses of every possible sort, from craft-supply megastores such as Hobby Lobby to homey storefronts that offer greeting cards, cakes, books, or office supplies with a Christian twist, one that usually reflects culturally conservative Protestantism. In this regard, the mere existence of Christian-identified security firms is not entirely surprising, especially in the Bible Belt. However, I am fascinated by how they fuse their religious and cultural beliefs with the language of securitization, creating a new, theologically infused mode of insecurity in the age of surveillance. These are scary times, these God-centric surveillance companies seem to say, but the answers are at hand. The challenge to secure the faithful against so many threats might seem overwhelming, but as one church-security handbook reminds its readers, there are many ways to "harden" a church's "soft" defenses against attack. The "good news" of securitization is available for those who will repent their complacent ways and feel the terrors of the time. As one Christian security professional puts it, perhaps inadvertently conflating himself with God: "Whoever listens to me will live in safety" (Proverbs 1:33).[15]

The Litany of Doom

The first commandment of sacred security is *Thou Shall Fear Thy Neighbor*, which is why the sales pitch begins and ends with fear. Hoping to scare the bejesus out of complacent congregations with terrifyingly vivid anecdotal evidence, the sales pitch leans heavily on what I call the "litany of doom," an extensive list of shocking crimes against sanctuaries in the United States. This grim catalog of murders, assaults, child abuse, rapes, and robberies provides the rationale for investing in an unprecedented degree of sacred security and surveillance. For instance, the NOCSSM, founded in Grapevine, Texas, in 2002, warns that "criminals come in all forms; sexual predators who prey on both children and adults, thieves who would steal in the dead of night or in broad daylight, and conmen who prey on the trusting. All of these criminals are attracted to the seemingly low risk environment of churches."[16] Another security firm warns: "An unfortunate aspect of our current society is that nothing seems to be sacred."[17] A rueful tone marks these assertions of an ever-present threat to personal and communal safety, which is then itemized in sensational detail.

"ANOTHER VIOLENT ATTACK IN A CHURCH" is one headline on the Gideon Protective Services website, though it could describe almost anything in these litanies of doom and destruction. "This will be the 32nd violent attack this year" (2010), Gideon reminds its readers, before listing many of these atrocities, often with links to news stories that emphasize the urgency of the crisis. Similarly, the Church Security Alliance features dramatic headlines on its website: "PASTOR SHOT IN THE HEAD WHILE HOSTING YOUTH GROUP EVENT ... MAN DRIVES CAR INTO CHURCH AND SETS BUILDING ON FIRE ... MURDER-SUICIDE AT TEXAS CHURCH ALTAR ... MINISTER BEATEN AFTER CLASHING WITH MUSLIMS ON HIS TV SHOW."[18] Or again in the Lone Star state, this time from a company called Safe at Church: "GUNMAN KILLS SEVEN, AND HIMSELF, IN TEXAS CHURCH."[19] To keep these warnings from seeming anecdotal, a few vendors add a veneer of social science, such as the security consultant who publishes a "comprehensive list of Ministry related deadly force incidents." His litany purports to describe hundreds of violent crimes committed on church grounds in the United States since 1999.

The purpose of these litanies seems obvious: they are designed to establish the urgency of the threat that churches face. Like all marketers, sacred-security firms work hard to overcome consumer passivity. "Our loved ones are dying, our churches are being burned down and the gifts that God has been so gracious to give us are being taken right from under our noses," writes one vendor before asking: "Where is the outrage?"[20] Of course, if the litany succeeds in providing outrage or fear, sacred-security firms will tend to those needs. Pastoral fear will find a productive outlet in the power of surveillance technologies, which will prevent a congregation from becoming another unfortunate statistic. The essential message is clear: you don't want to be the remorseful pastor who says to himself *if only we had invested in a surveillance system.* Instead, as one vendor encourages a reluctant minister, listen to Romans 13:4 and arm yourself against evil, for "God's minister" does "not bear the sword in vain ... he is ... an avenger to execute wrath on him who practices evil."

In the marketing materials for sacred surveillance, the attacker is inevitably male, the victim female. Horror stories in the litany of doom seem designed to arouse feelings of patriarchal responsibility for "their women." Quoting from the Book of Nehemiah (4:14), the Cops and Cross website reminds its customers to "Fight for your daughters, your wives." In this sense, one foundation of sacred security lies in the traditional roles that evangelical culture assigns to men and women. As with other religious conservatives in the contemporary United States, evangelicals favor traditional gender ideologies that charge "strong men" with the protection of women. Indeed, much of the sacred-security rhetoric sounds familiar to anyone who remembers the 1990s ascent of the Promise Keepers movement, whose "central theme" was that "current social problems are caused by a lack of appropriate male leadership." Their solution, as Becky Beal points out, was a call for men to "make a commitment to assume their 'rightful' obligations as leaders in our society."[21] Another scholar has explored the gender ideologies in Edwin Louis Cole's best-selling book *Maximized Manhood: A Guide to Family Survival* (1982), a Promise Keepers classic with almost a million copies in print. While women are stereotyped as emotional, responsive, and sensitive in Cole's worldview, men are understood as possessing a natural sense of "aggression, strength, and rationality." As Cole puts it: "A church, a family, a nation is only as strong as its men. Men, you are accountable."[22] Today, security firms make the same argument: strong men have a moral duty to protect their community. The founder of the Church Security Network even quoted the lyrics of a Christian rock band to inspire manly vigilance and to sell CCTV:

We were warriors on the front lines
Standing, unafraid
But now we're watchers on the sidelines

While our families slip away
Where are you, men of courage?
You were made for so much more.[23]

The patriarchal aspect is obvious. What is more nuanced is the racialization of the threat in the litany of doom. As Donald G. Mathews and other historians have shown, southern white males have long obsessed over the sexual purity of their wives, daughters, and sisters, in particular against the perceived advances of African American men. In most of the marketing material that I have studied, the racialization of the threat is subtle but persistent. The few faces of color that I came across in the sacred-security marketing materials were always suspects in custody, usually in a photograph linked to a TV news report about some heinous crime. Whereas the threat to churches is sometimes a person of color, the imagined victim is almost invariably white, as is the guardian figure. In other words, Christian-based security experts are almost invariably white men, often posed with guns, dogs, and other suggestions of military or law enforcement prowess, while their criminal litany tends to focus on white female victims and male perpetrators that are often African American—though women of color are also sometimes presented as threatening in the marketing materials. A few years ago, ABC News broadcast a story about a woman in Houston who stole money from purses during church services, even after exchanging the "sign of peace" with her victims. She was a woman of color, part of a worrisome pattern in these widely circulated news stories and the sacred-security marketing built around racialized villains. The news provides us with the church surveillance camera's POV: we gawk in judgment from above as the petty thief helps herself to someone's wallet. ABC's video footage, filled with standard-issue piety about holiness debased (perhaps not too different from my own), is then used by security companies to press their case for more cameras, more training, more guns in American churches.

The purpose of these emotionally resonant stories is clear: to overcome the second thoughts of clergy and congregants who are concerned not only about the high cost of surveillance systems, but also their appropriateness in a house of worship. As one security firm's website explained:

> One stumbling block for church surveillance systems is that they look, well, too much like surveillance systems. Many people do not want the place that others come to for worship and sanctuary, to look like it is a fortress. They want people to feel at ease [in] church, and [they might] not like [that] they are being watched. However, video surveillance systems these days are meant to provide tasteful design, while including a high-tech surveillance equipment.... Security cameras can be designed to look like they are meant to be there. In a church, people come to worship and feel closer to God, no one wants to feel like they are being monitored by the eye in the sky (and we are not referring to the big eye in the sky that people are there to worship).[24]

Many companies address this issue in their marketing materials, often returning to horror stories to overcome doubts. "Church leaders have been very reluctant to install church video surveillance systems because they believe it conveys distrust and sends a message of fear to the congregants," a website called SmartSurveillanceTips.com tells us. "The truth is, properly installed church video security monitoring systems will never affect the feeling of openness and trust that most congregations wish to experience." *Phew, what a relief! There are no side-effects to injecting another all-seeing eye into a small congregation.* The marketers explain away all doubts, even as they gin up the fear with long lists of atrocities committed on church grounds. Separating media hyperbole from actual danger is impossible in the welter of emotions that sacred security generates: fear, outrage, guilt, anger, vigilance, hope. Indeed, so much of this business works on an emotional level, where religion often flourishes as well. Because we have no compelling evidence that CCTV serves as a deterrent, churches are buying it "on faith" for *the feeling of security* that it presumably provides (and perhaps for the small satisfaction of being able to say after the next crime that "we did all we could"). In this sense, the proposition that "CCTV will make me safer" is no different in kind than "the Lord will provide" or "everything happens for a reason": investing in sacred security is an act of faith. (Of course, some vendors make unsupported claims that CCTV deters crime: "Don't hide your camera systems," one how-to book advises. "They serve as a deterrent. Let people know they are being watched. Place the camera in a secure location but out in full view.")[25] It sounds plausible enough at first glance, but the claim is never given much support, with the result being that I was quite doubtful about the claims being made for church surveillance systems.

Yet if the marketing rhetoric is any guide, I'm not the only skeptic. Doubt often remains in the hearts and minds of religious consumers, and they need something more than emotionally charged anecdotal evidence to overcome their skepticism. Again and again, I found a lingering question haunting the rhetoric of sacred security: *CCTV in a church? Really?* Almost every sales pitch for sacred security addresses this awkward question in some fashion. Often vendors answer this question not just with the fear-mongering and pop sociology of the litany of doom, but on theological grounds as well, opening up a surprising space in which surveillance studies and religious studies share a common interest.

What Would Homeland Security Do?
The Theology of Surveillance

The second commandment of sacred security is the theological justification for surveillance, or what is sometimes described as providing "biblical clearance." The reason is simple: many potential customers have qualms about the securitization of sacred space. Even a pastor in Fort Worth, Texas, who allows deacons to bring guns to church on Sunday, worries about taking things too far: "My ultimate conviction is what does the word of God say and what would Jesus do? Can you in your wildest imagination ever see Jesus packing a .38? I can't imagine Peter and Paul carrying .45s."[26]

No doubt, the proliferation of surveillance technologies is a source of deep conflict for many Christian conservatives. Evangelical conservatives have sometimes rejected CCTV and other security measures as diabolical tools that usurp divine judgment. In a book devoted to the topic, a "leading teacher in Bible Prophesy" has even claimed that surveillance technologies are "setting the stage for the rise of the Antichrist and world government."[27] Another Christian writer has fulminated against "the mind control that is coming under the 666 Surveillance System."[28] For some evangelical conservatives, CCTV is quite literally the mark of the beast—a sign of external control that is somehow related to the dark conspiracies of the "New World Order."

Yet something else might trump these vivid fears about security technologies: a strong desire to impose biblical order on contemporary society. Evangelical conservatives often express dismay about a "permissive" modern society that lacks supervision, if not outright control. In this context, surveillance technologies might enable fantasies of patriarchal control that would contain the criminality and waywardness associated with secular modernity. As this punitive antimodernism overshadows libertarian or even conspiratorial concerns about surveillance leading to "world government," so too does selective biblical quotation provide a means for winning over the theologically uncertain.

The selected Bible passages vary but the subtext is consistent: *be afraid, be aware, be vigilant, be strong, be a watchman.* In short, it's something like *In God We Trust — but pack a weapon just in case.* At the Call2Duty conference in Carrolton, Texas, in 2012, Jimmy Meeks, the previously mentioned founder of the Texas-based Cops and Cross, explicitly argued "the scriptural validity of the need for Church Security" as the core of his presentation.[29] Likewise, in its web pages devoted to church security, Christianet.com aims to dispel the myth that "Scripture never mentions a wireless security camera system." "False," we are told, although a skeptical reader might not be persuaded by the evidence from Mark 3:27: "No man can enter into a strong man's house, and spoil his goods, except he will first bind the strong man; and then he will spoil his house."

Not surprisingly, the vendors take some liberties with their Bible verses, relying on metaphorical understandings that they might find insufficiently literal in other contexts. NOCSSM's "founding scripture" is Chronicles 9:21, which describes "responsible men" who are "gatekeepers" around the "Lord's tent." There is the ubiquitous Nchemiah 4:9: "We prayed to our God and posted a guard." The Safe at Church firm attributes this nervous-making quotation to Jesus: "BEWARE OF MEN . . . THEY WILL HARM YOU IN THE SYNAGOGUE (Matthew 10:17)." Meanwhile, Gideon Protective Services offers a long list of "protective Bible verses" that seem to justify church security, while Church Risk Management gives several verses to augment its sales pitch: "Luke 10:19: Behold, I give you the authority to trample on serpents and scorpions, and over all the power of the enemy.... Luke 22:36-

... and he who has no sword, let him sell his garment and buy one.... 1 Peter 5:8- Be sober, be vigilant; because your adversary the devil walks about like a roaring lion, seeking whom he may devour."[30] And what could sell the enhanced vision of CCTV more effectively than the quotation from Zecharia 9:8 at the defunct website Church-Security-Training.com: "No more shall an oppressor pass through them. For now I have seen with my eyes."[31]

Sometimes the vendors engage their skeptics head-on, providing biblical chapter and verse that is intended to legitimize and even somehow consecrate their businesses. When one pastor suggested that security measures be left "in God's hands," a security expert shot back with a Bible verse that "each one should use whatever gift he has received to serve others," with the implication being that security consultants were using their God-given gifts in service of the Lord and thus should not be challenged. Then the consultant pushed further on the point of personal accountability, putting the moral onus on his questioner: "Are YOU being a good steward with the gifts that God has given YOU and your church?" As another company puts it, providing security is a "sacred charge," not something to be taken lightly.[32]

The conversation about sacred security spills over into various blogs and writings published elsewhere. One blog post from Church Security Alliance puts it this way: "I suspect Jesus was deeply saddened any church felt it necessary to hire security. But, thank God they did. Jesus and his followers faced many of the same threats churches face today. However, Jesus didn't face the threat of civil legal action for 'Failure to perform due diligence' our churches face today."[33] Another, from a journalist-politician in Canada, lamented in a letter to the editor of a provincial magazine: "When liberals destroyed faith in the real God, who watches everything we do and even think, the unintended but inevitable result was video-cameras. I agree it's a lousy substitute. But truth, and the whole truth, we must have, or nothing works."[34]

The upshot is clear: strong security is a grim necessity for these Christians. Pastors and deacons must embrace their moral duty of manly guardianship. Although the tide of sin cannot be stemmed, it can be slowed with the right technology and training—most often, practices that have weirdly devolved from the Department of Homeland Security to small suburban churches. In the meantime, pastors should use their CCTV to catch the sinners within the fold, such as teenagers having sex on the church grounds, or to protect the innocent charged with crimes on church property. One vendor points out that CCTV can clear the name of a minister falsely accused of child molestation—and thus one moral panic in twenty-first-century America fuels another.

The Architecture of Control: A Long History

Protestant churches are no strangers to the architecture of control, a culture of scrutiny that includes informal social networks, political rhetoric that centers on deviance and difference, and even designs for literally building surveillance into the church experience. From late-nineteenth-century church architecture that encouraged worshippers to scrutinize one another in pews that faced one another, to the incessant victimization rhetoric of the contemporary Christian right, American Protestants have kept a vigilant watch over their flocks' internal behaviors as well as their perceived external enemies. Writing about eighteenth-century Virginia, historian Don Mathews has described the intense scrutiny to which congregants were subjected: "Whether wanton or wanting, the world was a disorderly place, and Evangelicals were called out of it to establish proper social relations." This required "strict inquiry into the behaviors which affected only individuals" and "careful surveillance of antisocial behavior which threatened to disrupt the community or give it a bad name."[35] A well-established culture of ministerial scrutiny seems a natural foundation for the emerging culture of surveillance.

Historians have connected some of this fortress mentality to the racial politics of nineteenth-century southern white males, in particular their obsession with protecting the purity of white Southern women. In this sense, sacred security is interwoven with older ideas about sexual purity, racial threats, manly protection, and quasi-military vigilance, a kind of alert moral warrior posture that also animated the rhetoric of modern Promise Keepers as well as some recent politicians, such as former US senator Rick Santorum and others who cater to the conservative Tea Party.

Despite being the empowered majority throughout US history in most places and times, white Protestant conservatives have often imagined themselves as an embattled minority in the past century. The irony is obvious. Although a suburban mosque is probably a more likely target for vandalism and serious hate crimes, sacred-security firms are directing their energies toward Protestant churches in the rural and suburban South. Sacred security is endeavoring to reinforce the walls of the fortress, to train the "watchmen" to stand guard, and to explain away lingering doubts with the casuistry of the modern marketer. All for a price—and in a sales pitch that reveals a great deal about the relationship between religion and security in the contemporary Bible Belt. The friction is palpable at first, but with persistent marketing in a ripe environment, a smooth mutuality takes its place. And what this smoothness reveals, to my mind, is the underlying compatibility of old-fashioned southern Protestant religiosity, at least in its conservative form, and newfangled surveillance technologies. As one historian has put it, low-tech forms of human surveillance "undergirded evangelical morality" in nineteenth-century America. Now we have new technologies that boost the power of religious watchmen, whose gender is most certainly male and whose anxieties are most certainly real, even if their sense of imminent threat is often fueled by old habits and patterns of belief.

Fear Thy Neighbor: Religion and Social Trust

We prayed to our God and posted a guard.

—NEHEMIAH 4:9, QUOTED ON CARL CHINN'S WEBSITE

One of the best works of social science to assess contemporary religious life in America is Robert D. Putnam and David E. Campbell's *American Grace: How Religion Divides and Unites Us* (2010), whose subtitle has particular relevance here.[36] Religious identification seems to cut both ways when it comes to worrying about one's neighbors. Although the book does not deal explicitly with security issues, it does provide an invaluable guide to the diverse cultural landscape of American religious life, one that might help us to explain the appeal of sacred security to particular communities of faith that are hardly the fringe sects that some might imagine. Instead, these are faith communities with deep pockets and considerable influence in contemporary America.

Conducting an extensive Faith Matters survey in 2006–2007 with thousands of Americans, Putnam and Campbell found that churchgoing significantly increases "social trust" more than any other factor except education; they call churchgoing "the universal predictor of good neighborliness."[37] What is it about churchgoing that makes individuals more trusting, more optimistic, and happier than nonchurchgoers? These political scientists argue that the social networks that arise from active churchgoing, rather than from the nitty-gritty of theological doctrine, are the primary ingredient for social trust. In other words, making friends in church is more important than what is preached on Sunday morning, in terms of encouraging a more secure picture of the outside world—though theology is far from meaningless in this regard.

The great exception to the correlation between neighborliness and churchgoing is among fundamentalists, and herein lies the sweet spot for sacred security. Although it is often confusing to parse these seemingly fuzzy terms, fundamentalism is generally understood as a subset of the much broader category of evangelical Protestantism (those various denominations that fall outside the designation of "mainline" Protestantism, such as Episcopalians, Methodists, Lutherans, and Presbyterians). Compared to the sunnier evangelicals in the Billy Graham tradition, fundamentalists are more skeptical about engagement with the modern world, put great stock in biblical "inerrancy," interpret scripture with stringent literalism, and hold antiscientific positions on issues ranging from evolution to climate change. Perhaps we could argue that their seemingly paranoid view of security, one that requires arming oneself against an apparently exaggerated threat, is in keeping with this worldview, in which empirical data about crime can be trumped by a Bible quote. This is why I would suggest that sacred security is directed at evangelicals as its primary audience but that its strongest cultural resonance is within fundamentalism, that influential subset of evangelicalism.

Sacred security seems to gain little traction among religious liberals such as Quakers, Unitarians, and mainline Protestants, who seem almost entirely absent from this part of the security landscape. One reason for their presumably more trusting view of the world, if I can extrapolate from Putnam and Campbell's findings, is theological (though education is

surely relevant as well). "Religious liberals more often experience a loving God, and they are among the most socially trusting of Americans," they write, "whereas religious conservatives more often experience a judgmental God, and they are
the least trusting of Americans, especially if they are obser-
vant."[38] What Putnam and Campbell are suggesting is not
surprising: a theology focused on a loving God who smiles in
blessing and forgiveness of his children will result in a more
trusting view of other people as well, while a theological emphasis on original sin, the depraved "original" nature of human
beings, and constant divine scrutiny will result in a distrustful
view of other people. In other words, if one imagines God as
a frowning patriarch sitting in judgment over a universe filled
with sin-crazed miscreants, she is likely to adopt a similar perspective on humanity—which makes for a good potential customer for sacred security. By contrast, if one is a religious liberal with a sunny view of divine forgiveness as well as a belief
in innate human decency, she is probably not as worried about
arming deacons or keeping video cameras trained on Sunday-
school teachers. As Putnam and Campbell put it, our ideas
about God are interwoven with our ideas about other people:
"a comforting, avuncular God encourages social comity and
confidence."[39] While most Americans report feeling God's love
"very often" (62 percent), a minority (39 percent) experience
judgment very often—and this fretful minority is probably
where sacred security has its greatest appeal. Where does this
leave other faiths? Catholics, Jews, Mormons, Muslims, Buddhists, Hindus, and other believers may have security needs
as pressing as those of evangelical megachurches in Dallas,
even more so in the case of some mosques or synagogues, but I
found little public evidence of their security anxiety expressed
in books, brochures, or training manuals or on websites, nor
did I find a significant number of religiously identified firms
marketing specifically to these faiths.

As noted earlier, sacred security is a phenomenon kept afloat largely by middle-aged southern evangelical white conservatives who are concerned about personal and communal safety. Its vendors are not slick corporations staffed by Harvard MBAs, but rather former cops and part-time preachers from small towns in Arkansas, Texas, Missouri, or Florida—"God-centric" businessmen of modest educational attainment, which might include theological training at a small religious college or criminology courses at a community college (and often a combination of the two). Their small security companies are often homespun, even quaint, in their self-presentation, with clunky websites that could not have been designed professionally, each one chock-full of more Bible verses than a church newsletter. And with the litany of criminal threats warning customers of the inevitable tide of violence to come, sacred-security vendors seem to operate from a position of distrust toward those outside the congregation. Worried about the possibility of murder or pedophilia on their church's grounds, these men seem eager to reestablish a vision of old-fashioned, quasi-military authority and patriarchal control over an ostensibly vulnerable community. These are the men who are now promoting surveillance technologies for American churches in the Bible Belt.

Putnam and Campbell's work is relevant here as well. What their massive survey confirmed is that religious Americans are less tolerant of dissent and less supportive of civil liberties. While religious life seems to enhance civil engagement, social trust, and other forms of citizenship in general, these political scientists also describe the "darker side of religion's link to citizenship."[40] Indeed, their Faith Matters survey confirmed what many earlier studies suggested: that there is a "fundamental correlation between religiosity and intolerance."[41] Because this intolerance is often directed at "outsiders" who appear "different," whether because of sexual orientation or political affiliation, I suspect that this pervasive feeling of "stranger danger" is feeding the appetite for security, especially when it is combined with a strong emphasis on obedience. Referring back to earlier studies by Kenneth Wald, Stephen Mockabee, and others, Putnam and Campbell characterize the "authority-mindedness" of religious people who are "particularly concerned to safeguard authority."[42] Although Putnam and Campbell never mention security issues such as surveillance per se, and while "authority-mindedness" is not perfectly coterminous with "security-mindedness," I think they are inadvertently describing the cultural backdrop for sacred security: religious people who are suspicious of outsiders and who put authority and control above autonomy and privacy. In this sense, what I take from Putnam and Campbell's survey data is that sacred security is most likely to spring from, and speak to, evangelical conservatives who prize authority and fear disorder, for theological, cultural, and political reasons. Although the reassuring social networks formed during churchgoing may undercut the social distrust of even the most theologically conservative parishioner, thereby reducing the desire for high-tech security measures at church, "authority-minded" evangelical conservatives—and fundamentalists in particular—might be the ideal demographic for a faith-based security company's sales pitch, given their theological and cultural outlook.[43]

Still, obvious questions remain for those who wire up their sanctuaries for CCTV and train their ushers to scan the pews for terrorists: *Does it work? Does it make them safer? Does it even make them feel safer?* I'm not so sure, especially not when training manuals remind us that our security training and equipment will never suffice because "there is still a seasoned and determined enemy at the gate."[44] For church members who are nervous about personal safety, who circulate horror stories about church shootings, and who are theologically and sociologically disposed to social distrust, sacred security may not solve the problem, either in terms of preventing crime or in creating a secure feeling. One of the sad ironies about surveillance is that its efficacy has never been demonstrated to the satisfaction of sociologists, whose studies tend to suggest that CCTV, in particular, is almost useless in preventing crime. But even sadder is what may be happening on an emotional level, where surveillance may prove equally problematic for those who live under its inquiring gaze. Looking at Protestant Boston in the 1850s, historian John Corrigan argues that religious devotion was offered to the divine in exchange for protection and blessing—in other words, emotions were commodified in a contractual exchange that implied "if I feel a certain way, I will receive a certain reward."[45] In a similar manner, some contemporary Christians offer a particular emotional stance—paternal protectiveness, righteous vigilance—that yields a smaller reward, if any. According to the sacred-security firms, no level of vigilance can ensure the total safety of the congregation. The threats are too grave, too implacable for that. "Hey Pastor, I will fill you in on something," writes the head of the Church Security Network in response to one Doubting Thomas. "Security is never 100 percent, but no security is 100 percent vulnerability. I never said you can stop 100 percent of the active shooters." At its best, high-tech vigilance will minimize the threat, keep it *relatively* at bay, in a manner that will allow the sacred community to survive but not really thrive. Thus, even as they make a bargain with security companies, looking to find solace in surveillance technology and quasi-military training, evangelical conservatives are probably still bedeviled by insecurity, vulnerability, anxiety, and a sense of victimhood. Even with their ideological brethren at the center of political power—from Congress to the Supreme Court to the White House—evangelical conservatives seem to retain their deeply encoded sense of vulnerability. This is true even in moments of their greatest triumph, and even when enmeshed in the increasingly high-tech web of surveillance culture. This is the tragic bargain that security often asks us to make: we spend a great deal, both financially and emotionally, for a very uncertain result.

What are the emotional implications of converting the relatively open doors of churches into something approaching a high-security camp with locks, gates, and cameras? Such confinement would seem oppressive and alienating, not only to outsiders approaching the gates of the temple but also to those inside biting their nails in anticipation of the next imagined atrocity. As this emotional shift takes place, churches may assume the least pleasant aspects of the airport, the location par excellence of control societies.[46] Along with airports, gated communities, and schools, churches can now be added to the list of security-obsessed institutions in the contemporary United States. Although some forms of sacred security existed before 9/11, the ongoing war on terror seems to have been a catalyst for the expansion of the security state into every realm of American life. Two sociologists noted as much in 2005: "September 11th provided a convenient opportunity for the security establishment to lobby for increased surveillance capacity, despite lingering questions about whether such devices can achieve their professed goals."[47] Churches and other religious institutions are yet another front in the intensifying war of control, access, mobility, and identity that has marked the era of homeland security in America.

Of course, many American churches, temples, and mosques have resisted the encroaching militarization with courageous moral stands: they offer sanctuary to undocumented workers, meals to the homeless of all faiths, and a message of social hope and trust that applies equally to friend and stranger. Unafraid almost by principle, these religious institutions are small islands in the sea of insecurity in which we live our lives

today. Other churches, as I've described above, have submerged themselves in insecurity. We will see how religious institutions are able to survive the incorporation of a fortress mentality that seems more appropriate to Christian life in early modern Europe, when some churches were literal fortresses.

Cameras and Crosses

I sense the pain in the room, the heaviness of the obligation, and the burden of serving as a "sheepdog" to protect the "flock" whenever I meet people involved with sacred security. Like me, these are ordinary people with the ordinary pains of living that they are trying to soothe in the best ways they know. I have empathy and, I hope, some degree of understanding for people who turn to sacred-security firms to solve a problem that may be grounded less in criminological facts than in certain emotional, ideological, and theological assumptions. Nevertheless, I am troubled not to hear a single reference to root causes, in a sociological sense. Church surveillance is marketed, consumed, and deployed without a nod to structural issues such as gun laws, racialized and gendered poverty, the treatment of the mentally ill, or the ripple effects of living in an increasingly militarized culture. Instead, this segment of the Christian right dismisses such concerns by simply claiming that "evil" is at work, that their congregations are staring down an implacable force so potent that nothing can stop it except, perhaps, guns, locks, and security cameras. Such measures cannot stop the evil entirely, but they are better than nothing. Such strong feelings of anxiety, vulnerability, and protectiveness seem to lead evangelical conservatives to this strange place in which "better than nothing" is something legitimate to pursue.

I'm interested in my own feelings about CCTV as well, even

surprised by them. Until recently I didn't know I cared about cameras in sacred spaces at all. Yet I keep returning to religious angles that I've never pursued in the past. I often wonder: Who would want surveillance cameras above the pews glaring down at the worshippers? What could be so alarming to a roomful of gun-owning, God-fearing, middle-aged white people in a small town or midsize city run by other white Christian people? In other words, what is so damn frightening that you'd replace the free-flowing calm and compassionate welcome of the idealized church with an ominous sense of lockdown? What draws me to this topic is the sheer contrast between the *ideal* of hopeful refuge and shoulder-to-shoulder togetherness in a sacred space versus the insinuated, carefully marketed anxiety of the security business, in which the threat of looming violence is forever amped up, and the need for eternal vigilance is well established. *Must everything drip with fear?* Do we really need "rules of engagement" for church security teams, who must be told that "protection of the offering (theft) is not an appropriate use of deadly force"?[48]

After a few years of looking at this subject from various odd angles, I can hazard this much: logic and evidence cannot compete with strong feelings and lurid stories about whatever evil is lurking outside the blessed community. For many conservative evangelicals, the enemy has a potency that is difficult to convey in secular terms.

In this distressed vision of modern America, the black cloud of evil can settle anywhere, anytime. It is the rank stranger outside the gate whom they fear. It is the vile nature of strangers, of difference, of heathens, but also the evil within: what the pastor might do to the organist, what the children might allege in the nursery—and if they don't fear these things, the marketing of sacred security explicitly tells them that they should. Thank God—or Gideon Protective Services, or Watchman

Security, or Savior Protection—that video surveillance cameras, properly installed, will protect the innocent and ward off the wicked, even if it's only sometimes. Such is the sales pitch from the companies that I have been following in this complex economy of fear.

Deep down, I suppose what rattles me about sacred surveillance is the vague feeling of personal violation. That plastic camera near the roofline seems out of place, almost seeming to function like a rival to the crucifix—and one just as alive with potentiality. My father's broken-down Catholicism, my mother's stern Church of Christ, my own peevish teenage Lutheran apostasy and surreal exile to a Catholic boys' school—all tell me that I'm looking the wrong way, that *I'm responding to the wrong icon* when I look past the crucifix to stare at the CCTV camera. But that camera is why I feel watched and judged. I want it to stop looking, to simply trust me not to harm, whether I'm in a church singing hymns or in the Gap shopping for socks. But it never sleeps; it never closes its glassy eye; it never stops judging, recording, archiving the face that we present to the machinery of electronic security.

Queasy as I am about the blurring of cameras and crosses, of old theology and new technology, I also wonder if they have a certain affinity. Both are emblems of judgment from afar, of an inscrutable downward gaze. Along with other forms of tracking human behavior, increasingly ubiquitous surveillance cameras represent yet another encroachment on our privacy and liberty—yet I have come across very little opposition to CCTV in churches (or in most other aspects of American life). Perhaps we would find this encroachment more disturbing if the new eye of providence didn't feel so much like the old one—that is to say, if ancient patterns of belief hadn't prepped the ground for this new outgrowth of the security state.[49]

With the expansion of our control society into every realm

of American life, I fear that we're building a gaudy Las Vegas of the mind, a slick zone of mechanized distrust in which we're always under someone's watchful eye. In director Martin Scorsese's film *Casino*, Ace Rothstein, the savvy operator played by Robert De Niro, explains this culture of relentless scrutiny:

> In Vegas, everybody's gotta watch everybody else. Since the players are looking to beat the casino, the dealers are watching the players. The box men are watching the dealers. The floor men are watching the box men. The pit bosses are watching the floor men. The shift bosses are watching the pit bosses. The casino manager is watching the shift bosses. I'm watching the casino manager. And the eye-in-the-sky is watching us all.

Of course, the "all-seeing eye" used to refer to the divine. Now it is a small lens linked to a video monitor in the back room of a church, casino, shopping center, or office building. And therein lies the dismal bathos of the contemporary moment, in which the cross is not adequate protection, even for believers: *God's not dead—he's just been demoted.*

It's not for me to say whether CCTV eases or intensifies the fear of crime in a particular congregation—that will have to wait for an ethnographer who can track individual responses over many months, something I have not attempted here. Perhaps the cameras will be well received in some quarters, or perhaps they will be perceived (paradoxically) as unnerving symbols of insecurity, as reflections of a history of violence in a particular location that might otherwise seem benign. I'm interested in these perceptions, as well as the other psychological baggage that accompanies the proliferation of CCTV. For instance, I'm curious as to whether the addition of video surveillance enables a kind of comprehensive, unseen seeing that humans are not used to possessing, one that far exceeds the

imaging technologies of the twentieth century. Will the proliferation of small, powerful, and networked surveillance cameras represent an unprecedented expansion of vision, one that
approaches certain aspects of the all-seeing divine described
in Proverbs 15:3 ("The eyes of the Lord are in every place, be-
holding the evil and the good")? The theology of video surveillance is my ultimate destination here.[50]

Indeed, how we internalize video surveillance and the other
imperatives of a control society is, for me, the heart of the matter. Well before Jeremy Bentham made this internalization of
the guard's gaze a key aspect of his diabolically clever Panopticon, the fifteenth-century German monk Nicholas of Cusa dis-
ciplined an entire abbey with a single portrait of Jesus, whose
eyes had been painted to appear to follow the monks wherever
they went.[51] As much as it inspired a greater degree of piety in
the abbey, the constant gaze was also an irritant, an oppressive force for those who had to live with what I imagine as a
bug-eyed Jesus. A perverse parable emerged for Nicholas of
Cusa's brethren, in which the hunger for security begat a new
kind of insecurity, and I suspect that we will discover much
the same thing in our mania for technologies of control. What
should have offered comfort and calm (Jesus, CCTV) may
end up provoking discomfort and unease, if not painful self-
consciousness. Maybe we will feel clumsy and naked on this
perpetual stage, or maybe we will revel in it as we embrace
lives of carefree exhibitionism. Privacy be damned, some will
say, relishing the sense of being watched as a way to give meaning to their lives. Perhaps our deeds, both petty and grave, will
take on a greater depth of meaning that goes along with our
sense of being monitored.

I'm also interested in the flip side: being the divine watcher
must have its own perils. In his short story "Human Moments
in World War III," first published in *Esquire* magazine in July

1983, Don DeLillo imagined the God-like sensation that accompanies the rapid expansion of vision that an astronaut might experience:

> Earth orbit puts men into philosophical temper. How can we help it? We see the planet complete. We have a privileged vista. In our attempts to be equal to the experience, we tend to meditate importantly on subjects like the human condition. It makes a man feel *universal*, floating over the continents, seeing the rim of the world, a line as clear as a compass arc, knowing it is just a turning of the bend to Atlantic twilight, to sediment plumes and kelp beds, an island chain glowing in the dusky sea.

As we increasingly scrutinize other people on CCTV in our churches, homes, and offices, or from small flying drones equipped with surveillance cameras, will we not feel this God-like perspective of gazing down from above, sitting in judgment, convinced that *we* are the all-seeing "I"?[52] (I say "convinced" because the all-seeing eye—whether technological or theological—is always fantasy: knowledge and visibility are never coterminous.) Will we become God-like voyeurs in our desire to watch friends and neighbors, coworkers and students, studying each of them with a Stasi-like efficiency on an ever-expanding surveillance system? A popular app already enables the fantasy of anonymous global voyeurism, allowing us to tap into live surveillance feeds from around the world. *Look, it's snowing in Japan ... a man is jaywalking in Sweden ... a car has just been parked in Florida.* We can even move these far-away cameras, changing the angles, rotating the view. Perhaps the next generation of the app will let us speak to the jaywalker in Sweden: *Hey! You're breaking the law. I see you! Shape up!* And he will look up, suddenly flush with fear and trembling, scurrying away from this anonymous scolding. Eventually, the peep-junkies may be able to direct small bursts of foul odor or electric shocks in order to hassle the wicked souls appearing on their CCTV monitors, thereby adding an element of "gamification" to the disciplinary regime (I'm only half-kidding here). The possibilities are endless at the leading edge of surveillance technology.

Of course, more than petty scolding is at stake when surveillance technology allows us to watch and judge in secret— we are also being tempted to assume an authoritarian mindset that seeks to categorize and control human behavior from above, rather than remaining in the democratic fray. *To the Lighthouse*, Virginia Woolf's incomparable novel about a genteel English family on holiday, includes a passage in which she describes a young girl standing over a tide pool, playing God with its tiny marine inhabitants. As she becomes bored with the little universe at her feet, she begins to fantasize about her power over all that she surveyed:

> Brooding, she changed the pool into the sea, and made the minnows into sharks and whales, and cast vast clouds over this tiny world by holding her hand against the sun, and so brought darkness and desolation, like God himself, to millions of ignorant and innocent creatures, and then took her hand away suddenly and let the sun stream down.

Perhaps herein lies the future of CCTV, a world in which every petty soul can play God over some private puddle. As we sit in personal judgment, seeing without being seen in the machinery of surveillance, we have taken the "first step in the construction of God," as one of Bentham's explicators has suggested.[53] In my bleaker moments, I imagine us, increasingly, hunched over a bank of surveillance monitors in the back of a high school, private home, or church, surveying some little world through a lens as we munch on salty snacks and scratch ourselves. We'll spend the afternoon peering dyspeptically into every crevice of human behavior that can be displayed on screen, scouring the surface of things for the merest hint of danger. Dully obsessed with our seemingly limitless gaze—neither satisfied with our digital voyeurism nor able to give it up—we'll simply be *brooding* over our own little kingdoms of insecurity, struggling in vain to remember what privacy, security, and community felt like before the advent of the plastic all-seeing eye.[54]

CHAPTER SIX

The Business of Insecurity

On a cold November morning in midtown Manhattan, after passing through a surreal street lined with horse-drawn carriages and stables reeking of manure, I dart across 11th Avenue to the entrance of the ultramodern Javits Center. Gripping my coat shut, I pass under a massive billboard for a strip club that juts from the roof of the convention center, such that naked flesh consumes much of the horizon. Apparently the old stereotype about sex-crazed male conventioneers is alive and well, at least among the people who license the outdoor advertising around here.

Inside the convention center the atmosphere is a little more sober. In the unsexy confines of a vast new structure that looks like a futuristic airplane hanger is the 2013 International Security Conference (ISC), a huge trade show that features the latest breakthroughs in CCTV cameras, burglar alarms, fingerprint and facial recognition, and many other products and services.[1] Stepping into Javits on this particular weekend, I'm at ground zero of the new surveillance marketplace in more ways than one. It's a place that offers an inside glimpse at the booming business of surveillance in which smiling sales teams, slick brochures, expert testimony, and technological imperatives converge on customers hoping to safeguard homes, workplaces, and communities. No, PRUDENCE ÜBER ALLES isn't carved above the entrance to the convention center this weekend, but it might as well be. Grey, plastic, and eminently corporate in feel, the building is a monument to well-designed impersonality, which is well suited to the chilly abstractions of the new surveillance marketplace that has drawn multinational corporate vendors, smaller companies showing their wares, and thousands of potential customers and curious attendees here today.

Hundreds of middle-aged men in suits and a smattering of women are noshing on bagels in anticipation of the main event: a chance to explore Javits North and the latest in surveillance and security equipment. But for now, in the minutes before the grand opening, we huddle behind a velvet rope like anxious shoppers on Black Friday, making awkward small talk and taking in the enormity of the room where the two-day trade show will be held. Somehow there are enough vendors to fill the cavernous building to its rafters (literally, if one counts the enormous banners representing the big security companies in attendance). I really can't see to the other end of the hall, at least not without one of the ultra-high-resolution CCTV cameras that is being set up on the other side of the rope.

Clearly, the surveillance industry is in a bull market. As part of its surprisingly in-depth coverage of the surveillance economy, the *Wall Street Journal* has reported that the "new global market for the off-the-shelf surveillance technology" has exploded since 9/11, with the retail market for surveillance tools increasing from "nearly zero" in 2001 to $5 billion a year by 2011.[2] By the end of 2014, the global market for CCTV equipment and support exceeded $20 billion, while in the United States alone, video surveillance is projected to reach $15 billion in sales by 2020.[3] Reliable financial details are often elusive, with a single report costing $5,000 a pop and self-interested exaggeration always a risk, but surveillance is undoubtedly at the heart of a multibillion-dollar industry that is feeling quite good about its prospects.[4]

Looking around the teeming 100,000-square-foot convention hall confirms the massive scale of the business, yet I have to remind myself that this event is only the little brother of the bigger show out west. Even with 200 exhibitors and 8,000 attendees descending on the Javits Center, ISC East is dwarfed by the annual ISC West in Las Vegas. These two events are fundamental to the work of the Security Industry Association (SIA). Founded in 1969 to promote the design, manufacturing, and installation of security systems, SIA describes itself as the "leading trade group for businesses in the field of electronic physical security." The Washington, D.C.–based organization represents what it now calls a "$186 billion global industry," for which it hosts major trade shows in New York City, Las Vegas, Mexico City, Mumbai, Paris, London, Sao Paulo, and Abu Dhabi.[5] Flipping through one of their many well-designed brochures, I come across their bold slogan: "Keeping Society Safe." I look across the long expanse of the room and think: *if we are at war with insecurity, this is the arsenal.*

But something interrupts my reverie. From somewhere behind me, an improbable parade has started—the most sullen teenage marching band in the history of musical pageantry is trudging past the coffee and bagels. If their patriotic anthem connotes "victory," their tone suggests something darker and more exhausted in spirit, something that feels coerced and vaguely hung over. When the band finishes its ragged anthem to scattered applause, a middle-aged man who is a little too excited jumps on a makeshift stage, grabs a microphone, and welcomes us to the official opening of the show, which he promises will be *the best ever.* In a crazily upbeat voice that I never hear in faculty meetings, he speaks on behalf of his employer, the Security Industry Association, host of "the world's largest security trade shows and conferences."[6] After some cheerful razzmatazz about the many wonders of the security industry, he passes the microphone to some other white men in expensive suits who seem much less accustomed to public speaking. Less charismatic but equally reverential about the SIA's stated mission to serve as "a catalyst for growth within the global security industry through information, insight and influence," these men talk in a manner that would make an English professor depressed: motivational poster clichés and corporate buzzwords are uttered in the weary tone of someone who's been calling bingo for too long at a senior center.[7] But who needs charisma when you have real power? Based at Microsoft, Samsung, Bosch, Sony, and other major corporations, these SIA board members are described as "industry professionals who represent a broad spectrum of electronic security interests."[8] These are elite executives at the pinnacle of their industry, even if some of the biggest companies are not present this weekend at the ISC. GE, Honeywell, and IBM are marketing "sense making software" for "data-driven city management"—basically, the tools to create an urban command center linked to thousands of CCTV cameras—but I don't see them on the sales floor. Rather than buying for entire cities, the men and women at the conference are mostly shopping for universities, school districts, hospitals, apartment buildings, hotels, factories, and midsize businesses with expensive security needs. ISC provides one-stop shopping for all sorts of security professionals. Offering "direct access to technical reps from 200+ brands," the show floor is lined with hundreds of booths for companies from across the United States as well as some international players, each of which has a small store's worth of inventory on display.[9]

Some privacy activists in the United Kingdom have cut their hair short, put on pinstriped suits, and created fake business cards for imaginary companies in order to bluff their way into surveillance trade shows like this one, which sometimes are closed to scholars, journalists, and activists who might make a fuss. In a fascinating article headlined "MEET THE PRIVACY ACTIVISTS WHO SPY ON THE SURVEILLANCE INDUSTRY," I read about a representative of the London-based organization Privacy International: "Once he's infiltrated the trade show, he'll pose as an industry insider, chatting up company representatives, swapping business cards, and picking up shiny brochures that advertise the invasive capabilities of bleeding-edge surveillance technology" whose contents are rarely "ever marketed or revealed openly to the general public."[10] As for me, I simply registered and walked in the front door with notebook in hand. They even gave me a small bag of swag.

The proceedings are not unpleasant, as I discover once the SIA board members have stopped talking and opened the gates to the sales floor. Like most sales conventions with endless products vying for customers' attention, the show strains for liveliness and even a hint of the carnival in some places. Temporary putting greens made of AstroTurf and fully functional basketball hoops compete with dry presentations about high-resolution video monitors. Attendees might be worried about threat detection in their workplaces, but Elton John is blaring happily from the PA system, a reminder that two lucky attendees are going to win tickets to a concert at Madison Square Garden.

As I make my way through this grand bazaar of insecurity, I find myself in the middle of one long sales pitch. Everyone is handing out brochures, gimme caps, key chains, or candy to encourage customers to linger over their wares. Everyone is smiling at me and making that weird sort of eye contact that says *I have something to sell.* Everyone wants my contact information for a mailing list that promises special offers and incredible discounts, at least until they find out that I'm an academic with no purchasing authority for anything more pricey than a box of pencils, at which point I receive a glazed-over expression in which boredom, exhaustion, and disgust seem to comingle in equal measure, even in the hopeful first hours of the conference. Feeling bad for blocking their revenue stream for even a moment, I shuffle aside and wander down an aisle jammed with prospective customers, eager sales teams, and expensive new products, all coming together with the dull roar of a casino pit.

Banners promise "limitless possibilities for CCTV," which could serve as the motto for a convention that is crazy for security cameras and related devices. Looking like something that should be mocked on the Internet, one roving vendor is wearing an enormous vest that includes multiple cameras and monitors that simultaneously record and display everything he encounters. Even putting aside the strange postmodern spectacle of a man entombed in electronic media, I've never seen so many CCTV cameras and monitors in a single room: *everywhere I go, there I am, staring back at myself in unnervingly high resolution*. Despite my lack of purchasing power and what must be an evident lack of securitarian fervor, in one sense I fit in—the event is overwhelmingly white, male, and middle-aged. Some women are scoping out the products and making purchasing decisions, but a greater number are working the sales floor as representatives for various companies. Smiling from the booths and handing out brochures, these female workers, often young and attractive, field questions from guys who are geeking out over spec sheets. *What's the FPS on the 3.6mm fixed-lens camera? Can it do progressive scan? Dual stream? H.264 compression format? What about audio inputs?* These fellows are in their element, shopping for gadgets like they're cruising the Best Buy on Christmas Eve, but instead of video-game consoles or laptop computers, they're looking for deals on thermal imaging cameras and magnetic-field intruder detection systems for small factories in Connecticut or strip malls in Ohio. While I wonder if shopping centers really need all this James Bond stuff to ward off teenage vandals or the occasional shoplifter, everyone else seems hooked. As dozens of men gather around to see their heat signature on an over-sized monitor (female customers aren't falling for this gambit), it all seems like jolly good fun, like we're at a boat show fiddling with the throttle of a cool new Jet Ski without a care in the world. No second thoughts or reservations are expressed, only enthusiasm for the evident wow factor of the latest gadgets. No one seems uncomfortable with the implications of the securitarian smorgasbord that spills out of hundreds of booths, offering an endless supply of products and services for watching, sorting, sensing, and archiving that exceeds the wildest imaginings of Cold War spies. Now anyone can have the tools of professional spycraft in their own home or office.

Indeed, every tonic to soothe a nervous soul is on display: panic buttons, two-way radios, license-plate readers, forensic spyglasses, e-mapping solutions, 180-degree panoramic ceiling cameras, biometric scanners, long-range identification systems, metal detectors, massive CCTV data storage, RFID tracking tags for "laptops, servers, people" (people!), and even special insurance and accounting companies that focus their business on the surveillance industry. Like military contractors gathered around the trough of federal dollars, all sorts of ancillary businesses are profiting from the new wave of American insecurity. Even little companies that make the banners and stickers that say "THIS AREA UNDER SURVEILLANCE" have a spot in Javits North, next to boring old locksmiths, some with clunky doorknobs on a table, others with high-tech "solutions" that promise "security with style," which usually means a swipe card and a camera for "enhanced access control." As the ads for one big security company put it, "Control, monitor and defend your businesses with Access Control." The word choice seems oddly pugnacious: I'm not sure the language of "defending" a business has been heard since the nineteenth-century American frontier.[11]

Other booths have more unusual offerings than fancy locks. I rub my hands on the steel of the high-security architectural bollards that can spring from the pavement to block a truck. These thick steel shafts seem more suited to an embassy in a war zone than an office park in the suburbs, but people keep stopping to talk to the two middle-aged salesmen who seem quite jovial for people in the truck bomb deterrence business. Everyone seems keen on the massive fortification of a home or business. In a society in which soccer moms drive Hummers ripped from the dunes of Iraq, I shouldn't be surprised, but I am taken aback when I feel the military-grade seriousness of the equipment on display. I take a brochure for photoelectric beams designed to detect intruders at "borders, substations, solar fields, residential [buildings], and prisons," and walk away astonished that security guards and German Shepherds are no longer enough to "secure the perimeter," to use a bit of the demilitarized jargon that courses through the security industry's bloodstream like Viagra.[12]

Not everything is slickly produced or battle-hardened. While major corporations like Samsung and Tyco have expensive booths in which to promote themselves, a few mom-and-pop companies are here, too, elbowing for space in booths that seem much more homemade. One fellow seems right out of *This Old House*—sparks are flying as he noisily cuts metal for some kind of special lock. Down the aisle is a man with super glue that he's bonding to anything that will attract a crowd. He has the patter of a nineteenth-century patent-medicine salesman, which is entertaining but a little mystifying. What is the relationship between security and super glue? He doesn't volunteer an answer.

One small company has gone wild with patriotic imagery, draping its booth with red, white, and blue bunting that evokes a presidential campaign, but otherwise it's hard to spot an American flag. Wherever I look in the convention center, nationalism is surprisingly muted in favor of a bland corporate internationalism. Aside from the opening ceremony with its tepid national anthem, no one is using overt nationalism to sell his or her products. No one is talking about "defending the nation," "securing the homeland," or "stopping al-Qaeda." No one is talking explicitly about terrorism or mentioning what happened on 9/11 not far from where we stand. I suspect that the presence of multinational security companies, including several based in China, would make flag-waving an awkward enterprise, but even still—no American flag pins? No military insignia? No Ted Nugent books? The Tea Party would be disappointed by what passes for securing the homeland these days.

So what are the keywords? Instead of the nationalistic language of the war on terror, the show is filled with the calm rhetoric of corporate efficiency and technical mastery. Over and over I hear words like *scalable, compliant, secure, efficient, intelligent, integration, easy to use, plug and play,* and *future proof.* This flavorless discourse is woven into everything from marketing videos and sales brochures to casual conversations with sales reps, with nothing trumping the magic word that appears everywhere: *solutions*! It's uttered like a mantra— *solutions, solutions, solutions*—that everyone is either selling or seeking on the vast floor of Javits North.

And what needs a solution? Although some security professionals are worried about licenses and regulations, more often the problem is some sort of technical challenge that might undermine their job performance. Many people are fretting about what they call the "weakest link in the chain," like a high-resolution camera with an underpowered lens that keeps the overall system from optimal performance. Others are worried about data storage: the explosion of high-definition CCTV cameras, each one eating up more gigabytes than a teenager downloading the *Lord of the Rings* trilogy, is a constant headache for security professionals. But the main problem right now is "integration." The explosive growth of the surveillance infrastructure in the past decade has resulted in all sorts of gaps and misalignments between its various parts: cameras, cables, software, hardware, personnel, and other elements have to link up seamlessly for systems to reach full capacity. Because systems are not working as well as advertised in previous sales conventions, customers are clamoring for "solutions" that will blend analog and digital aspects of their surveillance feed into a harmonious symphony of information. Ideally, the solution will be "plug and play," "scalable," and "future proof," meaning that it will be simple to install, simple to expand, and simple to use for years to come. Although this might be rare, people seem confident that they'll find what they need to solve their security challenges. The only anxiety I can sense is the fear of missing out, the fear of having out-of-date software, or the fear of a glitch in a security system that will result in a subpar performance evaluation. If salespeople seem anxious about not making their quotas, attendees are worried about lacking the right tools to perform well in their jobs. Attendees are narrowly focused on one question: "Will this help me do my job with greater proficiency?"

People are so focused on technical issues, in fact, that explicit references to violent crime are surprisingly rare for a conference on security and surveillance. One small company created a clumsy poster for a metal detector that features a Latino prisoner in an orange jumpsuit, while on the other side of the room a presenter talked about the need for "ultra resolution" cameras to get "what we all want," which is, as he soon explained, "convictable evidence." One of the hour-long workshops had the scary title "Are You Prepared for a Boston Marathon–Like Event?," while another featured the chief of police from Newtown, Connecticut, talking about the tragic elementary school shooting in 2012. But these were exceptions to the corporate calm that reigned supreme in various workshops, publications, videos, websites, and verbal interactions. In general, worrisome references to the challenges of the world at large were absent or simply implied.

Because the event is suffused with the calm, rational, and apolitical rhetoric of tech-minded corporations, the mood on the selling floor is neither somber nor tense. Divorcing itself from burning questions of ethics and politics, the new surveillance marketplace trades on cooler feelings of inevitability, obligation, realism, prudence, foresight, duty, and concern. This trade show is not a place for deep passions and emotional intensities about our existential insecurities as a nation, community, or individual, nor is it about the vexing ethical dilemmas that are inherent to the use of most surveillance technologies. Rather, it is simply a place where sober professionals must make necessary preparations for unavoidable circumstances. No one seems interested in root causes or unintended consequences. No one is debating anything beyond technical "solutions" to very specific problems, narrowly defined. No one is challenging, no matter how subtly, the securitarian worldview that is on display at the trade show and in its various publications, signs, and videos. Admittedly, nuance, doubt, and misgivings are unmarketable qualities in most businesses, but the sheer seamlessness of the event is astonishing. Everywhere I look, people seem to have gotten the memo and internalized it: a firm, clear, and calm certainty is the industry's public face at all times, with its power of assertion overwhelming any second thoughts that might arise. Confused as to whether biometric scanners have a place in your small-town medical facility? Take a look at the article "WHY BIOMETRICS IS GOOD FOR EVERYONE'S HEALTH" in the trade magazine *Campus Safety* and rest assured. Trade magazines, brochures, and videos, all free for the taking, are filled with such confident assertions, all part of the industry's rush toward "CREATING THE FUTURE OF SECURITY . . . TODAY," as one advertisement explains.[13]

Indeed, education is a big part of the show in more ways than one. In the back of the room are "free education sessions" that promote products and services along with attitudes conducive to the industry. With titles such as "Ultra-Resolution Surveillance: Delivering Precision Detail at Extreme Distances" and "Three Megatrends Affecting the Future of Building Systems," these hour-long presentations take place in pseudo-classrooms with podiums, PowerPoints, and plenty of seats for an audience of prospective clients and other interested parties. Many attendees listen closely and take notes with free pens from their swag bags; some flip through the brochures and magazines that are free for the taking.

More than simple sales pitches or how-to manuals, the magazines are often quite revealing about the business of surveillance. Bound and printed in a format that resembles an academic journal, SIA's main trade magazine, *Technology Insights*, is filled with articles with titles like "MEGAPIXEL CAMERAS GO MAINSTREAM" and "SEEING THE BIG PICTURE: 360-DEGREE CAMERA TECHNOLOGY." Pressing for changes in "ways of thinking" about security, one writer celebrates the "ever-increasing clip" of innovation in surveillance systems. "Now systems can provide total control," he boasted, but only if the public embraces new technologies with a "yes, we can" attitude that allows "innovation [to become] exponential."[14] Although the exponential growth in technological change that leads to "total control" might seem like a plot element in a dystopian sci-fi novel, *Technology Insights* heralds this development with smiling technocratic calm.

Another article in *Technology Insights* explored the challenge to "total control" under the headline "ACHIEVING IP VIDEO MANAGEMENT SCALABILITY THROUGH AGGREGATION."[15] The article describes new tools for integrating CCTV feeds from multiple locations into a simple package with expanded reach over workplaces, hospitals, schools, and even mobile locations such as employees in their cars. The upshot for business owners, managers, and security professionals who are synchronizing data from previously distinct systems? "More and more, the oversight is extending beyond traditional security considerations and into operational ones," the author explains calmly, citing the example of a store manager who can remotely scrutinize his employees in various locations rather than driving out in person. In other words, a rapidly increasing amount of data in increasingly integrated systems is bringing the rhetoric of total control closer to reality every year, though the industry presents all of this expansion in the morally and politically neutral tone of technological inevitability: *The changes are coming—is your organization prepared to meet the challenge? Are you prepared to say "yes, we can" to "total control"? Are you ready for innovation to become exponential? Are you ready to submit to the will of the machine?* Okay, the last one was only implied, but something about the solemn technological determinism of surveillance marketing feels antithetical to the sort of liberties that people used to hold dear. Some lines from Keats pop into my mind as I consider "the inhuman dearth / Of noble natures, of the gloomy days, / Of all the unhealthy and o'er-darkened ways," which seem to describe what I'm finding inside the Javits Center, though English Romanticism is absurdly out of place in this cool technocratic landscape. Such deeper expressions of our humanity are verboten here, even when the subject is education.

Certainly, education is a pragmatic concern for SIA. More than informing potential consumers about products and services that will fulfill their fantasy of total control, their trade show takes aim at educational consumers who represent a burgeoning market for surveillance products. With a cover photo of a smiling first-grader clutching his lunch in front of his elementary school, *Campus Safety* is a trade magazine devoted to the educational security market that covers everything from preschool playgrounds to graduate-school seminar rooms. The all-American boy with his lunch is a symbol of what one ad calls "securing your most precious asset," while another ad explains how "a trusted name in campus surveillance for over 15 years" can provide a camera to watch over wholesome high-school students.[16] Of course, a few cameras are not enough to safeguard these precious assets—not when the security industry has dozens of interlocking products to satisfy anyone's security needs. One article explains how to turn the front of an ordinary high school into an impregnable fortress of learning, thereby hardening a soft educational target into something that resembles a county jail. In addition to installing CCTV cameras, fences, locks, and guards at major access points, schools need to build in "natural surveillance" techniques with the thought that "people are less likely to commit crimes if they feel they are being observed." This means designing school entrances to "maximize visibility" for the purpose of monitoring visitors, emphasizing "territoriality" to make the ownership of the space self-evident (i.e., sending a message to strangers that *you don't belong here*), and even minimizing the use of glass less than 72 inches from ground level in order to present "a more secure image [that] makes forced entry more difficult."[17] None of this is presented as an unfortunate reflection of a populace that feels unable to protect its own children. Rather it is presented as a neutral and somehow inevitable outcome that poses not a philosophical, historical, or sociological challenge but a surmountable technical one.

Another typical article in *Campus Safety* is "THE ISRAELI APPROACH TO SCHOOL SECURITY," which continues the emphasis on technical solutions at the expense of historical context or ethical implications. Under a grim photo of confined Israeli schoolchildren "playing soccer inside a fenced-in area under the watchful eyes of teachers and an armed guard just out of the view of this camera," the article extols the Israelis' mind-set as much as their firepower as useful models for school security in the United States. Rather than noting the profound differences between a small country subject to rocket attacks versus the average American school district in Ohio, California, or Florida, the article emphasizes the alleged "it can happen here" similarities between America and Israel, while providing tips on how to live efficiently in the crosshairs of insecurity.[18] If any of this high-tech freak-out sounds bad for actual learning in an actual classroom, think again: "Smart security makes for smarter students," one advertisement promises in *Campus Safety*, reminding us that teachers can do a better job when they are free from the distraction of security issues. Throughout these trade magazines, whether in the text of the articles, editorials, or advertisements, the underlying message is always the same: everything is going to work out fine for those who have armed themselves with the latest in surveillance equipment and training, along with the right mind-set for situational awareness of all potential threats. There is no point in asking questions or entertaining doubts, even on college campuses where professors might be inclined to raise the awkward subjects of ethics, history, and political theory with impressionable students. Such is the shoulder-shrugging technological inevitability of a society entering terminal lockdown.

Friction-Free

Here everything conspires to annihilate even the slightest form of political intensity.

— *THE INVISIBLE COMMITTEE*[19]

History, politics, ethics, sociology, and other modes of reflection are rarely glimpsed at trade shows for any industry, least of all the surveillance industry—though, as is often the case, these matters have a way of bubbling up and causing discomfort. I was seated in an hour-long workshop on high-resolution CCTV when a presenter dropped a small bomb from the podium. "You know, the Nazis invented CCTV during the Second World War to monitor rocket launches," he said, without shifting his sleepwalker tone. I was curious to hear more about the subject, but he brushed it off as quickly as he raised it. "Uh ... it wasn't necessarily an application [of the technology] that we like," he explained, seeming remarkably casual about the connection, no matter how distant, between his livelihood and the Third Reich. While I tend to take such connections a little more seriously, I suspect I was alone in expecting even a momentary engagement with history and ethics in the midst of a trade show where companies are trying to meet sales quotas and roll out new products. Not surprisingly for an industry with a problematic historical relationship to state power in both authoritarian and democratic contexts, the modern surveillance industry has to repress its own troubling past in order to expand its markets. No one wants to hear about Nazis—or J. Edgar Hoover's illegal wiretapping, or the Chinese government's suppression of the prodemocracy movement—while shopping for surveillance equipment. That much is not surprising. What is surprising—and quite disconcerting—is that no one seems to ask the obvious questions about this vast world of technology on display inside the Javits Center: *Does it work? Does it make us safer, freer, happier, or more productive? Is it worth the billions that we lavish on it? Does it have unacknowledged side-effects for the people who live in its midst? Does it reduce the feeling of insecurity or simply mask it behind a wall of technological bluster about "best practices" for "future proof" risk management?*

Of course, no one vocalizes such things at a trade show like ISC East, where technological determinism, corporate calm, and the slick repetitions of marketing departments conspire to overwhelm the natural functioning of the questioning mind. Yet this slick calm cannot hide a fundamental exclusion. Something is missing from the sober landscape of risk assessment where SIA has pitched its tent: buried in the blizzard of technical specifications and professional necessities is a strange omission that might unsettle the savvy consumer. While the surveillance industry presents itself with such serene assurance and cool rationality, it fails to provide evidence for its claims in even the most glancing fashion. Not once at the conference did I see empirical data to suggest that particular surveillance technologies were essential to reducing crime on a single campus, increasing productivity in a single company, or creating a sense of well-being in a single community. Instead of the hard facts that corporate America is supposed to prize while professors keep their impractical heads in the sky, I kept hearing blanket assertions about the need for ever-greater degrees of fortification in every human context: nursing homes, outlet malls, lumber mills, solar-panel arrays, high-school football stadiums, kindergarten playgrounds. *No one is safe. Everyone needs surveillance. End of story.*

Rather than ask hard questions, or even acknowledge the fact that someone else is asking them, the surveillance industry hides its head in the sand whenever questions of efficacy and impact arise. In this sense it suffers from what Leonidis Donskis and Zygmunt Bauman call the "virus" of *adiaphorization*—"an exemption from the realm of moral evaluation."[20] As they describe in *Moral Blindness: The Loss of Sensitivity in Liquid Modernity*, adiaphorization is a process in which we exempt ourselves from the moral calculus that we expect from others.[21] For example, we would want someone to think through the moral implications of their actions if they were intending to trample on our privacy, liberty, or autonomy, but we might exempt ourselves from the same kind of scrutiny if we suffered from a certain kind of moral blindness that allows self-interested and hypocritical behavior to flourish. In this sense, adiaphorization allows the security industry to grant itself a waiver, to suggest that politics and ethics are not central to its enterprise. At SIA's big annual event in New York City, this apolitical stance creates a frictionless marketplace of stainless-steel bollards and metal detectors, thermal sensors and biometric access control, far from the grit and muck of uncertainty and complexity that is inherent to the use of such technologies. What emerges, then, is a kind of moral cynicism that allows the industry to perceive its own behavior as somehow neutral or separate from potential complications. They are *merely technicians, merely merchants, merely marketers, nothing more.*

This mind-set is a boon to the surveillance industry, which can grant itself an exemption from difficult discussions about the impact of its technologies. In this sense, the fundamental amorality of capitalism is the real ground zero of the surveillance industry. The marketplace encourages this displacement of the moral aspect of selling surveillance, or any other technology with complex and often problematic uses that might, if examined closely, undercut soaring profits. After all, old companies have expanded, new ones have been created, and enormous revenues have been harvested—what fool would argue with such results? The operator of another surveillance conference made this point explicit when pressed about the problem of selling powerful technologies to authoritarian regimes abroad: "We don't really get into asking, 'Is this in the public interest?'" he told one reporter.[22] *Exactly.*

Meanwhile, the industry rushes forward into new markets, new technologies, and new contexts, seemingly unimpeded by any countervailing forces. Celebrated Lithuanian philosopher Leonidas Donskis has described the way in which technological possibility triumphs over ethical concerns: put simply, if we have the technological means to do something, it will be done. All other considerations are shunted aside by the imperative to achieve what is achievable, technologically and economically, rather than what is just and proper. "We can, therefore, we ought" is the formulation that he laments.[23] If we have the opportunity to expand the surveillance infrastructure into suburban elementary schools quaking from "stranger danger," or to oil-rich emirates that abuse foreign workers, then we must do so. Describing this compulsion at the nexus of culture and capitalism, Donskis writes, "It is obligatory to spy and to leak, though it's unclear for what reason and to what end. It's something that has to be done because it's technologically feasible."[24] As former New York City mayor Michael Bloomberg said about the prospect of surveillance drones over his city: "It's not a question of whether it's good or bad. I just don't see how you can stop them."[25] Actually, it *is* a question of whether it's good or bad—he just doesn't want to ask the more meaningful question. The business of surveillance dictates that ethical deliberations—which should be at the heart of democratic politics—be ruled out as irrelevant, impractical, a needless distraction from the serious work that must be done without a moment's reflection. What emerges, then, is "a moral vacuum" in which a "new evil" thrives. "Two of the manifestations of the new evil," Donskis suggests, are an "insensitivity to human suffering, and the desire to colonize privacy by taking away a person's secret, the something that should never be talked about and made public."[26] The relevance to surveillance is profound.

This is why the word *privacy* is radioactive on the sales floor. If people seem excited to talk to me when they think I'm a business owner, they are clearly uncomfortable when I tell them I'm an academic who might be thinking about the implications of their technological marvels. The first question I got from one salesman was, "Are you one of these people who is against surveillance?" I had said nothing to invite such a question, other than to mention that I was writing a book in the most neutral tones I could muster, yet the salesman went immediately on the defensive. Later in the day, again without me saying anything about my own views on privacy, another security professional told me that privacy zealots "should stay at home," keeping away from conferences such as SIA East. This strain of defensiveness, if not belligerence, suggests that the mind-set here is not merely one of blissful ignorance but rather conscious repression of anything that might wrinkle the smooth surface of the marketplace. Apparently, asking questions is bad for business.

As these exchanges might suggest, the surveillance industry is adamant about one particular kind of privacy: its own. As one privacy activist has complained about the lack of transparency and ethical slipperiness of the surveillance industry, "The complex network of supply chains and subsidiaries involved in this trade allows one after the other to continually pass the buck and abdicate responsibility."[27] While the sales conferences are promoting technologies that undercut individual attempts at maintaining privacy, the industry remains quite concerned about its own privacy. After noting that security conferences in Dubai and Washington, D.C. were not open to the public, the *Wall Street Journal* wrote that its own reporters were "prevented from attending sessions or entering the exhibition halls" at these events that were deemed more sensitive in nature than what I witnessed in New York.[28] So goes the strange and lucrative business of surveillance, even when the clients are not authoritarian regimes in the Middle East but simply midwestern retail chains worried about shoplifters. "Surveillance companies are developing, marketing, and selling some of the most powerful, invasive, and dangerous technologies in the world, ones that are keeping pace with the capabilities of the NSA and GCHQ," claims the London-based Privacy International in its report on the industry (referring to the UK Government Communications Headquarters). "What's more, companies are maintaining relationships to the repressive regimes it sells to, constantly upgrading their systems and making customer service representatives available 24/7 for dictators and their cronies to reach out to should anything go awry with their products."[29] Such is the messiness that exists beneath the slick surface of the new surveillance marketplace.

Surveillance after 9/11

I was born in Brooklyn in the 1960s and thought about New York City a great deal as I grew up in the 1970s and '80s in unglamorous New Jersey. From there the city appears across the water like the emerald kingdom in Oz, floating above the Hudson like a gritty beacon of cultural possibility. It seemed, and in many ways was, the center of everything. Inspiring extremes of love and loathing in the rest of the country, the city occupied a special place in the American soul—as it still does in ways that were reinforced, I suspect, on September 11, 2001. Would the national response to the destruction of skyscrapers in, say, Houston, Phoenix, or Portland have been fundamentally different? If we put aside the Pentagon attack and the crash of Flight 93 in the Pennsylvania countryside for a moment and imagine if Ground Zero had been in any other American city— would the loss of a building elsewhere have been enough to inspire the epic backlash that included the longest wars in US history, the calamitous erosion of long-cherished privacy rights, and the rapid expansion of government surveillance powers? Perhaps. But the World Trade Center was the nerve center of the American economy, not some second-tier outpost of Sun Belt capitalism. And its destruction so evoked the special effects that Hollywood has implanted in our collective consciousness for decades, with its airborne means of delivery so confounding to our love of technology, that it struck in a uniquely vulnerable place and in a uniquely potent way. Americans were collectively shot through the heart on 9/11, and the emotional impact lingers like that of no other event on US soil in the postwar era. The fiftieth anniversary of President Kennedy's assassination might suggest a possible point of comparison, but JFK was only one man, and Dealey Plaza has long since succumbed to tourist kitsch and conspiracy-minded circus sideshows. Thus 9/11 triggered a paroxysm of national grief and confusion that endures, making it difficult to this day to know how to respond meaningfully to what happened so quickly that surreal morning.

All of which raises the question: *What should a city do when its iconic buildings suddenly vanish?*[30] It is a question that no city should have to answer, yet it has haunted New York since the first months of its recovery from the attacks. The answer has taken many forms, some hopeful, some depressing. Too often, security bureaucrats and corporate allies, poised to profit off the technologies and techniques on display inside the Javits Center, have been the first to answer: *wire it up and lock it down!* Yet fortification and permanently heightened surveillance are not the only responses to the wounds of 2001, something I felt strongly on walks through Manhattan's Ground Zero that served as a kind of emotional counterbalance to the cold and mechanistic world of the security trade show and the self-righteous securitarian fury that has distorted our foreign and domestic policies since 9/11.

In autumn 2013, when I first visit, the Memorial pools are a newly finished part of what is otherwise a hallowed ground still under construction, complete with chain-link fencing and impromptu gates for its so-called interim operating period. In the parklike contours of the space around the pools, not far from where the 9/11 museum is still taking shape, young swamp white oak trees have been planted everywhere—but so have CCTV cameras. Somewhere along the northeast corner of the pools, I stand under six separate cameras that are clustered just out of arm's reach. Like crows on a low-slung telephone line, they loom above while I try to make sense of a place I haven't visited since watching the buildings fall during a TV broadcast while I was in central Oklahoma. It's not easy to stand here. For someone looking down into the chasms of the black waterfalls where the Twin Towers used to stand, the enormity of the buildings' footprints is almost unbearable to contemplate. The scale of the event registers in the gut and knocks you back, an emotional testament to the work of memorial architect Michael Arad and landscape architect Peter Walker.

I take a break and walk a city block. A truck-based police observation unit, the first I've ever seen, is parked across from the site like a mechanical guardian that can rise 20 feet above the ground for maximum visibility—one more reminder that the NYPD is keen to watch everything that moves. Though I'm hesitant to photograph the blacked-out windows of the truck while officers stand guard, I take a few quick shots before retreating to a nearby café, a touristy place with the worst of Nashville music blaring. Looking out the window at the Freedom Tower rising north of Ground Zero, I feel privileged to watch yellowed leaves raining onto the sidewalk on a quiet afternoon—but I don't feel particularly free. I'd seen fifty cops and dozens of security cameras while walking a few blocks, and people seem nervous and uncertain around them. A statement of overwhelming force is being made that no one can miss: it is a very blunt instrument that hits the innocent and guilty with equal force, with an indiscriminate quality that I find morally reprehensible in modern surveillance culture. Even worse than the subtle and not-so-subtle abuses of emotional liberty, and the ways that this can make some people feel (rotten and lost), these measures are costly examples of the *security theater* that serves a function more symbolic than practical. CCTV won't stop a theocratic psychopath with an exploding backpack, something that politicians, including progressives like former congressman Barney Frank, overlook in their praise for security cameras that provided after-the-fact evidence of, but not a shred of deterrence against, the Boston Marathon bombers.[31] In this sense our security theater is absurd, something I say wistfully and even with respect for those who perform rituals in its name—*take off the shoes, remove the hat, look at the camera.* And when absurdity is absent, irony rushes in: consider the fact that Ground Zero's next-door neighbor is Zuccotti Park, better known as home to the tents and chants of Occupy Wall Street that popped up around the tenth anniversary of 9/11. I don't suppose those young activists felt particularly free in the shadow of the Freedom Tower, already eighty-two floors of unfinished construction by the autumn of 2011, in what was so evidently Mayor Bloomberg's city. Even a year or two after the heyday of Occupy, metal plaques bear warnings to would-be squatters that the park is "public" (*but, you know, not really*), with cops on round-the-clock duty to reinforce the point. There is a limit to what is allowed in the shadow of the Freedom Tower.

Walking toward the building while it's still under construction in 2013, and once again when it's largely finished in 2015, I find myself wondering about the relationship between its exalted architectural rhetoric and the ordinary American reality that the surveillance industry addresses. In other words: *What is the nature of the freedom that is heralded by this 1,776-foot glass tower?* It must be a glittering beacon to something vital, something that speaks eloquently to the national soul in a moment of post-traumatic recovery. *Resilience, hard work, hope?* I don't doubt any of these qualities are present somewhere in its 1,776 symbolic feet of glass and steel. But freedom is a more nuanced proposition than what our politicians are generally able to conceive, a fact that feels obvious to someone who left a paranoia-inducing surveillance convention to roam the streets of a city filled with ubiquitous CCTV and legions of cops, all coordinated by Mayor Bloomberg's Microsoft-created Domain Awareness System in ways that can be painful and problematic for some citizens.[32] (Such civic pain is what interests the artist Josh Begley, whose piece *Plain Sight: The Visual Vernacular of NYPD Surveillance* was installed at the Open Society Foundation in Midtown Manhattan in 2015. A wall-sized collage of police surveillance photos of Muslims in the New York area, *Plain Sight* suggests that police mapping of Muslim neighborhoods was more than "systematic racial and religious profiling," as the artist statement explains—"it created a climate of fear and suspicion that encroached on all aspects of everyday life.")[33]

After spending time in a security trade show that heralds the brave new world of "total control" and provides the tools for an invasive culture of monitoring with disturbing racial dimensions, I have to ask another version of the question above: *What freedom, exactly, does anyone possess while standing in the shadow of the Freedom Tower?* It's hard to say. I suppose I have the freedom to admire the "Torch of Freedom," as former New York governor George Pataki dubbed the tower's 400-foot spire, along with the grit and intelligence of the workers who put up these imposing structures. I have the freedom to publish these words without government permission (although government oversight is another question altogether). But do I have the freedom to say "no" to Mayor Bloomberg's scrutiny (or that of his successor, Bill de Blasio)? Do I have the freedom to close my eyes and mouth on the subway platforms stenciled with the ominous wartime phrase "SEE SOMETHING, SAY SOMETHING"? Do I have the freedom to point my own camera at law enforcement agents and gather data about their behavior? Do I have freedom from dataveillance regimes that suck up my web-browsing history and credit-card habits without my knowledge (or only the most vaguely implied consent)? Do I have the freedom to opt out of the generalized panic of the post–9/11 era, to insist on my own privacy as sacrosanct, so long as I don't harm anyone else? No, I don't think so.

Maybe US citizens have never enjoyed such freedoms, not even those who enjoy certain privileges within society, but we certainly don't have it now that securitization has taken command with an analytical depth that exceeds anything that was feasible during the Cold War. What's happened since 9/11 puts us much closer to an Orwellian condition of constant exposure and monitoring than our self-congratulatory political rhetoric would ever suggest. "The idea that we can know and tell everything about another human being is the worst kind of nightmare as far as the modern world is concerned," the Lithuanian philosopher Leonidas Donskis writes, in mulling over Orwell's *1984*. "We believed for a long time that choice defines freedom; I would hasten to add that, especially nowadays, so does defense of the idea of the unfathomability of the human being and the idea of the untouchability of their privacy."[34] Nothing about Ground Zero, Zuccotti Park, or the ISC trade show makes me feel untouchable in regard to state power.

Yet I have a faith in people, a faith I do not have in state or multinational corporations. Once again joining the crowds around the memorial site in 2013 and again in 2015, I am heartened to see how gently they move around the Memorial pools. Visitors are sober, quiet, even decorous. By 2015 the temporary cameras have become more discreet in placement, with the new security regime pressing less ominously on the experience of place. Somewhat to my surprise, Ground Zero in its finished state doesn't have the nationalistic excess that it might have possessed, maybe because the Memorial pools represent such a sublime aesthetic choice, and maybe because the Freedom Tower is a little too much like any other bank tower hanging over any other downtown to inspire patriotic fervor. In spite of the Freedom Tower's obsessive built-in reference to the American War of Independence, the memorial site below is happily devoid of the dumb bombast and sanctimony that characterizes much of our hypersecuritized culture. Nothing here has the curdled self-righteousness of our reigning political class, nor of its big media counterpart. Instead, the Memorial pools have emerged with reserve and even grace, reflecting a kind of spiritual good health that I wasn't expecting to find within the tumult of the city. Certain details stick in my mind: The white roses left on engraved names. The kind sharing of camera duties between strangers. The Vietnamese Catholic priest casually picking up litter. The multicultural calm. All in all, it is a wonderfully affecting place, appropriately engineered to invite thoughtful contemplation and sober remembrance. It is one of the few spaces of modern American mourning that makes sense to me.

The same is true, to a somewhat lesser extent, of the museum itself. Opened next to the Memorial pools in summer 2014, the National September 11 Memorial & Museum is not a vindictive place. It is not rooted in fear, vengeance, or anger in the ways that I anticipated. Instead, it reflects our best instincts in responding to a civic wound of unimaginable proportions—even if some observers feel otherwise. Writing in *Esquire* magazine in January 2015, Scott Raab complained that inside the museum is "a pandemonium of grief, a mausoleum with escalators, complete with human remains, recordings of mass murder, and a gift shop where the commodified fetish of massacre fills the shelves and the cashiers are trained to beg each customer for an extra buck—on top of the twenty-four-dollar entry fee."[35] I don't share that view. Admittedly, some of the tchotchkes in the gift shop raise questions about de-

cency and taste. And something about displaying the wreck-
age of steel girders and burned fire trucks is unsettling as well,
as if dead things—like the human beings who perished that
day—are better off buried in a place where no guided tours, no
matter how sensitive, can gawk at them. But otherwise it is a
place that *resists* the worst temptations of surveillance culture:
heavy-handed security measures, a rhetoric of inevitability,
implied violence, and melodramatic victimhood that veers into
a belligerent self-pity that justifies any and all measures.

It's actually a quiet place filled with ordinary objects and
ordinary people whose lives came to a premature end that is
described, sometimes in grueling detail, in video and audio
recordings from family members that visitors can listen to.
Honoring the ordinariness, even banality, of their lives seems
appropriate here. "The banality of evil," to use Hannah Arendt's
formulation, never seemed to fit the tragedy of 9/11, no matter how many times pundits tried to wedge it into their on-air
musings. What the hijackers did was the opposite of banal:
it was a rare spectacle of mesmerizing, horrifying intensity—
just as it was intended to be. It was an attack on good, old-
fashioned, American banality, which, reassuringly, can still be
found at Ground Zero. The banality of such small pleasures
continues for the survivors, perhaps a little guardedly, a little
guiltily, on the exact spot where the planes struck the never-
quite-loved buildings that now receive so much curatorial respect. We miss these buildings more than we ever anticipated,
and we mark this fact with modest gestures of mourning—
listening closely, trying to remember, buying a trinket—that
I find quite hopeful as a mode of public (and private) feeling.

Not everyone responds this way, of course. "Weird vibe,"
complained an uptight white guy to his wife in the gift shop,
while he bought a picture book that honored the canine heroes
of 9/11; apparently he had just been touring Ground Zero and
was venting some discomfort.[36] It is a weird vibe indeed for

those expecting simple flag-waving and Disneyfied tears.[37] Instead, a very human vibe endures at Ground Zero, even in the controversial museum and its gift shop. Its shortcomings may come into view with the passage of time, but for now the site is a triumph of renewal and commemoration, a place of deep and profound sorrow that invites a dignified and appropriate response to the crimes that sent waves of insecurity rippling across this country. If "a nation in fear" sounds maudlin and overdrawn, it was an accurate description for many months after 9/11. Yet neither the museum nor its adjacent memorials exploit that painful fact in the ways that cynics—myself included—might expect.

By contrast, the security-industrial complex offers a response that blends the necessary and practical (yes, we need some degree of surveillance) with the grotesque and self-serving (the church of limitless surveillance). In a very real sense, the industry trades off post–9/11 insecurities, using our frayed nerves as its happy profit center, always selling a fantasy of eternal vigilance in which everyone—everywhere, all the time—keeps watch with the latest in threat detection equipment and the appropriate mind-set for endless combat on an insecure planet. While the 9/11 Memorial offers a space of democratic calm and dignity in the face of terror and uncertainty, it also marks the birthplace of modern surveillance culture and its spirit of rationalized panic. You can draw a straight line from Ground Zero to the packed surveillance convention on the other side of Manhattan—and many other points on the new American map of fear and insecurity. This includes suburbs where police departments use Homeland Security grants to turn themselves into quasi-military commandos. And the Canadian border, where Predator drones look for terrorists slipping into Idaho. And even college campuses that are wiring up for high-grade CCTV—whether they need it or not. Transcontinental lines of insecurity have spread across the country like a web since 9/11, covering a landscape upon which there are relatively few real threats compared to those that the security industry likes to conjure (often with help from the media). In many communities the primary dangers are more likely to be unemployment, domestic violence, racist cops, bad food, and mediocre health care. Yet no camera can protect anyone from the police in South Carolina or New York City. No biometric scanner can protect someone from fast food–induced diabetes. No drone can protect someone from a banker who is bundling securitized mortgages into something that benefits his Wall Street buddies. And no number of steel bollards can keep a psychotic ex-boyfriend from getting the last word in a failed relationship.

This is why ceaseless surveillance is the wrong kind of remembrance for 9/11, the wrong kind of response to such trauma. Yet what I found in the emotional life of the Memorial pools is the exception, not the rule, in a society that has made unprecedented investments in surveillance with little discussion of the implications. In 1998, the New York Civil Liberties Union located sixty-five surveillance cameras in Midtown. Today that number is impossible to tally—many thousands in Midtown alone, not counting tens of thousands of smartphone cameras. By one estimate, New York City had at least 6,000 "public sector surveillance cameras" by 2013, with the number, quality, and interconnectedness of the cameras increasing every year.[38] Wondering about these webs of visibility and what's getting caught up in them, I consulted an online map of security cameras in Manhattan that civil libertarians in the NYC Surveillance Camera Project have prepared.[39] A popular website reminded me that the maps were "not intended for use in the commission of any crime or act of war."[40] Really? We can't even note the location of cameras that are noting our location without worrying about getting in trouble? Because actual terrorists are not dissuaded by legal disclaimers, the sole function of the warning is to afford its authors some legal protection, something they might have learned at the "Reducing Liability" seminar at the ISC trade show. Adding the disclaimer to such a subversive map is a very strange gesture: a paranoid legalism applied to a paranoid geography. This is understandable, I suppose, since I'm in New York City just a year after Mayor Bloomberg announced "a sophisticated city-wide surveillance platform developed with Microsoft that centralizes data from many sources, and displays information in real-time."[41] "Envisioning a future where privacy is a thing of the past," Bloomberg boasted like a super-villain in a *Batman* movie, "it will soon be impossible to escape the watchful eyes of surveillance cameras and even drones in the city."[42] Like vendors at the ISC, such politicians present the future of insecurity with calm inevitability, as if no other future were imaginable for the United States. But what happens after we wire ourselves up for maximum security, learn all the passwords, submit to all the scans, and internalize the logic of high security and asymmetrical transparency? Which powerful forces view us through the one-way mirror that we come to expect and quietly accept? How do we live then?

After the trade show at the Javits Center in 2013, I stopped at an Italian restaurant whose small tables were pressed close together, causing me to overhear too much of a nearby conversation for someone fleeing from a surveillance conference. Investment bankers lunching at the next table were passionately arguing that altruism was always dependent on wealth, reminding each other that *"all good deeds require vast sums of money"*—and even evoking the Bill & Melinda Gates Foundation's fight against malaria as an implicit justification for whatever transpired on their Bloomberg terminals that morning. No doubt, we all have our justifications, and I'm sure surveillance professionals feel the same way: *necessary, logical, defensible, inevitable.* But the rest of us shouldn't be so sure—

especially those of us with the ability to ask the questions that the industry and its insider allies are unwilling to consider. If we ask the right questions, we might come to a very different conclusion than the average security professional or US senator: *Not everything needs watching, monitoring, sorting, and archiving.* Not everything can be solved by fortification of mind and body, home and city, office and nation, in ever greater layers. Some things—probably most things, when you get right down to it—require more nuanced solutions that speak to root causes and dehumanizing systems. Addressing those underlying problems will take us closer to true security than will any high-tech fortress of CCTV and smartlocks, retina scanners and personal drones, even if this isn't a saleable message for a security industry on the march toward total control.

Although it might seem a strange counterpoint to the trade show inside the Javits Center, the 9/11 Memorial nonetheless reminds me that it is possible to find a measured and dignified response to an act of extreme sadism, whose "success" was attributable more to accident and perverse good fortune than to anything else. In short, we didn't need to change the way we think and live because of a few homicidal theocrats; we didn't need to run to gated communities in the suburbs; we didn't need to retreat inside a high security fortress or *its mental equivalent*, whether we lived in a small town in Iowa or a city in Oregon or somewhere in between. We didn't need to feel differently about public life in America, taking on a new skepticism about strangers that was most often applied to people of particular hues and customs. We didn't need to institutionalize the panic of those first frantic moments on September 11 and the days that followed, except that it proved immensely rewarding to a cynical few in politics, media, and business. To be clear, I don't necessarily blame the ISC rank-and-file. Most are typical midlevel merchants seizing an opportunity to expand a marketplace that grows every year: Who can fault them for the sins of their industry? No more willing or able to confront the big picture than most Americans, they have internalized the apolitical mandate of their trade and others like it (oil, automotive, chemical, meat) and worked hard to make a living, pay the mortgage, maybe save a little for a college fund. Ethics, wisdom, beauty, truth, justice—these are matters for another place, not the floor of a trade show where deals must be struck and contracts signed. And perhaps not anywhere in an economic system that flaunts its own amorality as a virtue. Corporate apologists often quote the economist Adam Smith to this effect: "It is not from the benevolence of the butcher, the brewer, or the baker that we expect our dinner, but from their regard to their own interest." As the writer Jonathon Porritt explains, such a canard distorts Smith's own belief that "people of conscience" must guide the "invisible hand" of the market with sound moral judgments.[43] In this sense, even Adam Smith would frown on the amoral free-for-all that the new surveillance marketplace has become. Naturally, I don't think he would blame the eager sales teams and grinning marketers that I met at ISC East, who are simply cogs in the big business of American insecurity, not its driving force. Yet as they labor in an industry that artfully excludes questions of ethics and impact at every turn—thereby externalizing the true process of accounting upon which democracy depends—the rest of us are obliged to make sense of their operations in ways that transcend the easy calculus of dollars and cents.

Acknowledgments

This book would look very different without a particular set of friends and influences. Above all, I've been very fortunate to work with Robert Devens and his talented colleagues at the University of Texas Press: Colleen Devine Ellis, Robert Kimzey, Sarah McGavick, Gianna LaMorte, and Dave Hamrick, the very supportive director. I'm also indebted to the colleagues in my department at the University of Texas at Austin, especially Steve Hoelscher, who has shown an unflagging interest in this project over the past five years. Every time I've given a talk on campus, he showed up, with collegial good cheer. Friends elsewhere have shown me similar kindness: Elizabeth Engelhardt, Chad Seales, Karl Offen, Ralph Beliveau, Karen Umminger, Stephanie Jung, Craig Campbell, David Delgado Shorter, Kyle Schlesinger, and others. I owe a special thanks to Jason Borge and Sonia Roncador for their generous hospitality and true friendship (all I can say is that the wine, walks, and talks made a real difference). I've also benefited from conversations with graduate students at UT Austin, especially Carrie Andersen, Paul Gansky, Andrew Gansky, Sean Cashbaugh, and Jose Centeno-Melendez. Finally, a Humanities Research Award, a program launched by Dean Randy Diehl of the College of Liberal Arts, made an enormous difference in allowing me to travel to places that proved crucial to the book.

I'm also grateful to the Public Feelings writing group at UT Austin. Its artful ringleaders, Katie Stewart and Ann Cvetkovich, have created intimate workshops where some of these pages were first tested. These experiences encouraged me to look more seriously at the role of feelings in surveillance systems, something that has received relatively little attention in the literature devoted to the subject. This is not to suggest a deficiency in that literature—if anything, the work on surveillance is impressively vast and deep. This book would scarcely exist without the scholars affiliated with the Surveillance Studies Network, many of them sociologists whose writing deserves much greater currency in the humanistic fields that I call home.

Finally, on the most personal level, I've benefited enormously from the love and kindness of Miranda Lewis and Monti Sigg. Thank you to my two M's, who keep an eye on me in the best possible sense. I love you both.

Notes

Introduction

1. Although Americans might have to seek permission from the nursing home or risk doing it surreptitiously, families in the United Kingdom have a legal right to install cameras to monitor the care being provided to loved ones. Tom McTague, "Families Given Official Green Light to Use CCTV in Care Homes to Check If Staff Are Abusing Their Elderly Relatives," *Daily Mail* (November 19, 2014): dailymail .co.uk/news/article-2841115/Families-given-official-green-light-use-CCTV-care -homes-check-staff-abusing-elderly-relatives.html.

2. Sarah Jaffe, "Hyatt Surveils Its Workers via iPods," *In These Times* (October 24, 2012): inthesetimes.com/working/entry/14078/hyatt_monitors_workers _via_ipods.

3. Even our tone of voice is coming under scrutiny in the workplace, as Silicon Valley entrepreneurs are "producing software to monitor digitally the emotions of Indian call center workers." Winifred R. Poster, "Emotion Detectors, Answering Machines, and E-Unions: Multi-Surveillances in the Global Interactive Service Industry," *American Behavioral Scientist* 55 (2011): 868, abs.sagepub.com/con tent/55/7/868. While 75 percent of American workers are subjected to *regular* surveillance in their workplace, those who use the Internet for work are scrutinized even more closely, with 33 percent enduring *constant* workplace surveillance. Torin Monahan and John Gilliom, *SuperVision: An Introduction to the Surveillance Society* (Chicago: University of Chicago Press, 2012), 93.

4. *Huffington Post*, "Muslim Baby Ordered off Plane for Being on No Fly List" (May 10, 2012): huffingtonpost.com/2012/05/10/baby-ordered-off-plane-for-be ing-on-no-fly-list_n_1505648.html.

5. Kevin Haggerty, "Surveillance and Political Problems," in Sean P. Hier and Josh Greenberg (eds.), *Surveillance: Power, Problems, and Politics* (Vancouver: University of British Columbia Press, 2010), ix.

6. Poitros quotes these words in her 2014 documentary film *Citizen Four*.

7. William G. Staples, *Everyday Surveillance: Vigilance and Visibility in Postmodern Life* (Lanham, MD: Rowman and Littlefield, 2000), 5.

8. Spencer Ackerman and James Ball, "Optic Nerve: Millions of Yahoo Webcam Images Intercepted by GCHQ," *Guardian* (February 28, 2014): theguardian .com/world/2014/feb/27/gchq-nsa-webcam-images-internet-yahoo.

9. *Guardian*, "'Any Palestinian Is Exposed to Monitoring by the Israeli Big Brother'" (September 12, 2014): theguardian.com/world/2014/sep/12/israeli-in telligence-unit-testimonies.

10. Ali Winston, "License-Plate Readers Let Police Collect Millions of Records on Drivers," Center for Investigative Reporting (June 26, 2013): cironline.org /reports/license-plate-readers-let-police-collect-millions-records-drivers-4883; Brian Bennett, "FBI Has Been Using Drones Since 2006, Watchdog Agency Says," *Los Angeles Times* (September 26, 2013): latimes.com/nation/nationnow/la-na -nn-fbi-using-drones-2006-20130926-story.html.

11. ACLU, "Stingray Tracking Devices: Who's Got Them?" (n.d.): aclu.org /map/stingray-tracking-devices-whos-got-them.

12. Mackenzie Ryan, "Body Cameras Making Their Way into Iowa Schools," *Des Moines Register* (July 5, 2015): desmoinesregister.com/story/news/education /2015/07/05/body-cameras-burlington-schools/29746803.

13. Lily Hay Newman, "Some Banks Collect Voiceprints during Service Calls to Identify You," *Slate* (October 14, 2014): slate.com/blogs/future_tense/2014/10/14 /associated_press_reports_that_banks_collect_identifying_voiceprints_during .html.

14. *Guardian* (via AP London), "Millions of Voiceprints Quietly Being Harvested as Latest Identification Tool" (October 13, 2014): theguardian.com/tech nology/2014/oct/13/millions-of-voiceprints-quietly-being-harvested-as-latest -identification-tool.

15. Alistair Croll, "Big Data Is Our Generation's Civil Rights Issue, and We Don't Know It," *O'Reilly Radar* (August 2, 2012): radar.oreilly.com/2012/08/big -data-is-our-generations-civil-rights-issue-and-we-dont-know-it.html.

16. April Salazar, "The Pregnancy Is Gone, but the Promotions Keep Coming," *New York Times* Motherlode blog (February 2, 2014): parenting.blogs.nytimes .com/2014/02/02/the-pregnancy-is-gone-but-the-promotions-keep-coming.

17. "In the Privacy of Your Own Home," *Consumer Reports* (June 2015): 24.

18. For a very good book on this subject, see Daniel Trottier, *Social Media as Surveillance: Rethinking Visibility in a Converging World* (Burlington, VT: Ashgate, 2012).

19. Damon Bares, "Facebook Is Watching You, Even When You're Not Clicking on Stuff," *Huffington Post* (June 12, 2014): huffingtonpost.com/2015/06/12/face book-news-feed_n_7572130.html?ir=Technology; Robert Booth, "Facebook Reveals News Feed Experiment to Control Emotions," *Guardian* (June 29, 2014): theguardian.com/technology/2014/jun/29/facebook-users-emotions-news -feeds.

20. Aviva Rutkin, "Facebook Can Recognise You in Photos Even If You're Not Looking," *New Scientist* (June 22, 2015): newscientist.com/article/dn27761 -facebook-can-recognise-you-in-photos-even-if-youre-not-looking.html# .VYlfgRNVikq.

21. *Telegraph* (by AFP), "Brazilian Evangelicals Set Up a 'Sin Free' Version

of Facebook" (July 4, 2015): telegraph.co.uk/news/worldnews/southamerica/bra
zil/11718235/Brazilian-Evangelicals-set-up-a-shu-free-version-of-Facebook.html.

22. Dell Cameron, "CIA-backed Surveillance Software Was Marketed to Public Schools," *Daily Dot* (October 18 [n.d.]): dailydot.com/layer8/geofeedia-surveil
lance-software-high-school-chicago-social-media-monitoring; EJ Dickson and Molly Stier, "To Catch a Cheater: 6 Apps for Spying on Your Significant Other," *Daily Dot* (March 5, 2014): dailydot.com/debug/love-surveillance-spying-apps. More about the Duke University art professor appears here: Katie Rose Guest Pryal, "To the Creep Who Videoed Me and Called It Art" (October 17, 2016): katieroseguestpryal.com/2016/10/17/to-the-creep-who-videoed-me-and-called
-it-art. For more on drone security: Matt McFarland, "Forget Your Old Alarm System. This Drone Will Protect Your House," *CNN tech* (November 3, 2016): money
.cnn.com/2016/11/03/technology/drone-home-alarm-system/index.html.

23. Leo Hickman, "How I Became a Foursquare Cyberstalker," *Guardian* (July 23, 2010): theguardian.com/technology/2010/jul/23/foursquare.

24. Spencer Ackerman and Ewen MacAskill, "Privacy Experts Fear Donald Trump Running Global Surveillance Network," *Guardian* (November 11, 2016): theguardian.com/world/2016/nov/11/trump-surveillance-network-nsa-privacy.

Chapter 1: Feeling Surveillance

1. AMC, *Breaking Bad*, "Open House" (orig. air date: July 31, 2011; Vince Gilligan, exec. prod.).

2. Listener comment reported by Brooke Gladstone on the NPR program *On the Media* (orig. air date: October 31, 2013).

3. David Shultz, "When Your Voice Betrays You," *Science*, no. 347 (January 29, 2015): 494.

4. *World Bulletin*, "Airplanes to Track Halal Food Choices" (January 30, 2015): worldbulletin.net/europe/154078/airplanes-to-track-halal-food-choices.

5. Matthew Sparkes, "How Do You Spot a Terrorist in a Crowd?" *Telegraph* (August 13, 2014): telegraph.co.uk/technology/news/11031651/How-do-you-spot
-a-terrorist-in-a-crowd.html.

6. Suzy Strutner, "Hotels Can Track Those Towels That You Steal," *Huffington Post* (February 3, 2015): huffingtonpost.com/2015/01/31/stealing-hotel-towels
_n_6555486.html?ncid=fcbklnkushpmg00000063.

7. A phrase from Ben Highmore comes to mind: the "awkward materiality" of the body. See Melissa Gregg and Gregory J. Seigwort, *The Affect Theory Reader* (Durham, NC: Duke University Press, 2010), 119.

8. Daniel Akst, "This Computer Keyboard Knows Who You Are," *Wall Street Journal* (February 12, 2015): wsj.com/articles/this-computer-keyboard-knows
-who-you-are-1423773965.

9. Keith Woodward and Jennifer Lea, "Geographies of Affect," in Susan J. Smith, Rachel Pain, and Sallie A. Marston, *The Sage Handbook of Social Geographies*, 154–175 (London: SAGE Publications, 2010), 164, 169.

10. Slavoj Žižek, "In the Grey Zone," *London Review of Books* (February 5, 2015): www.lrb.co.uk/2015/02/05/slavoj-zizek/in-the-grey-zone.

11. Hille Koskela, "Fear and Its Others," in Smith et al., *The Sage Handbook of Social Geographies* 12: 389–408, 395.

12. Surveillance Camera Man, "Surveillance Camera Man 6," *Daily Motion* (October 22, 2014): dailymotion.com/video/x28epli_surveillance-camera-man-6_creation; and "Why Does Everyone Hate Surveillance Camera Man?" *Verge* (October 22, 2014): twitter.com/verge/status/546171948749697025.

13. Paul Joseph Watson, "Drones Shot Down over Texas," *InfoWars* (May 29, 2012): infowars.com/drones-shot-down-over-texas/

14. Claire Bishop, *Artificial Hells: Participatory Art and the Politics of Spectatorship* (New York: Verso, 2012), 105.

15. Surveillance could be understood as a form of what Lisa Marie Cacho calls "acts of transparent recognition" that marks individuals as "unlawful." In her book *Social Death: Racialized Rightlessness and the Criminalization of the Unprotected*, she explains that the "ontologized" are "abstracted from the social relationships that effect them, assumed to represent ways of being in the world, defined only by people's claims and conclusions about their nature." It is "integral to the processes that criminalize people" at the level of being. See Lisa Marie Cacho, *Social Death: Racialized Rightlessness and the Criminalization of the Unprotected* (New York: NYU Press, 2012).

16. Torin Monahan, *Surveillance in the Time of Insecurity* (New Brunswick, NJ: Rutgers University Press, 2010), 113.

17. Ginger Allen, "Female Passengers Say They're Targeted by TSA," *CBS DFW* (February 3, 2012): dfw.cbslocal.com/2012/02/03/female-passengers-say-theyre-targeted-by-tsa/#comments.

18. Marita Sturken and Lisa Cartwright, *Practices of Looking: An Introduction to Visual Culture* (New York: Oxford University Press, 2009), 76–78.

19. *YouTube*, "Powell Shooting (Cell Phone Camera)" (August 20, 2014): youtube.com/watch?v=j-P54MZVxMU&bpctr=1424889127; see also *CNET*, "Store Owner Installs Surveillance Cameras to Spy on Police" (November 22, 2014): cnet.com/news/store-owner-installs-surveillance-cameras-to-spy-on-police/; *The Source*, "Anonymous Claims to Have Released the Officers' Names Who Killed Kajieme Powell" (December 10, 2014): thesource.com/2014/12/10/anonymous-claims-to-have-released-the-officers-names-who-killed-kajieme-powell.

20. Conor Friedersdorf, "The Killing of Kajieme Powell and How It Divides Americans," *Atlantic* (August 21, 2014): theatlantic.com/national/archive/2014/08/the-killing-of-kajieme-powell/378899.

21. National Public Radio, "Reflections On The Black Panther Party 50 Years Later" (October 23, 2016): npr.org/2016/10/23/499042341/black-panther-party-50th-anniversary-groups-photographerreflects-on-misconceptio.

22. Ethan Zuckerman, "Why We Must Continue to Turn the Camera on Police," *MIT Technology Review* (July 11, 2016): technologyreview.com/s/601878/why-we-must-continue-to-turn-the-camera-on-police.

23. Andrea Brighenti, "Visibility: A Category for the Social Sciences," *Current Sociology* 55, no. 3 (May 2007): 323–334, 336.

24. Marcia Dunn (AP), "Story Time from Space: Astronauts Getting New Picture Books," *Fox 21 News* (October 26, 2015): fox21news.com/news/story.aspx?id=1169455#.VPERZLPF-5I.

25. privacyelectronics, "Nanny Cams . . . What Is Really Going on When You Are Away" (July 9, 2009): youtube.com/watch?v=6DFILiZyEDI&app=desktop; and NOLATAC, "Home Invasion in Millburn NJ Caught on Nanny Cam—Brutal Beating in Front of Daughter, June, 2013," youtube.com/watch?v=qUoEJS3cJIc.

26. Purrfectstranger, "Child Abuse—Nanny Caught on Tape" (September 27, 2009): youtube.com/watch?v=vKiCVBAFKcQ.

27. One criminologist has used FBI statistics to show that fewer infants were killed by babysitters in 2010 than in 1976. Such facts are often lost in the nanny-cam hysteria. Sarah Schweitzer, "Much to Check Before Entrusting a Child's Care," *Boston Globe* (January 23, 2013): bostonglobe.com/metro/2013/01/23/navigating-path-nanny-fraught-process-for-parents/skyiEb4IBPffG3sbaYbpIJ/story.html.

28. Jon Burstein, "Nanny Files Lawsuit Against Hidden-camera Company," *Sun-Sentinel* (June 14, 2006): articles.sun-sentinel.com/2006-06-14/news/06061 30569_1_claudia-muro-recording-system-camera; *ABC News*, "Nanny Cleared of Violently Shaking Baby" (March 21, 2006): abcnews.go.com/GMA/LegalCenter/story?id=1749672.

29. Tamara Mose Brown, *Raising Brooklyn: Nannies, Childcare, and Caribbeans Creating Community* (New York: NYU Press, 2009), 20.

30. Mary Romero, "Nanny Diaries and Other Stories: Immigrant Women's Labor in the Social Reproduction of American Families," *Revista de Estudios Sociales*, no. 45 (2013): 188.

31. Joanna Stern, "Nest Cam Review: High-Resolution Spying on Your House—or Puppy," *Wall Street Journal* (June 23, 2015): wsj.com/articles/nest-cam-review-high-resolution-spying-on-your-houseor-puppy-1435081751.

32. Mike Wheatley, "Watch Out for Those Nanny Cams!" *Reality Biz News* (September 15, 2014): realtybiznews.com/watch-out-for-those-nanny-cams/987 26035.

33. Celia Walden, "Celia Walden on the Dubious Joys of Nanny Cams," *Telegraph* (July 17, 2014): telegraph.co.uk/journalists/celia-walden/10966369/Celia-Walden-on-the-dubious-joys-of-nanny-cams.html.

34. Jack Smith IV, "Couple Wakes Up in Airbnb to Find Hidden Cameras Watching Them," *Observer* (January 1, 2015): observer.com/2015/01/couple-wakes-up-in-airbnb-to-find-hidden-cameras-watching-them.

35. J. G. Ballard, *The Kindness of Women* (1991).

36. Katie Utehs, "Nanny Cam Catches Woman Attacking Infant, Police Say," *ABC 7 Chicago* (November 4, 2016): abc7chicago.com/news/nanny-cam-catches-woman-attacking-infant-police-say/1589479.

37. Meredith Krause, "Vigilance Fatigue in Policing: A Critical Threat to Public Safety and Officer Well-Being," *FBI Law Enforcement Bulletin* (December 2012): leb.fbi.gov/2012/december/vigilance-fatigue-in-policing-a-critical-threat-to-public-safety-and-officer-well-being.

38. Asad "Ace" Dandia, "My Life under NYPD Surveillance: A Brooklyn Student and Charity Leader on Fear and Mistrust," *ACLU* (June 18, 2013): aclu.org/blog

/national-security-religion-belief-criminal-law-reform-technology-and-liberty
/my-life-under-nypd.

39. Phil Hubbard, "Fear and Loathing at the Multiplex: Everyday Anxiety in the Post-Industrial City," *Capital & Class*, no. 80 (2003): 35 (quoted in Frank Furedi's "The Only Thing . . ."). For a perceptive overview of fear as a sociological problem, see Frank Furedi's excellent "The Only Thing We Have to Fear Is the 'Culture Of Fear' Itself'" (April 4, 2007): spiked-online.com/newsite/article/3053#.VPYJ-rPF-5I.

40. For more on RFID tags on humans, see *RFID Journal*, "Two Stories Highlight the RFID Debate" (July 19, 2005): rfidjournal.com/articles/view?6294.

41. Colson Whitehead, "The 'Loser Edit' That Awaits Us All," *New York Times*, March 3, 2015: nytimes.com/2015/03/08/magazine/the-loser-edit-that-awaits-us-all.html?_r=0.

42. Jennifer Burris, "Surveillance and the Indifferent Gaze in Michael Haneke's *Caché*," *Studies in French Cinema* 11, no. 2 (2011): 152.

43. John Naughton, "Edward Snowden: Public Indifference Is the Real Enemy in the NSA Affair," *Guardian* (October 19, 2013): theguardian.com/world/2013/oct/20/public-indifference-nsa-snowden-affair; Henry Porter, "Perhaps I'm Out of Step and Britons Just Don't Think Privacy Is Important," *Guardian* (September 7, 2013): theguardian.com/commentisfree/2013/sep/07/britons-privacy-not-important.

44. Mary Madden, "Public Perceptions of Privacy and Security in the Post-Snowden Era," *Pew Research Center* (November 12, 2014): pewinternet.org/2014/11/12/public-privacy-perceptions.

45. November 2014 Pew Research survey: pewinternet.org/2014/11/12/what-americans-think-about-privacy.

46. Matthew Wilsey, "The Metropolis and Mental Life," *The Modernism Lab* (n.d.): modernism.research.yale.edu/wiki/index.php/The_Metropolis_and_Mental_Life; Georg Simmel, "The Metropolis and Mental Life," in D. N. Levine (ed.), *Georg Simmel on Individuality and Social Forms* (Chicago: University of Chicago Press, 1971), 324–339.

47. Simmel didn't talk about feelings in his famous essay, but adding feelings to the equation only makes it more understandable that we would want to remove ourselves from the turbulence of the securitarian experience.

48. In its survey of security cameras in Manhattan, the New York Civil Liberties Union complained that "surveillance cameras have been passively accepted as necessary for our personal safety": nyclu.org/node/930 (n.d.).

49. Scott Stossel, *My Age of Anxiety: Fear, Hope, Dread, and the Search for Peace of Mind* (New York: Random House 2014).

50. Comparative anxiety rates taken from a WHO survey in 2002, cited in T. M. Luhrmann, "The Anxious Americans," *New York Times* (July 18, 2015): nytimes.com/2015/07/19/opinion/sunday/the-anxious-americans.html.

51. Anxiety and Depression Association of America, "Facts & Statistics" (n.d.): adaa.org/about-adaa/press-room/facts-statistics.

52. Stossel, *My Age of Anxiety*, 114.

53. National Institutes of Mental Health, "Social Anxiety Disorder: More

Than Just Shyness" (n.d.): nimh.nih.gov/health/publications/social-phobia-social
-anxiety-disorder-always-embarrassed/index.shtml.

54. Patrick McGuinness, *The Last Hundred Days* (New York: Bloomsbury
USA, 2012), 21. Elsewhere the author says, "My novel has elements of autobiography in it: the narrator's youth, unformedness, his bystander-to-his-own-
life quality. But it's a highly exaggerated and poeticised version of the reality I
lived, which though it was quite extreme was often grinding and grey." Interview
at *Foyles*, "Patrick Mcguinness" (n.d.): foyles.co.uk/patrick-mcguinness. Why the
English are so prolific on the subject of surveillance is a fascinating question: Bentham, Orwell, Ballard, McGuinness. What is it in the national experience there
that incubates the simultaneous expansion and thoughtful denunciation of the
surveillance state?

55. McGuinness, *The Last Hundred Days*, 21.

56. Ibid., 72.

57. Ibid., 71, 72.

58. Ibid., 56.

59. Ibid., 54.

60. Ibid., 89.

61. Octavia Butler, *Kindred* (Boston: Beacon Press, 2004), 91.

62. Ibid., 177.

63. Max Ehrenfreund, "The Risks of Walking While Black in Ferguson," *Washington Post* (March 4, 2015): washingtonpost.com/blogs/wonkblog/wp/2015/03
/04/95-percent-of-people-arrested-for-jaywalking-in-ferguson-were-black.

64. Peter K. Carpenter, "Descriptions of Schizophrenia in the Psychiatry of
Georgian Britain: John Haslam and James Tilly Matthews," *Comprehensive Psychiatry* 30, no. 4 (July–August 1989): 332. See also John Haslam, *Illustrations of
Madness: Exhibiting a Singular Case of Insanity, and a No Less Remarkable Difference in Medical Opinion: Developing the Nature of Assailment, and the Manner of Working Events; With a Description of the Tortures Experienced by Bomb-
Bursting, Lobster Cracking, and Lengthening the Brain* (London: Hayden, 1810).

65. All quotes from Haslam, *Illustrations of Madness*: "infernal machine"
(page 6); "magnetic impregnations" and "pneumatic chemistry" (19, 22); "assailment" (28); "kiteing" and "lobster-cracking," (31, 32); while "lengthening the
brain" ... "thought-making" (29).

66. Ibid., 41.

67. Jerry Mander might have seen the air loom as a predecessor to modern
media technologies. In his 1975 classic, *Four Arguments for the Elimination of
Television*, Mander argued that "television does what the schizophrenic fantasy
says it does. It places in our minds images of reality which are outside our experience. The pictures come in the form of rays from a box. They cause changes
in feeling and ... utter confusion as to what is real and what is not." Also, it may
be that Matthews has a great deal in common with the schizophrenics profiled in
the *New Yorker* who suffer from "The Truman Show Delusion," in which a person becomes convinced that they are the center of a nonexistent reality show. See
Andrew Marantz, "Unreality Star," *New Yorker* (September 16, 2013): newyorker
.com/magazine/2013/09/16/unreality-star.

68. Haslam, *Illustrations of Madness*: "somewhat resembling the compression of a new wicker-basket ..." (54); "... bubble by bubble"(28).

Chapter 2: Welcome to the Funopticon

1. TED, "Ads Worth Spreading" (n.d.): ted.com/about/programs-initiatives /ads-worth-spreading.

2. Ibid.

3. Yiftach Chozev, "Real 'Security Cameras'—Coca Cola parody" (n.d.): vimeo .com/44027600.

4. A rare connection of the playful to surveillance appears in Thomas Y. Levin's "Surveillance and the Ludic Reappropriation of Public Space," *Open*, no. 6 (2004): 50–71, downloadable at onlineopen.org/download.php?id=316. This short article deals insightfully with contemporary artists who playfully challenge surveillance cameras, but it does not develop the playful qualities of the performances. I would also note that the UC Davis Humanities Innovation Lab is exploring what they call the "Relations of ludic culture with surveillance, securitization, and militarization": modlab.ucdavis.edu.

5. Gillian Rose, "A Politics of Paradoxical Space," *Feminism and Geography: The Limits of Geographical Knowledge* 137, no. 60 (1993): 184–202.

6. Ariane Ellerbrok, "Playful Biometrics: Controversial Technology through the Lens of Play," *Sociological Quarterly* 52, no. 4 (September 2011): 528–547. A brief but interesting discussion of play and surveillance can be found in Anders Albrechtslund and Lynsey Dubbeld, "The Plays and Arts of Surveillance: Studying Surveillance as Entertainment," *Surveillance & Society* 3, no. 2/3 (2005): 216–221. Likewise in G. T. Marx, "Electric Eye in the Sky: Some Reflections on the New Surveillance and Popular Culture," in D. Lyon and E. Zureik (eds.), *Computers, Surveillance, and Privacy* (Minneapolis: University of Minnesota Press, 1996), 193–233.

7. Vincent Pecora, "The Culture of Surveillance," *Qualitative Sociology*, 25, no. 3 (Fall 2002): 348. I highly recommend this article.

8. Nigel Thrift, "Lifeworld, Inc.—And What to Do About It." *Environment and Planning D. Society and Space* 29 (2011): 5–26.

9. Ash Amin, *Land of Strangers* (New York: John Wiley, 2013), 1993.

10. Jeremy Bentham, *The Works of Jeremy Bentham, Volume 4. Panopticon, Constitution, Colonies, Codification* (Edinburgh: William Tait, 1843), 39.

11. Michael McCahill and Rachel Finn, "The Social Impact of Surveillance in Three UK Schools: 'Angels,' 'Devils,' and 'Teen Mums,'" *Surveillance & Society* 7, no. 3/4 (2010): 273–289 (quote on 286).

12. David Lyon, *Liquid Surveillance* (Cambridge, UK: Polity, 2012), 52.

13. Anders Albrechtslund and Lynsey Dubbeld, "The Plays and Arts of Surveillance: Studying Surveillance as Entertainment," *Surveillance & Society* 3, no. 2/3 (2005): 216. The Marx in question is Gary Marx, "Electric Eye in the Sky: Some Reflections on the New Surveillance and Popular Culture," in Lyon and Zureik (eds.), *Computers, Surveillance, and Privacy*, 193–233. See also Matthew J.

Cousineau, "The Surveillant Simulation of War: Entertainment and Surveillance in the 21st Century," *Surveillance & Society* 8, no. 4 (2011): 517–522.

14. David Lyon's "Ideas" lecture was broadcast on ABC TV (Sydney, Australia) in April 2012. *Surveillance Studies Centre*, "David Lyon" (n.d.): sscqueens.org /davidlyon.

15. See Kevin D. Haggerty, "Tear Down the Walls: On Demolishing the Panopticon," in David Lyon (ed.), *Theorizing Surveillance: The Panopticon and Beyond* (Cullompton, Devon, UK: Willan, 2006). See also Torin Monahan and John Gilliom, *SuperVision: An Introduction to the Surveillance Society* (Chicago: University of Chicago Press, 2012), 21–22.

16. James Miller, *The Passion of Michel Foucault* (Cambridge: Harvard University Press, 2000), 234.

17. Michel Foucault, *Discipline and Punish: The Birth of the Prison*, trans. Alan Sheridan (New York: Vintage, 1977), 195–196.

18. Ibid., 202.

19. Ibid., 205, 214.

20. The biographer in question is James Miller, author of *The Passion of Michel Foucault*. For more on historians with reservations about Foucault, see Gary Gutting, "Foucault and the History of Madness," in Gary Gutting (ed.), *Cambridge Companion to Foucault* (Cambridge, UK: Cambridge University Press, orig. publ. 1994), 50–51, in which Foucault is described as "seriously wanting" as a historian even by his admirers. If Gutting's summation is correct, Foucault had a genius for the big picture and remarkable sloppiness with the details.

21. Michael Thomsen, "Video Games Are Making Us Too Comfortable with the Modern Surveillance State," *New Statesman* (rpt., *New Republic*) (September 30, 2013): newstatesman.com/games/2013/09/video-games-are-making-us-too-comfortable-modern-surveillance-state. See also Carrie Andersen, "Game of Drones: The Uneasy Future of the Soldier-Hero in *Call of Duty: Black Ops II*," *Surveillance & Society* 12, no. 3 (July 2014): 360–376. For more on *Watch Dogs*, see watchdogs.ubi.com/watchdogs/en-us/home or David Chandler, "Think the NSA Is Bad? Games Are Masters of Surveillance," *Kill Screen* (July 21, 2014): killscreendaily.com/articles/think-nsa-bad-how-games-have-their-eyes-you.

22. On social media as surveillance, see Daniel Trottier, *Social Media as Surveillance: Rethinking Visibility in a Converging World* (Surrey, UK: Ashgate, 2011). On the example of Egypt, see Sheera Frenkel, "Egypt Begins Surveillance of Facebook, Twitter, and Skype on Unprecedented Scale," *Buzzfeed* (September 17, 2014): buzzfeed.com/sheerafrenkel/egypt-begins-surveillance-of-facebook -twitter-and-skype-on-u. Of course, the flip side of the big party of the networked and notable is old-fashioned social anxiety and exclusion, the sense that *no one invited me to the party*. Or even worse: *no one even noticed I was at the party*. Andreas Kitzmann writes about the "anxiety of obscurity" in *Saved from Oblivion: Documenting the Daily from Diaries to Web Cams* (New York: Peter Lang, 2004), 168.

23. Charlie Sorrel, "Surveillance Shaker Shows CCTV Feeds on iPhone," *Wired* (May 29, 2009): wired.com/2009/05/surveillanceshaker-shows-cctv-feeds-on -iphone.

24. eBay Buying Guide, "Cool Surveillance Gadgets That Make Fun and Unique Gifts for Kids" (n.d.): www.ebay.com/gds/Cool-Surveillance-Gadgets -That-Make-Fun-and-Unique-Gifts-for-Kids-/10000000177630513/g.html.

25. Kevin Short, "24 Drone-Created GIFs That Show You the World Like You've Never Seen It Before," *Huffington Post* (August 4, 2014): huffingtonpost .com/2014/08/04/stunning-drone-videos_n_5579199.html.

26. Christina Zdanowicz, "How to Shoot Amazing Video from Drones," *CNN* (May 22, 2014): cnn.com/2014/05/22/tech/innovation/drone-uav-photography /index.html?c=tech.

27. Joseph Flaherty, "Disney Meets Orwell With These Super Cute Sur- veillance Cameras," *Wired* (May 14, 2014): wired.com/2014/05/disney-meets -orwell-with-these-super-cute-surveillance-cameras-are.

28. See Alan Bryman, *The Disneyization of Society* (Thousand Oaks, CA: Sage Publications, 2004), 136. The Shutterbug video is no longer on the Disney site but is available here: youtube.com/watch?v=1yw30WXXQbo&feature=youtu.be. Thanks to Alejandro Flores for sending me this video.

29. Michael Price, "I'm Terrified of My New TV: Why I'm Scared to Turn This Thing on—and You'd Be, Too," *Salon* (October 30, 2014): salon.com/2014/10/30 /im_terrified_of_my_new_tv_why_im_scared_to_turn_this_thing_on_and _youd_be_too/.

30. *IFSEC Global*, "Gamification of Security and Video Surveillance ..." (Sep- tember 27, 2012): ifsecglobal.com/gamification-of-security-and-video-surveil lance.

31. Jane Wakefield, "Comedy Club Charges per Laugh with Facial Recogni- tion," BBC (October 9, 2014): bbc.com/news/technology-29551380. Thanks to Carrie Andersen for this news story.

32. *RT*, "CCTVandalism: 'Camover' Game Pokes Big Brother's Eye in Ger- many" (February 16, 2013): rt.com/news/cctv-cameras-vandalism-protest-371.

33. Michael S. Schmidt, "On Children's Website, N.S.A. Puts a Furry, Smiley Face on Its Mission," *New York Times* (January 24, 2014): mobile.nytimes.com /2014/01/25/us/on-childrens-website-nsa-puts-a-furry-smiley-face-on-its-mis sion.html?_r-0.

34. Andrea Peterson, "How the NSA May Be Using Games to Encourage Digi- tal Snooping," *Washington Post* (June 18, 2014): washingtonpost.com/blogs/the -switch/wp/2014/06/18/how-the-nsa-may-have-used-games-to-encourage -digital-snooping.

35. Evan Perez, "NSA: Some Used Spying Power to Snoop on Lovers," *CNN* (September 27, 2013): cnn.com/2013/09/27/politics/nsa-snooping.

36. Jason Edward Harrington, "Dear America, I Saw You Naked," *Politico* (January 30, 2014): politico.com/magazine/story/2014/01/tsa-screener-confes sion-102912_full.html#.VXj4gGTBzGc.

37. Clive Norris and Gary Armstrong, "CCTV and the Social Structuring of Surveillance," *Crime Prevention Studies* 10 (1999): 157–178. The 5-to-1 statistic is on 174.

38. John Curran, "Atlantic City Casino Fined for Cameras," *USA Today*

(December 16, 2004): usatoday3o.usatoday.com/tech/news/surveillance/2004 -12-16-surveil-abuse_x.htm.

39. *BBC*, "Ciaran McCleave: CCTV Operator Jailed for Voyeurism" (September 26, 2014): bbc.com/news/uk-northern-ireland-29380697.

40. David Bell, "Surveillance Is Sexy," *Surveillance & Society*, 6, no. 3: 203–212 (quote on 204).

41. Dana Cuff, "Immanent Domain: Pervasive Computing and the Public Realm," *Journal of Architectural Education* 57, no. 1 (2006): 43–49, 49, quoted in Bell, "Surveillance Is Sexy," 209.

42. Bell, "Surveillance Is Sexy," 203.

43. Ellerbrok, "Playful Biometrics," 528–547.

44. David Sirota, "*The Game*: David Fincher's Lost Classic," *Salon* (September 17, 2012): salon.com/2012/09/17/the_game_david_finchers_lost_classic/.

45. Ibid.

46. In modernity "the natural world and all areas of human experience become experienced and understood as less mysterious; defined, at least in principle, as knowable, predictable and manipulable by humans; conquered by and incorporated into the interpretive schema of science and rational government." Richard Jenkins, "Disenchantment, Enchantment and Re-Enchantment: Max Weber at the Millennium," *Max Weber Studies* 1, no. 1 (2000): 12, maxweberstudies.org /kcfinder/upload/files/MWSJournal/1.1pdfs/1.1%2011-32.pdf.

47. Weber himself did not believe the "iron cage" was inevitable. On Weber's hope for an alternative future, see Gilbert G. Germain, "The Revenge of the Sacred: Technology and Re-Enchantment," in Asher Horowitz and Terry Maley (eds.), *The Barbarism of Reason: Max Weber and the Twilight of Enlightenment* (Toronto: University of Toronto Press, 1994), 248–266.

48. Jenkins, "Disenchantment," 13.

49. George Ritzer, *Enchanting a Disenchanted World: Revolutionizing the Means of Consumption* (Thousand Oaks, CA: Pine Forge, 1999).

50. Jenkins, "Disenchantment," 18.

51. Henri Lefebvre, *Toward an Architecture of Enjoyment* (Minneapolis: University of Minnesota Press, 2014), 132.

52. Michel de Certeau, *The Practice of Everyday Life* (Berkeley: University of California Press, 1984), 37.

53. Jason Farman, "Creative Misuse as Resistance: Surveillance, Mobile Technologies, and Locative Games," *Surveillance & Society* 12, no. 3 (2014): 377–388, library.queensu.ca/ojs/index.php/surveillance-and-society/article/view/misuse /misuses.

54. McKenzie Wark, "A Ludic Century? Games, Aesthetics, the Twenty-First Century," *Public Seminar* (November 22, 2013): publicseminar.org/2013/11/a -ludic-century/#.VDRv9SldVb5.

55. Playable City can be found at watershed.co.uk/playablecity/2014 /shortlist/vvtc.

56. Aaron Souppouris, "Happy Birthday George Orwell, Here's Your Surveillance Society," *Verge* (July 4, 2013): theverge.com/2013/7/4/4490058/front404 -orwells-birthday-cctv-cameras-with-party-hats.

57. Juggalos and Juggalettes are fans of the group Insane Clown Posse and often wear outlandish face paint. See Robinson Meyer, "Anti-Surveillance Camouflage for Your Face," *Atlantic* (July 24, 2014): theatlantic.com/features /archive/2014/07/makeup/374929/; Joanne McNeil, "Art, Activism, and CCTV," *Medium* (October 29, 2013): medium.com/art-and-technology-1/art-activism -and-cctv-90f21eff4506.

58. !Mediengruppe Bitnik, "Surveillance Chess" (2012): vimeo.com/46236909.

59. Spacewurm, *I Listen: A Document of Digital Voyeurism* (New York: Incommunicado Press, 1999).

60. Golnar Motevalli, "'Video Sniffers' Subverting Surveillance for Art," *Reuters* (May 27, 2008): uk.mobile.reuters.com/article/idUKL2770714720080527?irpc=932.

61. For more on the limitations of playful resistance to surveillance, see Jennifer R. Whitson, "Gaming the Quantified Self," *Surveillance & Society* 11, nos. 1/2 (2013): 163–176 (esp. 175).

Chapter 3: Growing up Observed

1. Alan Cumming, *Not My Father's Son: A Memoir* (New York: HarperCollins, 2014), 7–8.

2. Ibid., 4.

3. Ibid., 24.

4. Freud certainly knew the power of spying on his parents. As a child he voyeuristically glimpsed his naked mother (his *"matrem nudam"* as he put it) on a train trip and never quite recovered. Peter Gay, *Freud: A Life for Our Time* (New York: Norton, 1988), 11.

5. One of the best commentaries on the subject of childhood and surveillance is Valerie Steeves and Owain Jones, "Editorial: Surveillance and Children," *Surveillance & Society* 7, nos. 3/4 (2010): 187–191.

6. The human rights activist quoted above is Isabella Sankey, the policy director at the human rights group Liberty. See Robert Mendick and Robert Verkaik, "Anti-Terror Plan to Spy on Toddlers 'Is Heavy-Handed,'" *Telegraph* (January 4, 2015): telegraph.co.uk/news/uknews/terrorism-in-the-uk/11323558/Anti-terror -plan-to-spy-on-toddlers-is-heavy-handed.html.

7. Marx and Steeves suggest that "there is a slowly emerging literature on children and surveillance" and offer some helpful examples. Gary T. Marx and Valerie Steeves, "From the Beginning: Children as Subjects and Agents of Surveillance," *Surveillance & Society* 7, nos. 3/4 (2010): 192–230.

8. Mike McCahill and Rachel Finn, "The Social Impact of Surveillance in Three UK Schools: Angels, Devils and Teen Mums," *Surveillance & Society* 7, nos. 3/4 (2010); see ojs.library.queensu.ca/index.php/surveillance-and-society/article /view/4156.

9. *RFID Journal*, "Should We Be Tracking Kids with RFID?" (September 13, 2010): rfidjournal.com/blogs/rfid-journal/entry?7864; Torie Bosch, "He Sees You When You're Hitting Your Sister," *Slate* (December 14, 2011): slate.com/articles

/double_x/doublex/2011/12/elf_on_the_shelf_miracle_for_parents_or_tiny_op
pressor_.html.

10. Douglas Besharov, *Recognizing Child Abuse: A Guide for the Concerned* (New York: Free Press, 1990).

11. Steeves and Jones, "Editorial: Surveillance and Children."

12. S. J. Douglas and M. W. Michaels, *The Mommy Myth: The Idealization of Motherhood and How It Has Undermined Women* (New York: Free Press, 2004), 6.

13. George Orwell, *1984* (New York: Signet Classic, 1961), book 1, chapter 2, 24.

14. See Kelly Wezner's "'Perhaps I Am Watching You Now': Panem's Panopticons," in Mary F. Pharr et al. (eds.), *Of Bread, Blood and* The Hunger Games: *Critical Essays on the Suzanne Collins Trilogy* (Jefferson, NC: McFarland, 2012), 148–158.

15. David Robinson, "Jenni Fagan on Life in Care and Her New Novel," *Scotsman* (April 16, 2013): scotsman.com/lifestyle/books/jenni-fagan-on-life-in-care -and-her-new-novel-1-2896052.

16. Jenni Fagan, *The Panopticon* (London: Windmill Books, 2013), 1.

17. Richard Handler, *Critics Against Culture: Anthropological Observers of Mass Society* (Madison: University of Wisconsin Press, 2005), 156.

18. Melissa Gregg, "A Neglected History: Richard Hoggart's Discourse of Empathy," *Rethinking History* 7, no. 3 (2003): 285–306 (quote on 286).

19. Michael Bailey, Ben Clarke, and John K. Walton, *Understanding Richard Hoggart: A Pedagogy of Hope* (New York: John Wiley, 2011), 11, 68.

20. Richard Hoggart, *A Measured Life* (New Brunswick, NJ: Transaction, 1994), xii.

21. For a less sanguine view of Hoggart, see K. K. Ruthven's dyspeptic review, "Forgetting Richard Hoggart," *Cultural Studies Review* 19, no. 2 (September 2013): 307–313.

22. Richard Hoggart, *The Uses of Literacy: Aspects of Working Class Life with Special Reference to Publications and Entertainments* (Harmonsworth, UK: Penguin, 1963), 73.

23. Ibid.

24. Ibid., 34, 79.

25. McCahill and Finn, "The Social Impact of Surveillance in Three UK Schools," 283.

26. Rita Felski, "Nothing to Declare: Identity, Shame, and the Lower Middle Class," *PMLA* 115, no. 1, Special Topic: Rereading Class (January 2000): 33–45 (quotes on 39–40).

27. Carolyn Steedman, *Landscape for a Good Woman* (New Brunswick, NJ: Rutgers University Press, 1987), 13.

28. Kathryn Hughes, "Kathryn Hughes on Carolyn Steedman's *Landscape for a Good Woman*" (November 27, 2000): newstatesman.com/node/152461.

29. Joseph Menn, "Yahoo Secretly Scanned Customer Emails for U.S. Intelligence—Sources," *Reuters* (October 4, 2016): reuters.com/article/us-yahoo-nsa -exclusive-idUSKCN1241YT.

30. For instance, a search of more than a decade of *Surveillance & Society*, the

best journal on the subject, yields no hits for the words "anxiety" or "depression" between 2004 and 2014.

31. "Wartime and later Cold War civil defense programs had required self-scrutiny as well as spying on one's neighbors; atomic-age films and duck-and-cover drills had promoted a 'stay in your homes' isolationism and the fantasy of domestic safety in an atomic age." Anna Creadick, *Perfectly Average: The Pursuit of Normality in Postwar America* (Amherst: University of Massachusetts Press, 2010), 124.

32. Deborah Nicholson, "Paranoia Optimization for Our Modern Times," *Media Goblin* (August 23, 2013): mediagoblin.org/news/paranoia-optimization .html.

33. Steve Henn, "Hey, Why Did You Floor It? Tracking Junior Behind the Wheel," *NPR* (October 14, 2013): npr.org/blogs/alltechconsidered/2013/10/14 /234078630/hey-why-did-you-floor-it-tracking-junior-behind-the-wheel.

34. Steven Stosny, "Emotional Abuse in Committed Relationships: Effects on Children," *Psychology Today* (January 28, 2011): psychologytoday.com/blog/an ger-in-the-age-entitlement/201101/emotional-abuse-in-committed-relationships -effects-children.

35. Hille Koskela, "Video Surveillance, Gender, and the Safety of Public Urban Space: 'Peeping Tom' Goes High Tech?" *Urban Geography* 23, no. 3 (2002): 257–278.

36. José Esteban Muñoz, *Cruising Utopia: The Then and There of Queer Futurity* (New York: NYU Press, 2009), 39.

37. Tina G. Patel, "Surveillance, Suspicion and Stigma: Brown Bodies in a Terror-Panic Climate," *Surveillance & Society* 10, nos. 3/4 (2012): 216.

38. Patel, "Surveillance, Suspicion and Stigma," 216.

39. Alexander J. O'Connor and Farhana Jahan, "Under Surveillance and Over-wrought: American Muslims' Emotional and Behavioral Responses to Government Surveillance," *Journal of Muslim Mental Health* 8, no. 1 (2014): 105.

40. As individualistic as most Americans prefer to imagine themselves, we are still case studies of Bourdieu's concept of "habitus," "which he uses to explain how class identities become inscribed not only on the mind, but also on the body and include 'a way of walking, a tilt of the head, facial expressions . . . a tone of voice, [and] a style of speech.'" See Pierre Bourdieu, *Outline of a Theory of Practice* (Cambridge, UK: Cambridge University Press, 1977), 85–87. See also McCahill and Finn, "The Social Impact of Surveillance in Three UK Schools," 286.

41. William Todd Schultz, *Torment Saint: The Life of Elliot Smith* (New York: Bloomsbury, 2013), 1, 36, 38, 307, 312, 313.

42. Tonya Rooney, "Trusting Children: How Do Surveillance Technologies Alter a Child's Experience of Trust, Risk and Responsibility?" *Surveillance & Society* 7, nos. 3/4 (2010): 344.

43. Alex Santoso, "NSA Surveillance Children's Book," *Neatorama* (June 10, 2013): neatorama.com/2013/06/10/NSA-Surveillance-Childrens-Book.

Chapter 4: Watching Walden

1. The sheriff's office of Mesa County, Colorado, first invested in drones in 2009. It is worth noting that their office had few restrictions: as one report put it, the county's drone program "does not include any geographical limits, essentially letting law enforcement look into events across the entire country." *RT*, "Drone Surveillance Quickly Becoming Routine in Colorado" (December 19, 2012): rt.com/usa/drone-surveillance-mesa-colorado-433.

2. Colorado Parks & Wildlife, "Lory" (n.d.): parks.state.co.us/Parks/Lory/crit ters/Pages/CritterCam.aspx.

3. Lori Zimmer, "Sign Up to Help Capture Images of Remote Places with the Google Trekker Backpack," *Inhabitat* (July 1, 2013): inhabitat.com/sign-up-to -help-capture-images-of-remote-places-with-the-google-trekker-backpack.

4. Laura Westra, *Living in Integrity: A Global Ethic to Restore a Fragmented Earth* (Lanham, MD: Rowman and Littlefield, 1998), 100.

5. Mark Kingwell, *Concrete Reveries: Consciousness and the City* (New York: Viking, 2008), 93.

6. Such musings are inevitably indebted to the seminal "End of Nature" argument put forth by Bill McKibben. See his book *The End of Nature* (New York: Anchor, 1989). Another predecessor is Carolyn Merchant, *The Death of Nature: Women, Ecology, and the Scientific Revolution* (San Francisco: Harper & Row, 1980).

7. *Texas Observer* (podcast), "Observer Radio Episode 44: One Man's Survivalist Tale from the Texas Pines" (February 7, 2014): texasobserver.org/observer -radio-episode-44-one-mans-survivalist-tale-texas-pines.

8. *Editions Hatch*, "Industrial Society and Its Future" (1995): editions-hache .com/essais/pdf/kaczynski2.pdf. For a surprisingly sanguine look at Kaczynski on the right, see Keith Ablow, "Was the Unabomber Correct?" *Fox News* (June 25, 2013): foxnews.com/opinion/2013/06/25/was-unabomber-correct-about-horrors -technology-combined-with-government.

9. Paul Wapner, *Living through the End of Nature: The Future of American Environmentalism* (Cambridge, MA: MIT Press, 2010), 163.

10. For an interesting, perhaps analogous view of image-making from the air, see reconstruction.eserver.org/Issues/112/Kaplan_Caren.shtml. Caren Kaplan, "'A Rare and Chilling View': Aerial Photography as Biopower in the Visual Culture of 9/11," *Reconstruction* 11, no. 2 (2011).

11. Francis Jennings, *The Invasion of America: Indians, Colonialism, and the Cant of Conquest* (New York: Norton, 1975), 15.

12. For more on the wild as waste or danger, see Michael L. Johnson, *Hunger for the Wild: America's Obsession with the Untamed West* (Lawrence: University Press of Kansas, 2007), 42–54.

13. Ibid., 2, 5. The "maw of the unknown" comes from Richard C. Poulson, *The Landscape of the Mind: Cultural Transformations of the American West* (New York: Lang, 1992), 27, quoted in Johnson, *Hunger for the Wild*, 5.

14. Rudyard Kipling, *American Notes* (New York: Brown and Company, 1899), 93.

15. William Cronon, "The Trouble with Wilderness; or, Getting Back to the Wrong Nature," in William Cronon (ed.), *Uncommon Ground: Rethinking the Human Place in Nature* (New York: Norton, 1995), 69–90. See also his masterful look at the way a city impacts the surrounding "frontier" in *Nature's Metropolis: Chicago and the Great West* (New York: Norton, 1992).

16. Thoreau quoted in Robert Sullivan, *The Thoreau You Don't Know: What the Prophet of Environmentalism Really Meant* (New York: Harper, 2009), 251.

17. Tapahonso quoted in Johnson, *Hunger for the Wild*, 17.

18. The Conservation Drones home page is located at conservationdrones.org.

19. Mónica Mendes and Nuno Correia, "RTiVISS: Real-time Video Interactive Systems for Sustainability," 1437–1440 in *Proceedings of the 18th ACM International Conference on Multimedia* (New York: ACM, 2010): dl.acm.org/citation.cfm?doid=1873951.1874238.

20. Wapner, *Living through the End of Nature*, 146.

21. Doug Stanglin, "Surveillance Drone Helps Firefighters Battle Calif. Blaze," *USA Today* (August 29, 2013): usatoday.com/story/news/nation/2013/08/29/yo semite-fire-drone-national-guard/2726601.

22. Jon Hamilton, "Spy Drones Turning up New Data About Hurricanes and Weather," *NPR* (September 13, 2013): npr.org/2013/09/13/221723991/spy -drones-turning-up-new-data-about-hurricanes-and-weather?sc=17&f=1001.

23. Sean Patrick Ferrell, "A Drone's-Eye View of Nature," *New York Times* (May 6, 2013): nytimes.com/2013/05/07/science/drones-offer-a-safer-clearer -look-at-the-natural-world.html; *Inside GNSS*, "Predator UAV Provides Surveillance in Battle Against Yosemite Fire" (August 30, 2013): insidegnss.com /node/3678.

24. David Smith, "Saving the Rhino with Surveillance Drones," *Guardian* (December 25, 2012): theguardian.com/environment/2012/dec/25/saving-the -rhino-with-surveillance-drones; Vishwa Mohan, "India to Use Drones to Keep Eye on Poachers in Tiger Reserves," *The Times of India* (March 18, 2015): timesofindia.indiatimes.com/home/environment/India-to-use-drones-to-keep -eye-on-poachers-in-tiger-reserves/articleshow/46609261.cms.

25. "Brazil sets up special security force to protect Amazon," Phys.org (October 10, 2012): phys.org/news/2012-10-brazil-special-amazon.html.

26. April Tonta, "Gardening from the Sky" [or "The Future Comes to Our Gardens," via Erica at High Rocks], *Grow Appalachia* (April 1, 2013): growappalachia .berea.edu/2013/04/01/the-future-comes-to-our-gardens-by-erica-at-high -rocks.

27. Denver Nicks, "Surveillance Blimps Will Watch over East Coast," *Time* (January 23, 2014): swampland.time.com/2014/01/23/surveillance-blimps-will -watch-over-east-coast.

28. Madison Gray, "Surveillance Is So Dope: Google Earth Helps Bust Pot Farm," *Time* (October 22, 2013): newsfeed.time.com/2013/10/22/surveillance-is -so-dope-google-earth-helps-bust-pot-farm; Swiss story in *APC*, "Marijuana Farmers Caught on Google Earth" (January 30, 2009): apcmag.com/marijuana _farmers_caught_on_google_earth.htm.

29. Eric Hagerman, "Coming Soon: An Unblinking 'Gorgon Stare' for Air Force

Drones," *PopSci* (August 26, 2009): popsci.com/military-aviation-amp-space/article/2009-08/coming-soon-unblinking-gorgon-stare-air-force-drones.

30. Elizabeth Sheld, "Drone Surveillance Footage Sends Man to Jail," *Fox News* (January 28, 2014): nation.foxnews.com/2014/01/28/drone-surveillance-footage-sends-man-jail.

31. Post by BluntKilla, "Sheriff's Department Uses Google Earth to Pinpoint Marijuana Fields," *420* (October 16, 2006): 420magazine.com/forums/internat ional-cannabis-news/57392-sheriff-s-department-uses-google-earth-pinpoint-marijuana-fields.html.

32. See pixcontroller.com.

33. "Thousands Sign up for Virtual Border Patrol," *New York Times*, December 14, 2009.

34. Ben Romans, "PETA Selling 'Hunter Watching' Surveillance Drones," *Field & Stream* (October 28, 2013): fieldandstream.com/blogs/field-notes/2013/10/peta-selling-hunter-watching-surveillance-drones.

35. Michael McWhertor, "To Create the 'Ultimate Open World' Two Ex-Ubisoft Devs Are Scanning the Planet," *Polygon* (February 3, 2014): polygon.com/2014/2/3/5374012/reroll-drone-sourcing-planet-earth-pixyul-pc.

36. Ingrid Longauerová, "10 Beautiful, Remote Places Brought to You by Google Street View," *Epoch Times* (April 11, 2014): theepochtimes.com/n3/3742 54-10-beautiful-remote-places-brought-to-you-by-google-street-view.

37. Tom Chivers, "The Story of Google Maps," *Telegraph* (June 4, 2013): tele graph.co.uk/technology/google/10090014/The-story-of-Google-Maps.html. Any work on Google's cultural impact is indebted to Siva Vaidhyanathan's *The Googlization of Everything (And Why We Should Worry)* (Berkeley: University of California Press, 2011).

38. Chivers, "The Story of Google Maps."

39. Ibid.

40. "There is an established geographical tradition," writes geographer Agnieszka Leszczynski, of "understanding spatial information and its cartographic representation as inherently implicated in practices of securing and exercising power." Yet the shifting power over the wilderness, spread with surprising *complementarity* between state and corporate actors, is not sufficiently understood. See Agnieszka Leszczynski, "Situating the Geoweb in Political Economy," *Progress in Human Geography* 36 (February 2012): 76. This article also lays out the idea of state and corporate "complementarity" on 84. Thanks to geographer Karl Offen for this citation.

41. Jason Farman, "Mapping the Digital Empire: Google Earth and the Process of Postmodern Cartography," *New Media Society* 12, no. 6 (2010): 869–888.

42. Eric Shouse, "Feeling, Emotion, Affect," *M/C Journal* 8 (December 2005), quoted in Ruth Leys, "The Turn to Affect: A Critique," *Critical Inquiry* (2011): criticalinquiry.uchicago.edu/uploads/pdf/Leys,_Turn_to_Affect.pdf.

43. For Senator Rand Paul's unofficial transcript, see Morgan Little, "Transcript: Rand Paul's Filibuster of John Brennan's CIA Nomination," *Los Angeles Times* (March 7, 2013): articles.latimes.com/2013/mar/07/news/la-pn-transcript-rand-paul-filibuster-20130307/36.

44. Wapner, *Living through the End of Nature*, 94.

45. "Walking," thoreau.eserver.org/walking.html.

46. Robert E. Richardson, *Henry Thoreau: A Life of the Mind* (Berkeley: University of California Press, 1986), 228.

47. The "hermit" allusion comes from George Stewart, "Thoreau, the Hermit of Walden: A Paper Read Before the Literary and Historical Society of Quebec, March 7, 1882." Printed at the *Morning Chronicle* Office, 1882.

48. Richardson, *Henry Thoreau*, 277.

49. Philip Cafaro, *Thoreau's Living Ethics: Walden and the Pursuit of Virtue* (Athens: University of Georgia Press, 2004), 15.

50. Henry David Thoreau, *The Maine Woods* (Boston: Ticknor and Fields, 1864). He used the place name "Mt. Ktaadn."

51. Henry David Thoreau, *Reform Papers*, ed. Wendell Glick (Princeton: Princeton University Press, 1973), 164, 165, quoted in Jane Bennett, "Thoreau's Techniques of Self," in Jack Turner (ed.), *A Political Companion to Henry David Thoreau* (Lexington: University of Kentucky Press, 2009), 297.

52. Thoreau, *A Week on the Concord and Merrimack Rivers*, ed. Carl F. Hovde, William L. Howarth, and Elizabeth Hall Witherell (Princeton: Princeton University Press, 1980), 272, quoted in Bennett, "Thoreau's Techniques of Self," in Jack Turner (ed.), *A Political Companion to Henry David Thoreau* (Lexington: University of Kentucky Press, 2009), 302.

53. Shannon L. Mariotti, *Thoreau's Democratic Withdrawal: Alienation, Participation, and Modernity* (Madison: University of Wisconsin Press, 2010), 95.

54. Henry David Thoreau, *Walden: A Fully Annotated Edition* (New Haven: Yale University Press, 2004). See Thoreau, *Walden*, for three previous quotations: "human neighborhood" (141), "a considerable neutral ground" (152), and "The search for motives ..." (147). And ibid. (on 46) for "spectatordom" quote.

55. Hannah Arendt, *On Revolution* (New York: Penguin, 1990), 98. Thanks to Carrie Andersen for this cite.

56. Jack Turner, "Introduction: Thoreau as a Political Thinker," in Jack Turner (ed.), *A Political Companion to Henry David Thoreau* (Lexington: University of Kentucky Press, 2009), 2.

57. Thoreau, *Walden*, 121.

58. Ibid., 95.

59. Nancy L. Rosenblum, "Thoreau's Democrative Individualism," in Jack Turner (ed.), *A Political Companion to Henry David Thoreau* (Lexington: University of Kentucky Press, 2010), 16.

60. On Thoreau's "Resistance to Civil Government," see Mariotti, *Thoreau's Democratic Withdrawal*, xiv, xv.

61. Mariotti, *Thoreau's Democratic Withdrawal*, xvii.

62. Richard D. Brown and Jack Tager, *Massachusetts: A Concise History* (Amherst: University of Massachusetts Press, 2000), 115–116. Brown quoted in Mariotti, *Thoreau's Democratic Withdrawal*, 88.

63. H. Daniel Peck, *Thoreau's Morning Walk* (New Haven: Yale University Press, 1990), 124.

64. James Ball, "Angry Birds and 'Leaky' Phone Apps Targeted by NSA and

GCHQ for User Data," *Guardian* (January 28, 2014): theguardian.com/world
/2014/Jan/27/nsa gchq smartphone app angry birds personal data.

65. Henry David Thoreau, *A Writer's Journal*, ed. Laurence Stapleton (Mineola, NY: Dover, 1960), 87.

66. Marriotti, *Thoreau's Democratic Withdrawal*, 126. Her use of the phrase "wooden men" alludes to Thoreau's use of it in "Civil Disobedience." Henry David Thoreau, *Civil Disobedience and Other Essays* (Mineola, NY: Dover, 2012), 3.

67. Mariotti, *Thoreau's Democratic Withdrawal*, 125.

68. See ibid., 120–126, for an excellent discussion of Thoreau's walking.

69. Max Oelschlaeger, *The Idea of Wilderness: From Prehistory to the Age of Ecology* (New Haven: Yale University Press, 1991), 164.

70. David R. Foster, *Thoreau's Country* (Boston: Harvard University Press, 1999), 19.

71. "Most alive" quoted in Oelschlaeger, *The Idea of Wilderness*, 167.

72. Foster, *Thoreau's Country*, 211.

73. *Online Etymology Dictionary* is located at etymonline.com.

74. J. A. Cuddon, *A Dictionary of Literary Terms and Literary Theory*, 5th ed. (West Sussex, UK: Wiley-Blackwell, 2013).

75. Manuel Arias-Maldonado, *Real Green: Sustainability after the End of Nature* (Burlington, VT: Ashgate, 2012) 56.

76. For "nakedness" see Oelschlaeger, *The Idea of Wilderness*, 167.

77. Wapner, *Living through the End of Nature*, 145.

78. That quoted phrase comes from Laurence Buell, *The Environmental Imagination: Thoreau, Nature Writing, and the Formation of Culture* (Cambridge: Harvard University Press, 1996), 39. His book describes the exclusionary aspects of pastoral ideology, including examples in which Thoreau's admirers have pushed his ideas toward a problematic fantasy of "nature-as-elite-androcentric-preserve." (To my mind the pastoral represents a lesser degree of wilderness: it is a rural fantasy of returning to the soil, of going back to a land that is not quite wild but somehow on the way to wildness.)

79. Buell, *The Environmental Imagination*, 45.

80. Hille Koskela, "Video Surveillance, Gender, and the Safety of Public Urban Space: 'Peeping Tom' Goes High Tech?" *Urban Geography* 23, no. 3 (2002): 257–278.

81. Elizabeth Engelhardt, *The Tangled Roots of Feminism, Environmentalism, and Appalachian Literature* (Athens: Ohio University Press, 2003), 3.

82. Carolyn Merchant, *Earthcare: Women and the Environment* (New York: Routledge, 1995), 41.

83. Rachel Carson, *Silent Spring* (Boston: Houghton Mifflin, 1962), 297.

84. William Cronon, "The Trouble with Wilderness," 69–90.

85. Buell, *The Environmental Imagination*, 52.

86. USC Cinematic Arts, *Walden: A Game* (n.d.): cinema.usc.edu/interactive /research/walden.cfm.

87. Mick Smith, *Against Ecological Sovereignty: Ethics, Biopolitics, and Saving the Natural World* (Minneapolis: University of Minnesota Press, 2011).

88. For more on this concept, see Viktor Mayer-Schönberger, *Delete: The*

Virtue of Forgetting in the Digital Age (Princeton: Princeton University Press, 2011).

89. On technology's subtly urbanizing effects, see Christina Nippert-Eng, *Islands of Privacy* (Chicago: University of Chicago Press, 2010), 205.

90. Roy Coleman, "Surveillance in the City: Primary Definition and Urban Spatial Order," in Sean Hier and Joshua Greenberg (eds.), *Surveillance Studies Reader* (Maidenhead, UK: Open University Press, 2007), 232.

91. Barry Schwartz, "The Social Psychology of Privacy," *American Journal of Sociology* 73, no. 6 (1968): 741–752, quoted in Nippert-Eng, *Islands of Privacy*, 98.

92. Nippert-Eng, *Islands of Privacy*, 3.

93. Christopher Hitt, "Toward an Ecological Sublime," *New Literary History* 30, no. 3 (Summer 1999): 603.

94. Cronon, "The Trouble with Wilderness," 80–81.

95. Peter Heymans, *Animality in British Romanticism: The Aesthetics of Species* (New York: Routledge, 2012), 27.

96. Meghashyam Mali, "Poll: Public Backs More Surveillance Post-Boston," *The Hill* (May 1, 2013): thehill.com/blogs/blog-briefing-room/news/297109-poll -public-backs-more-surveillance-post-boston.

97. Staff Report, "Boston Marathon Bombing Expected to Boost Video Surveillance Spending," *Security InfoWatch* (April 29, 2013): securityinfowatch .com/news/10930493/boston-marathon-bombing-likely-to-spur-government -spending-on-surveillance-and-security.

98. Thoreau, *Walden*, 7.

99. Frieda Knobloch, *Culture of Wilderness: Agriculture as Colonization in the American West* (Chapel Hill: University of North Carolina Press, 1996), x.

100. Liz Climas, "See the Robotic Jellyfish Drone Equipped with Surveillance Powers—Seriously," *The Blaze* (March 29, 2013): theblaze.com/stories/2013/03 /29/see-the-robotic-jellyfish-drone-equipped-with-surveillance-powers -seriously.

Chapter 5: A Mighty Fortress Is Our God

1. For the home page of the New Life Church, see newlifechurch.org/new.

2. Jason Bivins, *Religion of Fear: The Politics of Horror in Conservative Evangelicalism* (New York: Oxford University Press, 2008), 3, 10.

3. Ibid., 221.

4. *Huffington Post*, "Jeanne Assam Says She Was Asked to Leave New Life Church After Coming Out" (February 25, 2011): huffingtonpost.com/2011/02/25 /jeanne-assam-says-she-was_n_828201.html.

5. Carl Chinn, *Evil Invades Sanctuary: The Case for Security in Faith-Based Organizations* (Monument, CO: Snowfall Press, 2012).

6. The story of a church security team using metal detectors hidden in their sleeves appears in Paul E. Engle and Robert H. Welch, *Serving by Safeguarding Your Church* (Grand Rapids, MI: Zondervan 2002), 68.

7. Super|Circuits, "Church Security: Is Your Church a Sanctuary or a Target?"

(September 1, 2011): supercircuits.com/resources/blog/is-your-church-a-sanctu
ary-or-a-target.

8. Zygmunt Bauman, *Society under Siege* (London: Polity Press, 2002), 68.

9. Zygmunt Bauman, "Living in the Era of Liquid Modernity," *Cambridge Anthropology* 22, no. 2 (2000/2001): 1–19.

10. For many insights about schools and surveillance, see Torin Monahan (ed.), *Schools under Surveillance: Cultures of Control in Public Education* (New Brunswick, NJ: Rutgers University Press, 2009).

11. Sheepdog Safety Training, "What We Do" (n.d.): sheepdogsafetytraining .com/what-we-do. The lower figure of twenty-eight people killed in US churches appears in Ron Aguiar, *Keeping Your Church Safe* (Maitlan, FL: Xulon Press, 2008), 71.

12. The documentary film *Faith under Fire* explores the Dangerfield murder (August 24, 2014): heartstonepictures.com/inspirational/faith-under-fire.

13. David and Marie Works, *Gone in a Heartbeat: Our Daughters Died … Our Faith Endures* (Carol House, IL: Tyndale House, 2009).

14. From back cover of Carl Chinn's *Evil Invades Sanctuary*.

15. Aguiar, *Keeping Your Church Safe*, 21.

16. National Organization of Church Security and Safety Management, "Three Strands of Church Security Seminar," nocssm.org/one-day-seminar.

17. CCTV Camera Pros (Lantana, FL), "Church Video Surveillance Systems" (n.d.): cctvcamerapros.com/Church-Surveillance-Systems-s/219.htm.

18. Glen Evans (Church Security Alliance), "Verdict: Church Security Teams Unbiblical" (January 29, 2012): networkedblogs.com/tj3Fd.

19. The original URL is no longer valid but is archived at safeatchurch.com /examples.asp.

20. The now defunct blog for Gideon Protective Services Inc., accessed in spring 2015, was available at churchsecurity-training.com/tag/church-risk-management.

21. Becky Beal, "The Promise Keepers' Use of Sport in Defining 'Christlike' Masculinity," *Journal of Sport and Social Issues* 21, no. 3 (1997): 274.

22. E. L. Cole, *Maximum Manhood: A Guide to Family Survival* (Springdale, PA: Whitaker House, 1982), 72, quoted in John P. Bartkowski, "Breaking Walls, Raising Fences: Masculinity, Intimacy, and Accountability among the Promise Keepers." *Sociology of Religion* 61 (2000): 33–53 (quote on 35).

23. The original URL is no longer valid but might be archived at christian securitynetwork.org/Views-Comments/blog-131.

24. CCTV Camera Pros (Lantana, Florida), "Church Video Surveillance Systems" (section "Blending Surveillance Systems in with a Church") (n.d.): cctv camerapros.com/Church-Surveillance-Systems-s/219.htm.

25. Engle and Welch, *Serving by Safeguarding Your Church*, 89.

26. *Fox News* (via AP), "Growing Number of Detroit Pastors Wear Handguns in Pulpit" (October 1, 2009): foxnews.com/story/2009/10/01/growing-number -detroit-pastors-wear-handguns-in-pulpit.html.

27. Grant R. Jeffrey, *Surveillance Society: The Rise of the Antichrist* (Toronto: Frontier Research Publications, 2000).

28. *Worldview Times* website (worldviewweekend.com/times).

29. The NOCSSM website is located at called2duty.org.

30. The original URL is no longer valid but was archived at churchsecurity -training.com/tag/church-risk-management.

31. Ibid.

32. Sentry One Consulting Group, Inc.'s website is located at sentryone consulting.com.

33. Joan Goodchild, "Why Your Church Needs a Security Plan," *CSO* (January 27, 2009): csoonline.com/article/478069/why-your-church-needs-a-security -plan.

34. Link Byfield, "The Only Alternative to Video Monitors Is an Intrusive and Demanding God," *Alberta Report* 23, no. 41 (September 23, 1996): 2.

35. Donald G. Mathews, *Religion in the Old South* (Chicago: University of Chicago Press, 1997), 43.

36. Robert D. Putnam and David E. Campbell, *American Grace: How Religion Divides and Unites Us* (New York: Simon and Schuster, 2010), 12–13.

37. Ibid., 472. The authors explain their research in this fashion: *"American Grace: How Religion Divides and Unites Us* is based on many surveys, but central to its analysis is the Faith Matters Survey that was conducted in 2006 on behalf of Harvard University by ICR. The original national survey interviewed roughly 3100 Americans in an hour-long phone survey both about their religion (beliefs, belonging and behavior) and their social and political engagement. In 2007, we re-interviewed as many of these respondents as we could in the Faith Matters 2007 survey, and asked them a subset of these questions again (as well as a few new questions)." See americangrace.org/research.

38. Putnam and Campbell, *American Grace*, 470.

39. Ibid.

40. Ibid., 479.

41. Ibid., 482.

42. Ibid., 489.

43. Yet here is the kicker that Putnam and Campbell's research suggests: with the exceptions of fundamentalists, most people of faith in the United States are *more trusting* than their secular peers, who, ironically, sometimes like to imagine paranoid Jesus freaks clinging to their guns in a panic-induced frenzy at the merest mention of Osama bin Laden, Marilyn Manson, or Kanye West. The truth is that with the exception of fundamentalist church members with irregular attendance, who combine a skeptical theology with low social networking, religious Americans are generally more trusting and probably less nervous about their security needs than the rest of the country.

44. Chinn, *Evil Invades Sanctuary*, 59.

45. John Corrigan, *Business of the Heart: Religion and Emotion in the Nineteenth Century* (Berkeley: University of California Press, 2002).

46. Two authors argue for the centrality of the airport to control societies: Bulent Diken and Carsten B. Laustsen, *The Culture of Exception: Sociology Facing the Camp* (New York: Routledge 2005), 65.

47. Kevin D. Haggerty and Amber Gazso, "Seeing Beyond the Ruins: Surveil-

lance as a Response to Terrorist Threats," *Canadian Journal of Sociology* 30, no. 2 (Spring 2005). 109.

48. Chinn, *Evil Invades Sanctuary*, 90–91.

49. It is important to note that Christian scripture also has been used to endorse an open-door policy of trust and compassion in other congregations and that some evangelical Christians express considerable hostility toward surveillance culture.

50. Not much has been written on the intersection of theology and surveillance culture, but I would highly recommend David Lyon's excellent essay "God's Eye: Surveillance and Watchfulness in the Twenty-first Century," *Transmission* (Summer 2010): biblesociety.org.uk/uploads/content/bible_in_transmission/files /2010_summer/BiT_Summer_2010_Lyon.pdf, as well as Eric Stoddard's *Theological Perspectives on a Surveillance Society: Watching and Being Watched* (Surray, UK: Ashgate, 2011).

51. Although it seems likely given the context, I've been unable to confirm that the portrait was of Jesus or someone else whose gaze would affect the monks so deeply. See Christopher M. Bellitto, Thomas M. Izbicki, and Gerald Christianson, *Introducing Nicholas of Cusa: A Guide to a Renaissance Man* (Mahwah, NJ: Paulist Press, 2004) 389.

52. "In such a world, deadly gadgetry is just a grant request away, so why shouldn't the 14,000 at-risk souls in Scottsbluff, Nebraska, have a closed-circuit-digital-camera-and-monitor system (cost: $180,000, courtesy of the Homeland Security Department) identical to the one up and running in New York's Times Square?" See Stephan Salisbury, "The Cost of America's Police State," *Salon* (March 5, 2012): salon.com/2012/03/05/the_cost_of_americas_police_state.

53. See Slovenian philosopher Miran Bozovic's introduction to Jeremy Bentham, *The Panopticon Writings* (London: Verso, 1995), 11.

54. Or perhaps we will feel safe at last behind our banks of video monitors, luxuriating in our own version of Total Information Awareness, like primates content to scour the horizon for predators? My hope is that future ethnographic data will shed some light on this difficult question.

Chapter 6: The Business of Insecurity

1. See the ISC East home page located at isceast.com/Show-Info.

2. Jennifer Valentino-Devries, Julia Angwin, and Steve Stecklow, "Document Trove Exposes Surveillance Methods," *Wall Street Journal* (November 19, 2011): online.wsj.com/news/articles/SB10001424052970203611404577044192607407780.

3. *PR Newswire*, "Global CCTV Market Forecast to 2014" (March 13, 2012): m.prnewswire.com/news-releases/global-cctv-market-forecast-to-2014-14245 6805.html; Leif Kothe, "North American Video Surveillance Market Poised for Rapid Expansion," *Security Systems News* (July 15, 2014): securitysystemsnews .com/article/north-american-video-surveillance-market-poised-rapid-expan sion.

4. Security Industry Association, "2015 Annual Report" (n.d.): securityindustry .org/annualreport/SitePages/index.aspx.

5. The Security Industry Association is based in Silver Springs, Maryland, just outside of Washington, DC.

6. Security Industry Association, "About SIA" (n.d.): siaonline.org/Pages/About SIA/Mission.aspx.

7. Ibid.

8. Security Industry Association, "Board of Directors" (n.d.): siaonline.org /Pages/AboutSIA/Board-of-Directors.aspx.

9. Security Industry Association, full-page ad, *Campus Safety* (Bobit Business Media), October 2013, 49.

10. Daniel Rivero, "Meet the Privacy Activists Who Spy on the Surveillance Industry," *Fusion.net* (April 6, 2015): fusion.net/story/112390/unveiling-secrets -of-the-international-surveillance-trade-one-fake-company-at-a-time.

11. ADT ad is located at adt.com/business/access-control.

12. The brochure is titled "Optex Photoelectric Beam and Tower Guide."

13. *Campus Safety* (October 2013), 2, 44.

14. Michael Kremer, "From Access Control to Building Control to Total Control," SIA's *Technology Insights* (Winter 2013–2014), 47.

15. Jonathan Lewitt, "Achieving IP Video Management Scalability through Aggregation," SIA's *Technology Insights* (Winter 2013–2014), 17–19.

16. IQ inVision ad in *Campus Safety* (October 2013), 5.

17. Brad Spicer, "11 Components of a Secure School Front Entrance," *Campus Safety* (October 2013), 16–17.

18. *Campus Safety* (October 2013), 14.

19. The Invisible Committee, *The Coming Insurrection* (Los Angeles: Semiotext, 2009), 11.

20. Zygmunt Bauman and Leonidas Donskis, *Moral Blindness: The Loss of Sensitivity in Liquid Modernity* (Cambridge UK: Polity Press, 2013), 43.

21. Ibid.

22. Valentino-Devries et al., "Document Trove."

23. Bauman and Donskis, *Moral Blindness*, 77.

24. Ibid., 7.

25. David Pierce, "Mayor Bloomberg Says Surveillance Drones Are Inevitable in NYC: 'Get Used to It,'" *Verge* (March 24, 2013): theverge.com/2013/3/24/4141526 /mayor-bloomberg-says-surveillance-drones-inevitable-in-nyc.

26. Bauman and Donskis, *Moral Blindness*, 7.

27. Valentino-Devries et al., "Document Trove."

28. Ibid.

29. See Matthew Rice (Privacy International), "The Surveillance Industry Index: An Introduction" (November 18, 2013): privacyinternational.org/node/403.

30. I remember seeing a version of this question raised by the architectural critic Paul Goldberger, but either I am misremembering or simply failed to find the passage in his writings.

31. Barney Frank was celebrating the power of dense networks of urban CCTV in a conversation about the Boston Marathon bombing trial on Lawrence O'Don-

nell's MSNBC program *The Last Word*, April 8, 2015, the night that Dzhokhar Tsarnaev was convicted.

32. *Guardian*, "NYPD and Microsoft Launch Advanced Citywide Surveillance System" (August 8, 2012): theguardian.com/world/2012/aug/08/nypd-microsoft -surveillance-system.

33. Josh Begley, "Plain Sight: The Visual Vernacular of NYPD Surveillance," *Moving Walls 22, Watching You Watching Me* (catalog) (New York: Open Society Foundation, 2015), 12.

34. Bauman and Donskis, *Moral Blindness*, 77.

35. Scott Raab, "The Freedom Tower Is an Absolute Miracle," *Esquire* (January 12, 2015): esquire.com/news-politics/a32322/freedom-tower-world-trade-cen ter-miracle-0115.

36. This was the official gift shop attached to the site before the museum opened. I returned a year and a half later to explore the museum, its gift shop, and the memorial pools once again.

37. For a more critical take on the commodification of grieving, see Marita Sturken, "Tourism and Sacred Ground: The Space of Ground Zero," in N. Mirzoeff (ed.), *The Visual Culture Reader* (New York: Routledge, 2012), 412–427.

38. Jane C. Timm, "Drop a Bag in NYC? Cue the Bomb Squad," *MSNBC* (April 22, 2013): msnbc.com/morning-joe/drop-bag-nyc-cue-the-bomb-squad. Manhattan total appears in Tina Moore, "'We're Going to Have More Visibility and Less Privacy': Mayor Bloomberg Admits Soon NYPD Surveillance Cameras Will Be on Nearly Every Corner and in the Air," *New York Daily News* (March 22, 2013): nydailynews.com/new-york/bloomberg-new-york-eventually-surveillance-city -article-1.1296103.

39. On the New York City Surveillance Camera Project, see mediaeater.com /cameras.

40. See "Maps of Publicly Installed Surveillance Cameras in New York City" (n.d.): notbored.org/scp-maps.html.

41. Francis Lachance, "Getting 'Big-City Surveillance' with Small-City Budgets," *GSN* (September 26, 2012): gsnmagazine.com/node/27396?c=video_sur veillance_cctv.

42. Moore, "'We're Going to Have More Visibility ...'"

43. Jonathon Porritt, *Capitalism as If the World Matters* (New York: Routledge, 2005), 43.

Index